Essentials of
Health Care Compliance

Shelley C. Safian, MAOM/HSM, CCS-P, CPC-H, CHA

DELMAR
CENGAGE Learning™

Australia • Brazil • Japan • Korea • Mexico • Singapore • Spain • United Kingdom • United States

DELMAR
CENGAGE Learning™

Essentials of Health Care Compliance
Shelley C. Safian

Vice President, Career and Professional
Editorial: Dave Garza

Director of Learning Solutions:
Matthew Kane

Senior Acquisitions Editor: Rhonda Dearborn

Managing Editor: Marah Bellegarde

Product Manager: Natalie Pashoukos

Editorial Assistant: Chiara Astriab

Vice President, Career and Professional
Marketing: Jennifer McAvey

Marketing Director: Wendy Mapstone

Marketing Manager: Kristin McNary

Marketing Coordinator: Erica Ropitzky

Production Director: Carolyn Miller

Production Manager: Andrew Crouth

Senior Content Project Manager: Jim Zayicek

Senior Art Director: Jack Pendleton

For product information and technology assistance, contact us at
Cengage Learning Customer & Sales Support, 1-800-354-9706

For permission to use material from this text or product,
submit all requests online at **www.cengage.com/permissions**
Further permissions questions can be emailed to
permissionrequest@cengage.com

Library of Congress Control Number: 2008936174

ISBN-13: 978-1-4180-4921-8

ISBN-10: 1-4180-4921-2

Delmar
Executive Woods
5 Maxwell Drive
Clifton Park, NY 12065
USA

Cengage Learning is a leading provider of customized learning solutions with office locations around the globe, including Singapore, the United Kingdom, Australia, Mexico, Brazil, and Japan. Locate your local office at **www.cengage.com/global**

Cengage Learning products are represented in Canada by
Nelson Education, Ltd.

To learn more about Delmar, visit **www.cengage.com/delmar**

Purchase any of our products at your local bookstore or at our preferred online store **www.cengagebrain.com**

Notice to the Reader
Publisher does not warrant or guarantee any of the products described herein or perform any independent analysis in connection with any of the product information contained herein. Publisher does not assume, and expressly disclaims, any obligation to obtain and include information other than that provided to it by the manufacturer. The reader is expressly warned to consider and adopt all safety precautions that might be indicated by the activities described herein and to avoid all potential hazards. By following the instructions contained herein, the reader willingly assumes all risks in connection with such instructions. The publisher makes no representations or warranties of any kind, including but not limited to, the warranties of fitness for particular purpose or merchantability, nor are any such representations implied with respect to the material set forth herein, and the publisher takes no responsibility with respect to such material. The publisher shall not be liable for any special, consequential, or exemplary damages resulting, in whole or part, from the readers' use of, or reliance upon, this material.

Printed in the United States of America
2 3 4 5 6   23 22 21 20 19

Contents

Chapter 4   **Legal and Ethical Considerations**   **55**

Preface

Our health care system is in great need of help. There is never enough money and this shortage fuels concerns regarding the ability of facilities of all sizes to continue to provide quality services. Some erroneously feel that compliance eats away at the insufficient reimbursement amounts available. This is why I wrote this book. More often than not, health information management compliance, whether with regard to the Health Insurance Portability and Accountability Act (HIPAA) or coding and billing claims, has been shown to improve revenues.

My hopes are that this book can promote compliance and assist health information professionals to guide their departments and organizations to legally obtain optimal reimbursement and develop systems for all aspects of protecting our patients, our facilities, and ourselves.

Audience

This book is meant for any post-secondary and graduate school with a health information management program: certificate, diploma, associate's, bachelor's, or master's degree. These programs may be called: health information technology, health information management, or medical billing and coding.

The book can also be used in high schools with health care magnet programs. Health care facilities (physicians' offices, clinics, ambulatory care centers, nursing homes, and hospitals) can benefit those developing and running internal training programs.

Organization of this Text

The book is organized in a fashion that logically walks the reader through the process of developing a successful compliance program.

Chapter 1 explains the rationale for developing a program, and is followed by chapter 2, which details the role of the compliance officer.

Chapter 3 outlines the components of an effective program, while chapter 4 establishes the foundation of the program with reviews of applicable laws and regulations and ethical considerations.

Chapters 5, 6, and 7 investigate specific details regarding compliance with patient consent, documentation, and reporting, respectively.

Chapter 8 walks the reader through methodology for creating organizational policies and procedures, followed by chapter 9, which discusses educating and training staff for compliant behaviors.

Chapters 10 and 11 review processes for conducting both internal and external audits, respectively.

Chapter 12 discusses the importance of keeping the program current and provides insights for staying up-to-date on new laws and regulations.

Finally, chapter 13 outlines the importance of dealing with non-compliance and shares methods for determining effective and appropriate enforcement actions.

Features

- *Case Studies* are included in every chapter. These are all excerpts from actual cases investigated by the Office of the Inspector General, the Federal Bureau of Investigation, the Internal Revenue Service, Blue Cross Blue Shield Fraud Task Force, and more.
- *It's The Law* features excerpts from laws and regulations written by Congress or any of the many administrative agencies that oversee health care compliance
- *Sticky Notes* provide tips and short insights
- *Examples* are peppered throughout the text to illustrate the actual application of those concepts and strategies presented.
- *Chapter Review Quizzes* are located at the end of every chapter to help measure learning of key concepts.
- *Chapter Research and Discussion Activities* provided at the end of each chapter give the reader additional, hands-on learning opportunities to help take learning to the next level.

Supplements

The student learning package includes appendices with:

- Health Care Compliance Association (HCCA) Certified in Healthcare Compliance (CHC) Examination: Test Outline and Map to Text
- Abbreviations and Acronyms
- Professional Associations
- Professional Designations
- Reference Websites
- Glossary

The teaching package includes a separate instructor's manual with:

- Answer keys for all chapter review quizzes
- Sample lesson plans for both 8- and 16-week length courses
- Mapping to the HCCA national certification exam

About the Author

Shelley C. Safian is an associate professor of health information technology at Central Florida College in Winter Park, Florida.

Shelley was asked to investigate the requirements to be a coding and billing specialist for a special project many years ago. The results of that research led her to go back to school to study and become a nationally certified coding specialist. When asked about going back to school more than 25 years after getting her bachelor's degree, she says, "You are never too old to learn something new and get excited about it!" And she means that. In the last several years, Shelley went on to get a Graduate Certificate in Health Services Management, a companion to her master's degree in Organizational Management. She is also a certified HIPAA administrator, and is now certified in coding for both hospital and physician services. She is currently in the process of earning her PhD in Health Care Administration.

Since July 2005, Shelley has written four other books in the health information management genre: *Insurance Coding and Electronic Claims for the Medical Office, The Complete Procedure Coding Book, The Complete Diagnosis Coding Book,* and *You Code It! A Case Studies Workbook.*

Shelley is an enthusiastic, passionate, and knowledgeable educator who uses humor, real-world experiences, and current events to make learning enjoyable for her students.

Acknowledgements

This book is dedicated to my parents, Harriet and Jack Safian, who taught me to be diligent, to work hard, and to always try. I am who I am as a direct result of who they are . . . and I appreciate that.

I also want to thank Casa Price and Rhonda Dearborn for bringing me into the Cengage family. This is an honor for me.

Avenue for Feedback

Questions? Comments? Ideas to share? Contact the author at professorsafian@embarqmail.com.

Shelley C. Safian
Shelley C. Safian, MAOM/HSM, CCS-P, CPC-H, CHA

Reviewers

Patrice Jackson
Health Information Instructor
Heald College
Mililani, Hawaii

Myra L. Allen
Department Chair, Healthcare Management Technology
Fayetteville Technical Community College
Fayetteville, NC

Kristyn Rodvill, MHA, RHIA
Program Chair, HIT
DeVry University
Decatur, GA

Debbie Long, MS, RHIA, RHIT, CCS
Lamar Institute of Technology
Beaumont, TX

Debra Tymico, BA, RT(R)
Allied Health Department Chair
Brown Mackie College
Akron, OH

Nena Scott, MSEd, RHIA, CCS, CCSP
Program Director, Health Information Technology
Itawamba Community College
Tupelo, MS

Valerie Schmidt-Prater, MBA, RHIA
Program Director, HIM
DeVry University
Chicago, IL

Mary A. Bowman, MPA, RHIS
Devry University
Chicago, IL

Deb Honsted
Instructor, HIT Online Program
San Juan College
Farmington, NM

Sandra K. Rains, MBA, RHIA
Chairperson, HIT program
DeVry University
Columbus, OH

Chapter 1

Introduction to Compliance Programs

Learning Outcomes

- Determine the importance of a compliance program
- Distinguish between myth and fact when it comes to compliance
- Explain the value of a compliance program to a health care facility
- Identify the components of an effective compliance program
- Classify the benefits of implementing a compliance program

Key Terms

alleged / thought to have happened, but not yet proven

audit / an official review of work product for correctness

certificate of medical necessity (CMN) / a document, signed by the attending physician, that supports a medical reason for a patient requiring equipment, such as a wheelchair or cane

CMPL / civil monetary penalty laws

compliance / the act of obeying, or following rules

conspiracy / a plan between two or more people to commit a crime

defendants / persons or organizations accused of wrongdoing in a civil or criminal legal action

durable medical equipment (DME) / health care equipment designed to assist a patient with continued care, such as a nebulizer, or with improved quality of life, such as a wheelchair. These items are long-lasting or can be used for more than one patient

incarceration / imprisonment or confinement; putting someone in jail or prison

joint and several / each individual involved is responsible for the entire amount of the debt, judgment, or penalty

laws / the rules of behavior as determined by an authority

repercussions / consequences or results of one's actions

respondeat superior / a legal concept assigning responsibility and liability to a supervisor or person in charge for the actions of an employee

restitution / paying back money received fraudulently

unbundled / the practice of coding several services individually rather than using one combination code

Chapter Case Study

"On March 4, 2008, in Toledo, Ohio, Paul M. Neumann was sentenced to 37 months in prison to be followed by three years of supervised release. Timothy D. Neumann was sentenced on February 25, 2008, to 33 months in prison to be followed by three years of supervised release. Both defendants were each ordered to pay $1,710,725 in restitution, a $75,000 fine, a $200 special assessment fee, and $550,000 for the cost of prosecution. Paul and Tim Neumann were charged in August 2005 with one count of conspiracy to commit health care fraud and one count of conspiracy to commit money laundering. The charges related to the defendants' ownership and/or operation of the former MedBack chiropractic/medical clinics in Toledo, Oregon, Bowling Green, Fremont, Findlay, Bryan, and Sandusky. The Informations alleged that, from June 1997 to October 2000, the defendants caused the MedBack clinics to submit $4,860,017 in false billings for non-covered chiropractic services to Medicare, Medicaid, BWC, Medical Mutual of Ohio, Anthem, TriCare, and other health care benefit programs. The Informations further alleged these health care benefit programs paid the MedBack clinics $1,710,725 based on the allegedly false bills. The Informations also alleged that the defendants conspired to commit money laundering by using money derived from the alleged fraudulent billing scheme to make $1,589,439 in salary payments to the MedBack medical doctors, thereby allowing the fraudulent billing scheme to continue." (http://www.irs.gov)

Introduction

There are many government agencies charged with overseeing the provision of health care services in the United States. Federal and state legislatures write and enact statutory **laws**. In addition, administrative agencies have been given the authority to enact regulations, known as administrative laws, that have the same force as statutory laws focused on their specific area of expertise, such as the Internal Revenue Service (IRS), the Department of Health and Human Services (HHS), or the Centers for Medicare and Medicaid Services (CMS).

The agencies, and the legislatures, enact laws and regulations to guide the various members of the health care industry as to their responsibilities. And the problem is just that: there are *so many* laws and regulations that a clear understanding of exactly what each of us should do in a particular situation may become almost impossible.

Once the laws have been written, they need to be interpreted and translated into a language that all health care staff can be familiar with. This is the basis for a **compliance** program—to interpret the laws and provide each staff member with an unmistakable understanding of what should and should not be done in the course of their job performance.

Myths About Compliance

Health care administrators around the country, in facilities of all types and sizes, deal in some manner with the challenge of getting managers, clinicians, and staff to care about following the rules and regulations. So, let's begin with some common myths that are being heard in the hallways of physicians' offices, hospitals, nursing homes, and all other types of health care facilities, and investigate their basis in fact—or not. The Office of the Inspector General (OIG) website publishes many examples of cases that have gone through the courts along with the result of actual charges being filed.

Myth #1: Our company is too small to get caught—they only go after big health care facilities like hospital corporations.

False, according to the Office of the Inspector General:

*"April 2007: In Ohio, a former owner of a home health agency was sentenced to 97 months in prison and ordered to pay $2.7 million in **restitution** pursuant to her conviction for her scheme to defraud the Government. The investigation revealed that, from October 2001 through May 2003, Medicaid was billed for skilled nursing services that were not rendered as claimed. The woman billed for 14 hours of services per week when actually only 1 hour or less of services was provided per week. During the trial, it was also revealed that the woman instructed employees to falsify nursing notes."* (http://www.oig.hhs.gov)

*"April 2007: In Washington, D.C., a physician was sentenced to five months **incarceration** and ordered to pay $155,000 in restitution for health care fraud. From October 2001 through March 2003, the physician submitted claims to Medicare for Reteplase injections that were not given. Reteplase is a drug generally given in a hospital emergency room within the first three hours of a patient experiencing myocardial infarction (commonly referred to as a "heart attack"). The doctor submitted claims for one patient who purportedly had been injected 119 times."* (http://www.oig.hhs.gov)

These are good examples of individuals, not part of any large hospital, who surely thought they would never get caught. Services were provided to patients in their private homes where no one could see. Certainly, the patients themselves couldn't tell the difference, so how would anyone know? It is hard to believe, but the physician mentioned in the second case is certain to have thought that no one would notice that he injected this same patient so many times.

Just because the services are provided to indigent patients in their homes rather than in health care facilities does not mean that no one will discover the deceit.

As technology becomes increasingly involved in every aspect of health care, computers make assessment quite simple. Comparisons and statistical analyses of data are much easier than ever before because it no longer takes several individuals reading through hundreds of claim forms. One click of a mouse and an investigator can have a software program run through thousands of claim forms in a matter of hours, producing a report of patterns in inaccurate coding, overcoding, or other potential violations.

Myth #2: They only go after the physicians.

False, according to the Office of the Inspector General:

"March 2007: In Virginia, a personal care aide, who devised a scheme to defraud the Medicaid program, was sentenced to five months in jail and ordered to pay $58,000 in **joint and several** *restitution. Three co-defendants were previously sentenced for their involvement in the fraud scheme and held jointly liable for the restitution amount. The personal care aides caused the Medicaid program to pay for services not rendered by falsifying time sheets and personal care aide logs."* (http://www.oig.hhs.gov)

"March 2007: In Tennessee, the owner of a Texas **durable medical equipment (DME)** *supplier was sentenced to 18 months in prison and ordered to pay $432,000 in restitution for violating the anti-kickback statute. Investigation revealed that the owner paid kickbacks of $1,000 for each* **certificate of medical necessity (CMN)** *she received. The CMNs were then used to bill Medicare for motorized wheelchairs for patients who had no need for the wheelchair. Patients either received no wheelchair at all or were provided with a less expensive scooter."* (http://www.oig.hhs.com)

Every health care worker is either a part of the problem or the solution. Every individual involved in the health care team is equally responsible for complying with the laws, and this includes the physician, the office manager, the biller, and anyone else involved in participating in illegal behavior or trying to cover it up. In the case from Tennessee, the OIG and the state attorney general prosecuted a business owner who probably never took any health care courses, much less graduated from medical school. As you look through the many cases prosecuted throughout the United States, you will see that clerks, assistants, coders, billers, laboratory technicians—anyone who breaks the law—can be charged.

If you have ever taken a course in law, you might be familiar with the legal term **respondeat superior**. The original Latin phrase translates literally to "Let the master answer," and it has come to mean that the physician is responsible for the behaviors of his or her employees in our legal system. While this is often true, it does not remove the legal liability of the staff member. A criminal is a criminal and the government does not discriminate. Laws have been expanded to find that everyone on the health care team involved in fraud is responsible. So, for example, if the coder consistently submits claims containing codes for procedures not properly documented, both the coder and the physician can be charged with fraud.

Myth #3: They are not going to bother with a small physician's practice.

False, according to the Office of the Inspector General:

"February 2007: In Florida, a physician was sentenced to 24 months incarceration and ordered to pay $727,000 in restitution for his involvement in a health care fraud scheme. For cash payments, the physician signed blank prescriptions and certificates of medical necessity for patients he never saw. In turn, co-conspirators submitted claims to Medicare for DME and other items or services that were either not medically necessary or were not provided to beneficiaries." (http://www.oig.hhs.gov)

"January 2007: In Arizona, a podiatrist sentenced for theft of Government money was ordered to pay $55,000 in restitution. The podiatrist provided non-covered routine foot care services to beneficiaries but billed Medicare as if he performed nail avulsions or debridements." (http://www.oig.hhs.gov)

It does not require a large practice with many physicians to commit fraud. Actually, employees of small practices may be more susceptible to getting caught because they believe their size keeps them under the radar of government agencies. Very often, the conversations between defendants like these begin with a phrase like, *"Come on, who's going to know?"* These cases clearly answer this question.

There have also been discussions heard between professionals when the topics of non-compliance and the potential penalties that can be faced come up. They have said, "It's true that the law says we might be penalized or go to jail, but that hardly ever happens." The question to ask yourself, and your co-workers, is: Are you really wanting to roll the dice? If there is a 1-in-100 chance that you will be caught, 99 people have confirmed that it won't happen to them. What if you are the one—the *one*—who gets caught?

Smaller companies may, inadvertently, open themselves up to greater liabilities. When a practice is understaffed and desperate to bring in additional personnel, a thorough background check or legitimate credentials confirmation may not get done. Another concern may be the closeness between members of the staff. While it is very gratifying to work in a place where people trust each other, legally this can result in problems. For example, just because Janice is the physician's sister does not mean she knows the laws and guidelines affecting reimbursement. Janice's willingness to help in the family business could unintentionally result in charges of fraud.

Myth #4: They only go after facilities in big cities like New York or Los Angeles.

False, according to the Office of the Inspector General:

"January 2007: In South Dakota, an attorney was sentenced to three months incarceration and ordered to pay $9,000 in restitution for health care fraud and false claims. The attorney falsely claimed to be part Native American Indian so she could receive free health care services from the Indian Health Service." (http://www.oig.hhs.gov)

"January 2007: In Idaho, a man was sentenced to four months imprisonment, four months home confinement and ordered to pay a $5,000 fine for **conspiracy***. The man, who worked for*

a DME supplier, orchestrated a Medicare fraud scheme that included falsifying and forging certificates of medical necessity for oxygen services and supplies." (http://www.oig.hhs.gov)

The OIG works together with the attorney general and law enforcement agencies of each state, as well as other agencies, to investigate health care facilities and their **alleged** failure to comply with any of the many laws and regulations that govern the business of health care. Those in small towns and out-of-the-way places are not exempt from the law.

The federal False Claims Act (FCA) has a provision called *Qui Tam*. This portion of the statute, also known as the Whistleblower statute, permits an individual to bring suit against a company based on his or her knowledge of the fraudulent activity. In addition to doing the right thing, the informer, usually a former employee, filing the suit can receive up to 30 percent of the monies recovered by the government as a reward.

CASE STUDY

"Qui Tam Plaintiff filed an action in the United States District Court for the Western District of Washington, captioned as *United States of America ex tel. Steven T. Hubbard v. Fire Protection District No. 5, Mason County, et al.,* No. C94-5454RJB (hereafter "the Litigation") alleging that Defendants submitted invoices for payment by the United States from 1989 to the present which involved three types of false or fraudulent claims: (i) co-payment waivers, (ii) billing Medicare and Medicaid for Advanced Life Support services when Basic Life Support services were provided or where Advanced Life Support services were not medically necessary, and (iii) billing Medicare and Medicaid for transportation services provided by other entities. *Qui Tam* Plaintiff alleged that these false claims gave rise to a civil action under the False Claims Act, 31 U.S.C. §§ 3729-3.

"1. **Payment by Defendants.** In settlement and compromise of the above-referenced claims, Defendants agree to pay to the United States, within seven days of entry of the Order set forth in Exhibit A, the sum of Eighty Thousand Dollars ($80,000). This sum shall be delivered to Michael F. Hertz, Director, Commercial Litigation Branch, Civil Division, Department of Justice, P.O. Box 261, Ben Franklin Station, Washington, D.C., 20530, in the form of a cashier's or certified check made payable to the United States Treasury. In addition, pursuant to 31 U.S.C. § 3730(d)(2), Defendants agree to pay to *Qui Tam* Plaintiff the sum of Eighty Thousand Dollars ($80,000) for attorneys' fees and costs."

(http://www.usdoj.gov)

Myth #5: They only go after issues of malpractice when patients get hurt.

False, according to the Office of the Inspector General:

"May 2006: In North Carolina, an ambulance company and its owner were sentenced related to billing Medicare and Medicaid for dialysis patient transports that were not medically necessary. The owner was sentenced to 120 months in jail for health care fraud and to an additional 31 months in jail (to be run consecutively) for obstruction. The company and the owner were also ordered to pay $604,000 in joint and several restitution. Investigation revealed that emergency medical technicians were instructed to enter false information on ambulance reports falsely indicating patients required an ambulance when, in fact, they did not and could have

been transported by other means. The owner also instructed billing personnel to submit claims indicating that patients were bed-confined when, in fact, they were not bed-confined. In addition, prior to an audit, the owner and the billing manager changed records to indicate medical necessity. The owner also intentionally withheld subpoenaed documents. The billing manager was previously sentenced and was ordered to pay $30,000, a portion of the joint and several restitution amount." (http://www.oig.hhs.gov)

"February 16, 2006: Two south Florida pulmonologists agreed to pay $65,066 and $57,030, respectively, and enter into a three-year Integrity Agreement to resolve their liability under the Anti-Kickback Statute provision of the **CMPL** and the Stark Law. The OIG alleged that the physicians violated those laws by accepting gifts, including Miami Dolphins tickets and meals, from a durable medical equipment (DME) supplier in exchange for patient referrals." (http://www.oig.hhs.gov)

There are many laws and regulations that can result in civil and/or criminal actions against individuals and/or the facility other than malpractice. In addition to the anti-kickback statute in the case above, licensure regulations regarding the practice of the physician, nurse, and other professionals, and laws governing confidentiality, such as the Health Insurance Portability and Accountability Act (HIPAA)'s privacy rule, are examples of laws, other than malpractice, that can be violated.

While "following the rules" can be perceived as interference in the day-to-day business of caring for patients, the laws serve a purpose. If nothing else, compliance ensures that the facility can continue to care for its patients, and no one will have to go to jail or prison, and thousands of dollars will not have to be paid out in fines, penalties, and restitution.

Myth #6: Only those facilities that work with Medicare patients have to worry.

False, according to Blue Cross Blue Shield of Nebraska:

"A pharmacist was found guilty of billing for brand name prescription drugs when generic equivalents were supplied. He was given a one-year deferred sentence and ordered to pay a $5,000 fine and restitution to the victims." (http://www.bcbsne.com)

"A psychologist was sentenced for five counts of forgery, false information claims, and grand theft. He served a 30-day prison term and two years probation, and paid restitution to the victims. The psychologist admitted to billing one patient for 57 sessions when the patient had only seen the psychologist once." (http://www.bcbsne.com)

Unfortunately, fraud is not only perpetrated against the federal government. There are individuals who file false claims with the intent to steal money from state agencies and private insurers as well.

The state of Georgia, like most other states, has established the State Health Care Fraud Control Unit (SHCFCU). This agency is responsible for investigating and prosecuting physicians, dentists, hospitals, nursing homes, and other health care providers that treat Medicaid recipients. The Georgia Bureau of Investigation, the Georgia State Attorney General's Office, and the Georgia Department of Audits and Accounts work together to run the SHCFCU.

The Blue Cross Blue Shield Association has an active National Anti-Fraud Department (NAFD) in charge of coordinating a national multi-jurisdictional strike force that works to detect, prevent, and investigate health care fraud, as well as to get restitution for monies paid out improperly.

In addition, the OIG established the Partnership Plan to work with state auditors conducting joint reviews of health care facilities that provide services to Medicaid beneficiaries.

Most organizations have created departments or divisions whose sole purpose is to investigate health care facilities of all sizes with the intention of diminishing the amount of money that is paid out in false claims. Fraud is a crime, regardless of the target.

Myth #7: We've been doing it for years this way and we have never had a problem.

False. Take a careful look at the first two cases under Myth #1, copied from postings on the OIG website dated April 2007. You can see that the fraudulent behaviors occurred from 2001 through 2003. It takes a long time to do an investigation.

An investigation begins when a sequence of fraudulent behaviors is identified. For example, an **audit** will not be opened if your office **unbundled** one or two claims. They understand human error. The claim will be rejected or denied with the expectation that you will correct the error and learn not to do this again. As you will learn later in this textbook, one of the benefits of a compliance program is to give your department the opportunity to catch errors and prevent them from happening again.

Once a few errors have been earmarked, the investigative unit, whether it is internal, such as Blue Cross Blue Shield's NAFD, or the OIG may then monitor your facility's claims over the course of the next 12–24 months to watch for a continuing pattern. When there is evidence of a continuous submission of claims with unbundled codes from your office going on for a year or two, then an official investigation will be initiated.

Even at this point, the individuals in the health care office are not typically aware of the investigation. Documentation may be gathered from past years. Once a fraudulent behavior is suspected, the investigator will often go back over claims submitted in previous years, adding evidence to the suspicion that the fraud is not an innocent human error but instead intentional fraudulent behavior. In addition, affiliated facilities (such as hospitals at which your office has admitted patients, or an imaging center often used for patient X-rays) will possibly be contacted with a request for documentation related to the suspicious cases. The data in their documentation will be compared with the data on the suspected officer's claims. The investigators may also contact the patients, looking for their confirmation or denial of specific conditions or procedures in regard to the questioned claims.

By the time your facility is notified of the investigation, it has been well underway for quite some time.

The Truth About These Myths

In 2000, the federal government collected $717 million resulting from health care fraud and abuse cases, of which more than $577 million was returned to the Medicare Trust Fund, and $27 million was recovered as the federal share of Medicaid restitution. In 2001, the Department of Justice (DOJ) reported that the federal government won or negotiated more than $1.2 billion from health care fraud cases and proceedings.

During 2006, the Federal Bureau of Investigation (FBI) probed 2423 cases of suspected health care fraud that resulted in 588 indictments and 534 convictions of health care fraud criminals, as well as collecting $1.6 billion in recoveries, $373 million in restitutions, $172.9 million in fines, and $24.3 million in confiscated items such as equipment.

The Miami office of the FBI announced on May 25, 2007 that they were indicting the defendants with criminal charges for allegedly billing Medicare fraudulently for approximately $101 million. That's just one case and the FBI is only one of the agencies of the federal government responsible for these types of investigations.

CASE STUDY

"On May 22, 2007, a Miami federal grand jury returned a 46-count indictment against eight defendants in United States v. Mabel Diaz, et al., No. 07-20398-Cr-Ungaro. The indictment charges Mabel and Abner Diaz, wife and husband, with operating All-Med Billing Corp. (All-Med), a Miami medical billing company, and executing a scheme to submit tens of millions of dollars in fraudulent claims to Medicare from 1998 to 2004 for reimbursement for durable medical equipment (DME) and related services. The indictment alleges that All-Med submitted approximately $80 million in false claims on behalf of 29 DME companies. The claims were allegedly fraudulent in that the equipment had not been ordered by a physician and/or had never been delivered to a Medicare patient. As a result of the submission of the fraudulent claims, Medicare paid the DME companies approximately $56 million. The indictment also seeks forfeiture of the fraud proceeds and substitute assets, including real estate of the Diazes. The Diazes were additionally charged with conspiracy to launder the proceeds of the alleged All-Med billing fraud scheme. Also charged in the All-Med billing fraud scheme was All-Med employee Suleidy Cano."

(http://miami.fbi.gov/dojpressrel/pressrel07/mm20070525.htm)

These statistics show that investigating and prosecuting health care fraud is very worthwhile. These numbers are cumulative, meaning that these huge sums are totaled from small charges here and there. One claim form submitted by a small physician's office for an extra $85 may be thought of as "no big deal" and not worth an investigation. But, multiply that $85 by ten patient claims per week and one physician has fraudulently gained over $44,000 in just one year.

What Is a Compliance Program?

It may be reasonable for a business to expect its professionals to know and obey the laws that govern its activities. However, having expectations is not enough. A formal compliance program is a written document designed to clearly express

> A successful compliance program is an on-going active awareness campaign for everyone involved with the organization to follow the laws, rules, and polices put in place by the federal and state governments, as well as the company itself.

what laws affect the facility, what behaviors are expected as a result of the law's directives, the company policies and procedures related to these legal behaviors, and the consequences that can be expected from not behaving in accordance.

The Benefits of a Compliance Program

The business of health care becomes more and more complex every day. New technology and research help individuals live longer, and preventive medicine protocols enable professionals to identify health care concerns early enough to enable a better quality of life. With all of this, health care must respond to an increase in federal and state laws and regulations. The government and the media scrutinize every aspect of the process. The creation of a compliance program helps health care practices and facilities of all sizes and types manage these issues more easily by breaking each law into manageable pieces and laying out clear guidelines.

The written documentation of this program is critical to:

- Ensure the complete understanding of all staff members;
- Provide consistent interpretation of the laws;
- Dismiss myths;
- Establish clear guidelines for behaviors;
- Create safe methods for the reporting of alleged violations internally;
- Enact corrective behaviors before the authorities get involved;
- Institute groundwork for internal audits.

Let's review some of the key benefits.

Create a Framework for Success

The structure supplied by a compliance program can help the members of the department or facility adjust to policies and procedures more easily. Outlines and templates providing step-by-step instructions for what actions should be taken when handling particular situations give all staff members the confidence and sense of empowerment to do the right thing. This works to protect the staff, the patient, and the organization.

The OIG states that health care organizations should:

- Concretely demonstrate to employees and the community at large the hospital's strong commitment to honest and responsible provider and corporate conduct;
- Provide a more accurate view of employee and contractor behavior relating to fraud and abuse;
- Identify and prevent criminal and unethical conduct;
- Tailor a compliance program to a hospital's specific needs;
- Improve the quality of patient care.

It is the actions of the organization that speak loudest to the staff and the patients about caring, ethics, and legal behaviors. The most effective way to "concretely demonstrate" the importance of "honest and responsible" behavior is to enforce policies and rules, promote openness for the reporting of violations, and reward good behavior. A formal compliance program can accomplish all these things.

Generate a Foundation of Knowledge

If everyone understood the laws involved, as well as the importance of following these laws and doing the correct thing all the time, rules and regulations would not be necessary. However, humans are not perfect, so these controls must be put into place. When it comes to health care, the first problem may lie with the fact that not all health care workers (clinicians, professionals, managers, and staff alike) know enough of the specifics of the laws to actually follow them. There are far too many individuals working in physician's offices, nursing homes, and hospitals that do not know about anti-kickback statutes, and far fewer understand the actual parameters of fraudulently coding for coverage. Many health care professionals do not fully understand the details of the federal False Claims Act or how it can impact their facility if they are found to be guilty of non-compliance.

Ignorance of the law is not a defense. As a matter of fact, virtually every law is written including the phrase *"knows or should know."* This means that the obligation to know and understand all applicable laws and regulations relating to the particular job one is doing is included in the requirements of the laws themselves. HIPAA, for example, actually requires each health care facility to educate their staff completely about their responsibility under the Privacy Rule. Failure to provide evidence of this education, when requested by an investigator, is actionable.

Realistically, if the staff does not know the law, how can they be expected to make the right decisions? In an industry like health care, things change so quickly. Organizations that don't value continuing education and training are not only practicing bad business, they may be contributing to the decline of the quality of the care they provide and increasing their liability. Virtually every aspect of the industry has changed dramatically over the last few decades, and these transformations continue at a rapid pace. Think about it . . . computers barely interacted with health care just fifteen years ago, and now these incredible machines assist in performing surgery, keeping a heart pulsing regularly from within a patient's body, and transmiting the billing and payment transactions. HIPAA wasn't active ten years ago, and Present on Admission codes, and the Physician's Quality Reporting Initiative (PQRI) didn't exist until 2007.

Awareness both of current issues and those still under evaluation must provide a framework for the organization to promote an atmosphere that encourages ongoing learning. These positive elements contribute dramatically to the success of the organization.

Establish an Environment of Honesty

Being proactive with your staff about these legal concepts, having this supported by company policies and procedures for compliance, and reinforcing the policies with clearly stated **repercussions** for non-compliance demonstrate that the organization is dedicated to providing care to its patients in an honest and responsible manner.

Written standards of conduct are important components of the organization's ability to establish that it takes its legal obligations seriously. Additionally, these policies provide the guidelines or templates for decision-making by all members of the company so that being in compliance and protecting the patients, the staff, and the facility is a known common course of action.

Typically, one important manifestation of these written standards is that ensuring compliance becomes everyone's job, not just the responsibility of the compliance officer or upper management. Everyone within the organization will be able to identify and prevent (or help to prevent) criminal and immoral conduct. When staff members know that their management will back them up, they will work to reinforce the rules. An environment that promotes ethical and legal behaviors is one that will encourage employees to report potential problems internally, enabling the facility to correct the problem before a violation or complaint is filed.

Improve Service to Patients

The substantive nature of most of the laws and regulations affecting health care organizations actually seeks to improve the level of care provided to patients. For example, the Joint Commission provides guidelines for the completion of documentation after each patient encounter.

Complying with this directive will not only make the next audit go more smoothly but work toward patient safety because the next health care professional will have all the pertinent information necessary to make better diagnostic and treatment decisions.

When documentation is completed in a timely manner, the information is available to ensure better continuity of care. It is access to these notes that will ensure that the assistant at the front desk processes the referral for a diagnostic test. The Joint Commission includes in its patient safety goals that *"Effective communication, which is timely, accurate, complete, unambiguous, and understood by the recipient, reduces error and results in improved [patient] safety."*

The Annuals of Internal Medicine reported in their October 2006 issue that 48 percent of physician errors were due to *"too little knowledge."* This makes sense, doesn't it? How can a physician hope to care for a patient properly without critical information, such as current medications and previous conditions—information found in the patient's chart. How can a treatment plan be implemented for a patient without the test results?

Health information management is an integral part of patient care excellence. It is this department that enables all of the individuals on a health care team—the attending physician, the specialist, the therapist, the nurse, the medical assistant, the lab technician, the radiology technician, the radiologist, the pathologist, the family members— to know what is necessary to help the patient maintain and reattain good health.

> **EXAMPLE** Dr. Thomas told Nurse Samms that Benita must be NPO (nothing by mouth—no food or water) because he might need to take her into surgery in the next few hours, depending upon the results of her CT scan. Dr. Thomas did not write this on Benita's chart. Nurse Samms

was busy with another patient when Denise, the patient care technician, came into Benita's room to check on her. Benita begged for some water because she was so very thirsty. Denise checked her chart, and upon seeing no orders to the contrary, gave Benita a cup of water. Surgery had to be delayed because of this, endangering Benita's health. The flow of information is critical to patient care.

Minimize Loss

When the system of documentation (information) flows smoothly, claims can be created and submitted to third-party payers for reimbursement sooner. Coders have the necessary amount of time to read the physician's notes and operative reports, abstract them properly, and ask the attending physician for clarifications. Having this system in place increases the percentage of claims being paid. This reduces the number of claims rejected or denied, making sure the organization will get the money it earned. This revenue can then be available to fund capital expenses, such as new equipment, necessary medical supplies, additional staff, or perhaps the annual bonuses.

Think about the cases from the OIG shown earlier in this chapter. A total of $4,897,096 (four million, eight hundred ninety-seven thousand, ninety-six dollars) in monetary judgments from only ten cases! This is just the beginning of the financial impact because each of these facilities lost more money from employee hours spent gathering information, sitting for depositions, and appearing in court rather than doing their jobs. They also had to potentially pay attorneys' fees, administrative costs, civil damages and penalties. Future revenue is lost if the physician and/or facility are excluded from participating with Medicare, Medicaid, or any other third-party payer.

Reduce Liability

There are many ways a compliance plan can actually reduce a health care facility's liability from non-compliance.

1. The internal audit section of the compliance plan will help identify areas of concern early and give the administration of the facility the opportunity to correct the problems before a complaint can be filed or an investigation ensues. It is logical, and good business, to find out if one of your coders is not doing a very good job, or if the person working in patient records never asks for signed releases before handing over copies of patient information, before a federal investigator shows up at your door.

2. When management creates an environment of proper corporate conduct, staff members tend to follow their lead and work in a positively oriented atmosphere to not only avoid illegal actions, but to stay out of those gray areas of concern. Educating staff members about the specific requirements of laws that affect them, and supporting that with a corporate attitude of honesty, will automatically reduce the number of times a law or rule is broken. Subsequently, there will be fewer opportunities to be found guilty of fraud and abuse, thereby reducing those occasions where the organization may be financially fined, penalized, or be required to return monies received improperly.

Preventive medicine's purpose is to keep healthy patients healthy and to restore health to the sick more quickly and at a lower cost. The same concept works here. The implementation of a compliance program will contribute to a reduction in unlawful or unethical conduct and reduce the facility's liability from the outset. Fewer violations within the organization translate into fewer investigations from government and legal regulators.

3. In some cases, a compliance program can be used to establish the intent of an organization to work within the law and result in lower penalties if found guilty. While this is not guaranteed, it has been known to be a positive point of consideration in the assessment of fines and other penalties. Federal Sentencing Guidelines, promoted by the United States Sentencing Commission, will apply good corporate behavior "credits" to organizational **defendants** that can prove the existence and implementation of a compliance program designed to detect and deter fraud, waste, and abuse. A facility found guilty of violating federal criminal laws that has an active compliance program created according to the seven elements of a compliance program, as put forth by the U.S. Sentencing Guidelines for Organizations, may have its assessed penalties cut by as much as 70 percent against the fines that the law requires, according to the Health Care Compliance Association.

Mandatory Compliance Programs

Deficit Reduction Act

Section 6032 of the Deficit Reduction Act of 2005, which took effect on January 1, 2007, compels health care organizations that receive payments from Medicaid of $5 million or more per year to create and implement a compliance program. The law specifies that the program must provide written policies for all employees and contractors detailing their responsibilities under the False Claims Act, including:

- Clearly understandable policies and procedures for preventing fraud, waste, and abuse
- Methods for exposing non-compliance
- Internal, civil, and criminal penalties for false claims and statements
- Protections for whistleblowers

In addition, this law requires that health care organizations' employee handbooks include their specific protections for whistleblowers, as well as a reiteration of the facilities' policies and procedures for the prevention of fraud, waste, and abuse.

Pay for Performance

The concept of pay for performance (P4P) programs is not new to business and has been merged into health care reimbursement plans since 2005, when Medicare released its P4P initiative. These policies, now adopted by many public and private agencies and insurers, are designed to encourage quality improvement in patient care and enhance health outcomes.

The Centers for Medicare and Medicaid Services provide financial rewards for those physicians who meet or exceed their established performance standards in clinical delivery systems and patient outcomes in their care of Medicare beneficiaries. The essence of P4P systems is to directly connect compensation with work quality and goal-based achievements.

The evolution of P4P programs may mature as time goes by and standards and goals are refined and more closely identified. This program, along with other bonus payments programs such as the Physicians Quality Reporting Initiative (PQRI) instituted by CMS, all have accurate data and efficient reporting methods—the management of the information—at their core.

Medicaid Fraud Control Units (MFCU)

In 1977, federal funding was authorized for the creation of State Medicaid Fraud Control Units (SMFCUs) by the enactment of the Medicare and Medicaid Anti-Fraud and Abuse Amendment. Each state's unit, like the one in Georgia discussed earlier, is responsible for the investigation, and prosecution, of providers who allegedly abuse and neglect Medicaid beneficiaries, or enable fraud against these patients.

> **EXAMPLE** "The Alaska Medicaid Fraud Control Unit (MFCU) has been part of the Attorney General's Office since January 1992. The unit is located in Anchorage and has statewide jurisdiction. It has the responsibility for investigating and prosecuting Medicaid fraud and the abuse, neglect or financial exploitation of patients in any facility that accepts Medicaid funds. The Director of the MFCU is Assistant Attorney General Donald R. Kitchen, a career criminal prosecutor with more than a quarter century of experience in the criminal justice system. There are 47 MFCUs across the U.S." (http://www.law.state.ak.us/department/criminal/mfcu.html)

CASE STUDY

MEDICAID FRAUD CONTROL UNIT RECOVERS $100,000 IN SETTLEMENT WITH WESTCHESTER MENTAL HEALTH CENTER

The Medicaid Fraud Control Unit (MFCU) of the Office of the Attorney General today announced that the Mental Health Association of Westchester County, Inc. (MHAW), has agreed to repay more than $100,000 to taxpayers for services that the organization failed to properly document as having provided to Medicaid recipients.

"The taxpayer-funded Medicaid program was designed to assist citizens in need," said Thomas F. Staffa, Acting MFCU Co-Director. "This financial recovery will go a long way in ensuring that those needs are being properly met."

The settlement is based on an audit conducted by the MFCU. In reviewing the Medicaid billing records for MHAW, the audit revealed that, between January 1996 and October 1999,

(Continues)

CASE STUDY (*Continued*)

the organization received Medicaid reimbursement for outpatient clinic services that either were not supported by entries in recipients' charts or that were for services different from those documented in the charts. As a result, MHAW has agreed to make restitution of $108,414 to the Medicaid program.

"Once the problem was brought to the attention of the organization, it cooperated fully with the investigation and readily agreed to reimburse the State," said Acting MFCU Co-Director Karen I. Lupuloff.

In 1999, MFCU redirected resources by putting greater emphasis on fulfilling the unit's statutory mandate of identifying those health care providers who were improperly billing the state's $28 billion Medicaid program. Over the last three years, this new approach to enforcement has resulted in the recovery of more than $58 million, a 300 percent increase in restitution.

(http://www.oag.state.ny.us/press/2002/jun/jun06c_02.html)

Chapter Summary

Investigations followed by civil and/or criminal convictions have led to billions of dollars being returned to the accounts of Medicare, Medicaid, third-party payers, and most importantly, to the people who pay premiums to these programs so they can receive care.

Many health care employees have come to believe the myths that they will not be discovered and are lulled into a false sense of security, only to end up penalized or in jail.

A compliance program can serve as a detailed road map to help prevent incidents of fraud and abuse within your department and your organization.

As you venture out to begin your new career, be a professional who looks to implement *best* practices, not *common* practices!

CHAPTER REVIEW

Multiple Choice Questions

1. Health care facilities that are exempt from fraud investigations include
   a. private physician practices.
   b. clinics and short-term acute care facilities.
   c. none; all facilities are subject to the law.
   d. hospitals with more than 500 beds.

2. If found guilty of fraud, an individual may be ordered to
   a. go to jail or prison.
   b. pay restitution.

   c. pay fines and penalties.

   d. all of the above

3. Virtually every law includes the phrase
   a. "admits to knowing."
   b. "knows or should know."
   c. "proven to be known."
   d. "may know."

4. Compliance in a health care organization is the responsibility of
   a. the physician.
   b. the president.
   c. the compliance officer.
   d. all employees, volunteers, and interns.

5. A formal compliance program may
   a. lessen fines and penalties.
   b. get in the way of good patient care.
   c. cost more money than it is worth.
   d. increase liability.

6. The Partnership Plan includes state auditors working with the
   a. OIG.
   b. FBI.
   c. DOJ.
   d. CMS.

7. SMFCU are delegated to investigate providers of
   a. Medicare services.
   b. Blue Cross Blue Shield services.
   c. Medicaid services.
   d. durable medical equipment.

8. The National Procurement Fraud Task Force prosecutes alleged violations of
   a. licensing and certification.
   b. conflict of interest.
   c. Joint Commission standards.
   d. embezzlement.

9. Anyone falsifying health care information is subject to
   a. possible jail time.
   b. possible monetary fines and penalties.
   c. exclusion from program participation.
   d. all of the above

10. A law is a(n)
    a. diagnostic statement.
    b. act of obeying.
    c. determination of the rules of behavior.
    d. corporate policy.

11. Health information professionals are responsible for
    a. following the law.
    b. doing as directed by the physician or manager.
    c. getting the facility paid above all else.
    d. getting claims out quickly.

12. *Restitution* is the order to
    a. pay penalties and late fees.
    b. place someone in prison.
    c. return all documents to their proper files.
    d. pay back money received fraudulently.

13. Physician's offices can be investigated by agents from
    a. the OIG.
    b. the FBI.
    c. the IRS.
    d. all of the above

14. If the office manager tells the coder to do something fraudulently, and the coder does it because she doesn't want to lose her job
    a. only the office manager can be charged with fraud.
    b. only the coder can be charged with fraud.
    c. only the physician can be charged with fraud.
    d. the coder is at the greatest risk for being charged.

15. A *Qui Tam* lawsuit is also known as the
    a. Premium recovery act.
    b. Whistleblower statute.
    c. Partnership provision.
    d. Fraud control unit.

Research and Discussion Project

1. Go to the website for your state, or another state of your choice, and review the information regarding that state's battle against health care fraud and abuse.
    a. In what ways are individuals able to report suspected violations?

    _____

    _____

    b. What types of cases have been successfully prosecuted?

    _____

    _____

    c. Compare and contrast one state's efforts to control health care fraud to another's.

    _____

    _____

    _____

2. How do the federal and state governments' efforts compare to those of private organizations such as Blue Cross Blue Shield, Prudential, Humana, or Aetna?

_____

_____

_____

3. What would you do if you discovered you were working for an individual or a company that did something similar to one of the cases you have seen in this chapter?

_____

_____

_____

4. Case Study Analysis: Research and discuss the key points of the case study below. What would you do if you were the compliance officer working for Otsuka American Pharmaceutical, Inc.?

_____

_____

_____

CASE STUDY

Monday, March 31, 2008

Japanese drug company will pay $4 million to settle FCA charges

Otsuka American Pharmaceutical Inc., the U.S. subsidiary of Japanese pharmaceutical manufacturer Otsuka Pharmaceutical Co., Ltd., will pay more than $4 million to resolve allegations that it marketed Abilify, an atypical antipsychotic drug, for "off-label" uses.

The Corporate Crime Reporter said that the Food and Drug Administration had approved Abilify to treat adult schizophrenia and bi-polar disorder but that the company promoted it for pediatric use. While physicians are allowed to prescribe drugs for "off-label" uses, companies are prohibited from promoting drugs for uses that aren't FDA approved.

The whistleblower in the suit will receive $348,000 as his relator's share.

Chapter 2

The Compliance Officer

Learning Outcomes

- Identify the major functions of the compliance officer
- Explain the need for the compliance officer's full authority
- Determine the qualifications for a compliance officer
- Assess the responsibilities of the compliance committee
- Enumerate the competencies of the HIM compliance officer

Key Terms

ambiguity / something that can be interpreted in more than one manner
analyze / to study something in great detail with the intent of better understanding its contents
auspices / the realm of responsibility of a job title, a department, or an organization
determine / to decide something conclusively
ethical / in agreement with accepted moral conduct
implement / to put into action
integrity / the personal characteristic of high moral principles and professional standards
retribution / a punishment for something someone has done
sanction / a punishment for failing to obey a law or rule
synthesized / the combining of different ideas into a new, cohesive unit

Chapter Case Study

"January 2007: In Michigan, a dentist was sentenced to 15 months in prison and ordered to pay $147,000 in restitution and a $50,000 fine for health care fraud. The dentist's husband was ordered

to pay almost $10,000 for making a false statement. The dentist submitted or caused to sub-
mit claims to insurers for services that were not rendered. The investigation revealed that
claims were for services rendered when the dentist was on travel or purportedly rendered by
the former owner of the practice who had been deceased since January 1996. In addition to
the fraud scheme, it was revealed that the dentist, who had been diagnosed with hepatitis, did
not disclose her condition to patients or take certain precautionary measures when treating
patients." (http://www.oig.hhs.com)

Introduction

Assuring that all members of a facility's health information management department
are compliant with legal and **ethical** standards is a complex job. Therefore, it is important to have one person designated as the health information management compliance
officer. The size of the department will **determine** whether or not this responsibility
becomes a full-time position or part of the job tasks assigned to someone already in
the department.

Health information management is a segment of the health care industry that has
many ethical and legal standards with which to comply. The individual in charge
must fully understand the day-to-day factors related to following the official guidelines of diagnosis and procedure coding (using all coding data sets), as well as those
issued by each and every third-party payer, federal and state laws, and the codes of
ethics set forth by our professional organizations, the American Health Information
Management Association (AHIMA) and American Academy of Professional Coders
(AAPC).

Primary Responsibilities

According to the Federal Register (Vol. 63, No. 35), every hospital should identify one
person to oversee and coordinate compliance within the organization. This mandate
for hospitals is not carried over to physician practices. However, the recommendation
for individual and small group physician practices is strong. The compliance officer's
responsibilities include:

- Creation and **implementation** of a detailed compliance program
- Maintenance of the program's effectiveness; making revisions as necessary
- Coordination of professional qualifications compliance for each appropriate staff
  member
- Education and training of all appropriate staff members
- Confirmation of compliance from outside vendors, as necessary
- Supervision of activities under the **auspices** of the program
- Development of internal reporting systems which encourage staff to report sus-
  pected violations without fear of **retribution**
- Performance of regular internal audits to assure compliance
- Investigation of reported violations

- Enforcement of penalties for non-compliance
- Taking corrective action when fraud and/or abuse is discovered
- Reporting to the organization's governing committee on a regular basis

The primary aspect of the compliance officer position is to serve as the heart of the entire compliance program. This is not solely a function of police work, figuratively ticketing those who jaywalk across the lines. This person should be one who stands as an icon of the department's, and the facility's, dedication to maintaining an honest, ethical business while still standing by their most important obligation—to care for their patients.

The best person for this job is one who understands the laws and ethics of the health information management industry and is able to create and communicate policies and procedures that make "doing the right thing" a normal part of the way to get the job done. There is an aspect of psychology involved in this. When designing the program, for example, it would be beneficial to predetermine how each compliant behavior involved will fuse into each staff position's regular workflow.

> **EXAMPLE** HIPAA's Privacy Rule requires patients to sign a release of information form before any data may be disclosed (with certain exceptions). The compliance officer should make certain these forms are easily accessible to staff. This may mean placing the forms in boxes near each workstation or including an electronic folder containing forms that can be printed out in a minute or two on everyone's computer desktop.

Many offices simply put their forms in a central location so that everyone has to walk down the hall to get what they need. However, this can provide a handy (though weak) excuse for non-compliance. It probably sounds ridiculous to think walking down a short hallway would actually stop someone from following the law, but it happens every day.

The flow of information through the office—from the clinicians to transcription to chart completion to coding to billing to appeals—should be smooth and include the components necessary to comply with various rules.

> **EXAMPLE** Richard, the coder, finds Dr. Jackson's notes from his encounter with Renee Zoneman to be incomplete, therefore preventing him from coding her diagnosis accurately. Richard should have a pre-existing format for querying Dr. Jackson for clarification.

The compliance officer should work with the clinical staff to work out an amenable system so questions can be answered quickly and accurately and the documentation can be amended appropriately. This can be accomplished using in/out boxes, or faxes or e-mails (which can be printed out and placed in the patient's record). A method should be found that is preferred by the physician, so the action needed can occur with the least amount of delay. Once the physician updates the documentation, the coder can do his or her job properly (and legally) and the claim can be filed for honest reimbursement. When it is a part of the normal flow of business, it is easier to comply with the law. (More on developing a proper query process in Chapter 6.)

It is not enough for the successful compliance officer to write down a list of things that the staff should do and expect that to be adequate. While policies and procedures must be written and distributed for everyone to read, this is not sufficient. How many people do you know who actually read and memorize their employee manuals? Exactly. The written manual is there to protect the organization when something goes wrong, so that it can be referenced to support a challenge or a **sanction**. In addition to these written policies, an effective compliance program must include the implementation of systems to encourage the practice of these policies.

The Authority to Enforce

A compliance officer without the authority to assess penalties for violations, to adjust or promote updates to the corporate compliance program, or to impact the policies of the organization, is ineffective. In order to actually protect the health care facility, and the professionals and staff that work within, from serious legal problems, this individual must have autonomy.

The OIG states that this authority is an important factor in the success of the program:

"Designating a compliance officer with the appropriate authority is critical to the success of the program, necessitating the appointment of a high-level official in the hospital with direct access to the hospital's governing body and the CEO." (http://www.oig.hhs.gov)

After all, what impact can this person have if they are afraid to report an alleged violation to their manager for fear of getting fired?

The compliance officer will be ineffective if he or she is in a position to be intimidated by profitability issues or stockholder reports. A company acting illegally will not be able to stay profitable for long. This individual must be permitted to review all documentation within the facility, including patient charts, claims and billing records, and contractual agreements with third parties such as clearinghouses, remote coders, and software companies. The compliance officer will need access to perform background checks on all department members, including certification confirmation. The organization should facilitate open communication between the compliance officer and the facility's legal counsel, as necessary.

Compliance Officer Competencies

Personal Integrity

As someone with the influence as described previously, a compliance officer must have great **integrity**. The Health Care Compliance Association (HCCA) issued their professional code of ethics in 1999 (Figure 2-1). As most professional organizations do, this code outlines the key factors that should be a part of the compliance officer's belief system. The AHIMA and AAPC have also issued Codes of Ethics (Figures 2-2 and 2-3, respectively) to help guide health information managers and coders to understand their role in keeping their health care activities honest and above-board.

CODE OF ETHICS FOR HEALTH CARE COMPLIANCE PROFESSIONALS

ADOPTED SEPTEMBER 15, 1999

PREAMBLE

Health care compliance programs are ultimately judged by how they affect, directly or indirectly, the delivery of health care to the patients, residents and clients served by the health care industry and, thus, by how they contribute to the well being of the communities we serve. Those served by the health care industry are particularly vulnerable, and therefore health care compliance professionals (HCCPs) understand that the services we provide require the highest standards of professionalism, integrity and competence. The following Code of Ethics expresses the profession's recognition of its responsibilities to the general public, to employers and clients, and to the legacy of the profession.

The Code of Ethics consists of two kinds of standards: Principles and Rules of Conduct. The principles are broad standards of an aspirational and inspirational nature, and as such express ideals of exemplary professional conduct. The rules of conduct are specific standards that prescribe the minimum level of conduct expected of each HCCP. Compliance with the code is a function both of the individual professional and of the professional community. It depends primarily on the HCCP's own understanding and voluntary actions, and secondarily on reinforcement by peers and the general public.

A Commentary is provided for some rules of conduct, which is intended to clarify or elaborate the meaning and application of the rule. The following conventions are used throughout the code: "Employing organization" includes the employing organization and clients; "Law" or "laws" includes all federal, state and local laws and regulations, court orders and consent agreements, and all foreign laws and regulations that are consistent with those of the United States; "Misconduct" includes both illegal acts and unethical conduct; and "Highest governing body" of the employing organization refers to the highest policy and decision-making authority in an organization, such as the board of directors or trustees of an organization.

PRINCIPLE I: OBLIGATIONS TO THE PUBLIC

Healthcare compliance professionals should embrace the spirit and the letter of the law governing their employing organization's conduct and exemplify the highest ethical standards in their conduct in order to contribute to the public good.

PRINCIPLE II: OBLIGATIONS TO THE EMPLOYING ORGANIZATION

Health care compliance professionals should serve their employing organizations with the highest sense of integrity, exercise unprejudiced and unbiased judgment on their behalf, and promote effective compliance programs.

PRINCIPLE III: OBLIGATIONS TO THE PROFESSION

Compliance professionals should strive, through their actions, to uphold the integrity and dignity of the profession, to advance the effectiveness of compliance programs and to promote professionalism in health care compliance.

Figure 2-1   HCCA Professional Code of Ethics

The following ethical principles are based on the core values of the American Health Information Management Association and apply to all health information management professionals. Health information management professionals must

1. Advocate, uphold, and defend the individual's right to privacy and the doctrine of confidentiality in the use and disclosure of information
2. Put service and the health and welfare of persons before self-interest and conduct themselves in the practice of the profession so as to bring honor to themselves, their peers, and the health information management profession
3. Preserve, protect, and secure personal health information in any form or medium and hold in the highest regard the contents of the records and other information of a confidential nature, taking into account the applicable statutes and regulations
4. Refuse to participate in or conceal unethical practices or procedures
5. Advance health information management knowledge and practice through continuing education, research, publications, and presentations
6. Recruit and mentor students, peers, and colleagues to develop and strengthen a professional workforce
7. Represent the profession accurately to the public
8. Perform honorably health information management association responsibilities, either appointed or elected, and preserve the confidentiality of any privileged information made known in any official capacity
9. State truthfully and accurately their credentials, professional education, and experiences
10. Facilitate interdisciplinary collaboration in situations supporting health information practice
11. Respect the inherent dignity and worth of every person

Figure 2-2   AHIMA Code of Ethics

Members of the American Academy of Professional Coders shall be dedicated to providing the highest standard of professional coding and billing services to employers, clients and patients. Behavior of the American Academy of Professional Coders members must be exemplary.

American Academy of Professional Coders members shall maintain the highest standard of personal and professional conduct. Members shall respect the rights of patients, clients, employers and all other colleagues.

Members shall use only legal and ethical means in all professional dealings, and shall refuse to cooperate with, or condone by silence, the actions of those who engage in fraudulent, deceptive or illegal acts.

Members shall respect the laws and regulations of the land, and uphold the mission statement of the American Academy of Professional Coders.

Members shall pursue excellence through continuing education in all areas applicable to their profession.

(Continues)

Figure 2-3   AAPC Code of Ethical Standards

Figure 2-3   *(Continued)*

This job is focused on keeping an entire department, or organization, honest—sometimes in the face of strong-willed co-workers determined to take short cuts around the law.

The determination to fight for what is right is more than a core competency—it is a personal characteristic that will help an individual successfully accomplish the responsibilities of the job. This is not necessarily "a calling." To be successful as a compliance officer, however, one should begin with a firm belief in the premise of this job—that obeying the law is the right thing to do.

Organization and Coordination Skills

There are a multitude of laws, regulations, and guidelines that must be monitored and overseen at the center of this job. The ability to stay organized is mandatory in order to juggle the federal and state governments' directives, the policies and procedures mandated by each third-party payer that is dealt with by the facility, plus meet coding compliance for diagnosis codes, procedure codes, the up-coming implementation of ICD-10, and more.

Each individual has her own way of staying organized. An excellent filing system may be established electronically or a new, more efficient database software program may be implemented. Staff may be encouraged to join listserv communities to keep them updated on laws and regulations. Other staff members may prefer file folders in cabinets just an arm's length away. The act of being organized simply means that each individual can maintain massive quantities of information up-to-date and at her fingertips for quick reference.

The ability to coordinate the behaviors of the members of the HIM department, clinical staff, admissions/reception, and administration is critical to assuring that the HIM department stays compliant. This is not to imply that a workforce is made incapable of making decisions. Quite the opposite. Instead, disperse the information; evaluate systems to confirm that all members of the team promote—not interfere with—compliance; encourage teamwork; and ensure open, two-way communications.

Leadership Skills

There is a big difference between being a manager and being a leader. For this particular position, leadership skills are needed to motivate staff and administration alike to agree with the details of the compliance program and to abide by its guiding principles. So many individuals fear change, and jarring staff out of their comfort levels and changing their routines can cause resentment. It takes a leader to guide them to accept new policies and procedures and help them find comfort in the new, more compliant processes.

Being a compliance officer does not mean that you have to act like an elementary school hall monitor. Theodore Roosevelt said: *"The best executive is the one who has sense enough to pick good men to do what he wants done, and self-restraint to keep from meddling with them while they do it."* Train them thoroughly so there are no misunderstandings about what should be done in different circumstances, support them by working to help them mesh compliance smoothly into their daily routines, listen to their ideas about how to make the systems better, encourage teamwork, communicate with them, and give them positive feedback every now and then.

Figure 2-4 lists some key leadership skills successful managers need to possess.

---

1. Situational analysis/evaluation
2. Problem solving
3. Decision-making
4. Planning: present, short-term, and long-term
5. Communication
6. Delegation
7. Basic psychology: understanding motivation
8. Meeting organization
9. Change management

Figure 2-4 Key Leadership Skills

Analysis and Implementation

The compliance officer needs to **analyze** policies in two phases: before implementation, and after. This provides perspective of the process of complying with the law.

Before the organization can write policies and procedures for obeying the laws relating to health information management, these regulations must first be analyzed and key components formulated into segments that can be understood clearly by the entire staff. This analysis will be used as the foundation for each company policy and procedure sequence.

Once created, these policies and procedures must be implemented by passing along the information to your employees. Educational programs should be designed to teach staff how to easily merge new policies into their current work systems to reduce resistance to any changes involved.

After policies have been in place, data from completed audits need to be analyzed and **synthesized** into a report to be used within the department as well as submitted to the governing board, and, sometimes, regulatory agencies. These results should be used to implement corrective actions, as necessary, so the facility can avert the continuation of non-compliant behaviors. At times, the analysis will reveal the need for the execution of new and/or reformulated policies.

Planning Skills

Once a law is enacted or a regulation updated, the new requirements may result in subsequent changes within the department, the way information is processed, and the manner in which work flows. On occasion, a new system may need to be designed to comply. This might be as simple as redesigning a form, or it might be multifaceted and necessitate creating an entirely new system and engaging in total retraining.

This may sound overwhelming, but it doesn't have to be. The compliance officer does not have to do this all alone. More often, these changes involve a team of professionals within the organization. However, you will need the ability to plan out the sequences for new policies and procedures so that you can participate in the overall process.

Communication Skills

The compliance officer has to communicate effectively with all members of the HIM department as well as those in other related departments, including clinical staff and admissions or reception. This is why he or she needs to have excellent written and oral communication skills. The ability to avoid **ambiguity** when writing directives is critical in this job. The actual laws and rules of ethics can be very confusing to team members, leaving gray areas open to individual interpretation. This can lead to errors and misjudgments that might put the department and facility at risk. Therefore, it is an important part of the job to be able to interpret the formal wording of laws and regulations and translate them into terms that can be easily understood.

Figure 2-5 shows a list of key communication skills necessary for success in management positions of all types.

1. Reading comprehension
2. Listening
   a. Directions
   b. Feedback
3. Writing
   a. Formal proposals
   b. Business letters
   c. Memos
   d. E-mails
4. Speaking
   a. Expressing new ideas
   b. Negotiating
   c. Giving feedback
   d. Public speaking, speaking within a group, one-on-one
   e. In-person and on the telephone

Figure 2-5 Key Communication Skills

The Compliance Committee

In most types of health care facilities, the HIM compliance officer will sit on a committee with the compliance officers from other departments in an effort to form a cohesive compliance program that covers all aspects of the facility. The group as a whole can support the individual compliance officers and share strategies for plans and implementation. This focus should include the promotion of the entire organization as one of honesty and compliance.

The committee can share responsibility for elements of the compliance program, including creating and manning a hotline reporting system and doing presentations at training seminars.

Some systems and processes will carry over from one department to another, requiring the departmental compliance officers to work together to assure seamless standards. The committee should also perform a regular assessment of the industry, including any political and legal areas that have arisen since the last evaluation, to determine if any existing policies and procedures in the facility's compliance program should be changed or amended. There are several laws that cross over and impact all departments within the facility, such as HIPAA.

Some organizations may have members of the corporate board of directors and/or governors of the facility sit on the compliance committee. The Organizational Sentencing Guidelines support the responsibility of corporate boards to participate more actively in the implementation and enforcement of compliance programs. Larger organizations may establish executive compliance committees composed of internal and external company directors, in addition to the committee of the department compliance officers and possibly department heads. In any event, the two committees must practice open and legitimate communications with each other, the staff, the governing board, and the regulatory agencies.

The *Federal Register* (Vol. 63, No. 35) identifies six key functions of the compliance committee:

1. Analysis of the legal requirements with which the organization must comply

2. Assessment of current policies and procedures to assure all applicable areas are included

3. Interaction with each department to produce standards of conduct and encourage conformity with the program

4. Development of internal systems and controls, as part of the day-to-day operations, to carry out the compliance program

5. Establishment of effective strategies for detecting and investigating alleged violations, including the launching of hotlines, protection for whistleblowers, and other reporting systems

6. Encouragement of the reporting of and prompt investigation and response to any and all complaints and identified concerns

The committee's involvement is not necessarily limited to these elements. Instead, this list should serve as an outline for the creation of the committee's agenda.

Chapter Summary

The health information management compliance officer is the individual designated to guide all the other members of the HIM team in methodologies they can use to perform their individual jobs ethically and legally.

The compliance officer of each department, the compliance director of the organization, and the compliance committee should all work together to establish an organizational culture of legal and ethical behaviors. These staff members are charged with the responsibility of coordinating and promoting the proper methods and systems for excellence in health care delivery while maintaining solid legal standing. This works to protect the facility, the staff, and the patients.

CHAPTER REVIEW

Multiple Choice Questions

1. Health information management departments
   a. do not require their own compliance officer.
   b. do not have specific laws with which to comply.
   c. should have a dedicated HIM compliance officer.
   d. should have their own attorney.

2. An HIM compliance officer is
   a. responsible for implementation of the compliance program.
   b. responsible for all staff members becoming certified.
   c. responsible for firing employees who step out of line.
   d. responsible for the entire facility.

3. Compliance officers must do all except
   a. create a detailed compliance program.
   b. report to the governing board.
   c. file lawsuits against non-compliant staff members.
   d. investigate allegations of violations.

4. Creating a written compliance program is
   a. all that is required by law.
   b. the first step to implementation.
   c. a requirement of certification.
   d. the responsibility of the facility's attorney.

5. A compliance officer should have the authority to
   a. assess penalties for violations.
   b. adjust financial reports.
   c. send an individual to prison.
   d. hire and fire anyone in the facility with no exceptions.

6. *Integrity* is a personal characteristic of someone who is
   a. good at math.
   b. understands diversity.

    c. is a leader.

    d. has high moral standards and professional ethics.

7. *Retribution* is the act of
   a. rewarding good behavior.
   b. vengeance.
   c. promotion.
   d. retaking a certification exam.

8. Good communications skills are necessary to avoid writing policies that are
   a. ambiguous.
   b. analytical.
   c. clear and precise.
   d. compliant.

9. Compliance procedures should
   a. mesh smoothly into daily job routines.
   b. be implemented by the court.
   c. be separate from regular job responsibilities.
   d. be the job of one person per department.

10. Before policies and procedures can be written, the laws must be
    a. altered.
    b. analyzed.
    c. localized.
    d. appealed.

11. According to the sample job descriptions in Figures 2-1 through 2-5, most HIM compliance officers need a
    a. master's degree in compliance.
    b. license to practice law.
    c. knowledge of ICD and CPT.
    d. experience with the OIG.

12. The primary responsibilities of an HIM compliance officer include
    a. good written communications skills.
    b. strong oral communications skills.
    c. excellent analytical skills.
    d. all of the above

13. According to the professional code of ethics, compliance professionals should
    a. understand the details of the laws.
    b. assess the intent, or spirit, of the laws.
    c. have the education necessary to rewrite the laws.
    d. a and b only

14. The HIM compliance officer should
    a. sit on the corporate compliance committee.
    b. report directly to the stockholders.
    c. be a member of the board of directors.
    d. be responsible for the hotline reporting system.

15. Organizational skills are important due to the
    a. requirement to file patient records.
    b. governmental paperwork.
    c. massive amounts of information.
    d. need to keep your office neat.

Research and Discussion Projects

1. Review the Codes of Ethics from the HCCA, AHIMA, and AAPC.
   a. What areas are covered by all three organizations? Why do you think these organizations have pinpointed these factors as so important?

   _____

   _____

   _____

   _____

   b. What element(s) do you notice mentioned in one Code of Ethics but not the others? Why do you believe this is worthy of mention by one and not all three?

   _____

   _____

   _____

   _____

2. Compare the lists of responsibilities shown in the sample job descriptions on pages 34–37 (Figures 2-6 through 2-9) with the competencies identified for compliance officers and directors.

   _____

   _____

   _____

   _____

   _____

   a. If you were interviewing for the position of Compliance Officer, how would you support the skills and abilities necessary to do the job?

   _____

   _____

   _____

   b. What experiences would highlight the necessary characteristics?

   _____

   _____

   _____

c. How would the job responsibilities change for a compliance officer in the HIM department of a hospital versus the compliance officer in a smaller physician's office? How would the job description change for the compliance officer in a nursing home?

_____

_____

_____

_____

3. Review the lists of qualifications on each of the job descriptions.
   a. How do they differ?

_____

_____

_____

   b. What characteristics and/or skills are consistently required? Why do you think this is?

_____

_____

_____

4. Call a local health care facility and make an appointment to interview their compliance officer.
   a. Write three or four questions you would ask about the position and the responsibilities involved.

_____

_____

_____

_____

   b. Did any of the responses surprise you? If so, which ones?

_____

_____

_____

_____

   c. Discuss the interview and what you got out of this experience.

_____

_____

_____

_____

Position Title: Compliance Officer

Immediate Supervisor: CEO

General Purpose: The Compliance Officer establishes and implements an effective compliance program to prevent illegal, unethical, or improper conduct. The Compliance Officer acts as staff to the CEO and Governing Board by monitoring and reporting results of the compliance and ethics efforts of the company and in providing guidance for the Board and senior management team on matters relating to compliance. The Corporate Compliance Officer, together with the Compliance Committee, is authorized to implement all necessary actions to ensure achievement of the objectives of an effective compliance program.

Responsibilities:

- Develops, initiates, maintains, and revises policies and procedures for the general operation of the compliance program and its related activities to prevent illegal, unethical, or improper conduct. Manages day-to-day operation of the Program.
- Develops and periodically reviews and updates Standards of Conduct to ensure continuing currency and relevance in providing guidance to management and employees.
- Collaborates with other departments (for example, Human Resources, Chief Security Officer, Health Information Management Director, and so on) to direct compliance issues to appropriate existing channels for investigation and resolution.
- Consults with General Counsel as needed to resolve difficult legal compliance issues.
- Responds to alleged violations of rules, regulations, policies, procedures, and Standards of Conduct by evaluating or recommending the initiation of investigative procedures.
- Develops and oversees a system for uniform handling of such violations.
- Acts as an independent review and evaluation body to ensure that compliance issues and concerns within the organization are being appropriately evaluated, investigated, and resolved.
- Monitors, and as necessary, coordinates compliance activities of other departments to remain abreast of the status of all compliance activities and to identify trends.
- Identifies potential areas of compliance vulnerability and risk, develops and implements corrective action plans for resolution of problematic issues, and provides general guidance on how to avoid or deal with similar situations in the future.
- Provides reports on a regular basis, and as directed or requested, keeps the Compliance Committee of the Board and senior management informed of the operation and progress of compliance efforts.
- Ensures proper reporting of violations or potential violations to duly authorized enforcement agencies as appropriate or required.
- Establishes and provides direction and management of the compliance hotline.
- Institutes and maintains an effective compliance communication program for the organization, including promoting: (a) use of the compliance hotline, (b) heightened awareness of Standards of Conduct, and (c) understanding of new and existing compliance issues and related policies and procedures.

(Continues)

Figure 2-6 Compliance Officer Sample Position Description

- Works with the Human Resources Department and others as appropriate to develop an effective compliance training program, including appropriate introductory training for new employees and ongoing training for all employees and managers.
- Monitors the performance of the Compliance Program and relates activities on a continuing basis, taking appropriate steps to improve its effectiveness.

Qualifications:

- Education: Bachelor's degree required; master's desired
- Experience: A minimum of 10 years experience in a health care organization
- Skills: Demonstrated leadership ability
- Ability to communicate effectively orally and in writing
- Knowledge: Familiarity with healthcare laws, regulations, and standards
- Understanding of coding and reimbursement systems, risk management, and performance improvement helpful

Figure 2-6 *(Continued)*

Position Title: HIM Compliance Specialist

Immediate Supervisor: Corporate Compliance Officer

Responsibilities:

- Oversees and monitors implementation of the HIM compliance program
- Develops and coordinates educational and training programs regarding elements of the HIM compliance program, such as appropriate documentation and accurate coding, to all appropriate personnel, including HIM coding staff, physicians, billing personnel, and ancillary departments
- Maintains attendance rosters and documentation (agenda, handouts, and so on) for HIM training programs
- Ensures that coding consultants and other contracted entities (for example, outsourced coding personnel) understand and agree to adhere to the organization's HIM compliance program
- Conducts regular audits and coordinates ongoing monitoring of coding accuracy and documentation adequacy
- Provides feedback and focused educational programs on the results of auditing and monitoring activities to affected staff and physicians
- Conducts trend analyses to identify patterns and variations in coding practices and case-mix index
- Compares coding and reimbursement profile with national and regional norms to identify variations requiring further investigation
- Reviews claim denials and rejections pertaining to coding and medical necessity issues and, when necessary, implements corrective action plan, such as educational programs, to prevent similar denials and rejections from recurring
- Conducts internal investigations of changes in coding practices or reports of other potential problems pertaining to coding

(Continues)

Figure 2-7 HIM Compliance Specialist Sample Position Description

- Initiates corrective action to ensure resolution of problem areas identified during an internal investigation or auditing/monitoring activity
- Reports noncompliance issues detected through auditing and monitoring, the nature of corrective action plans implemented in response to identified problems, and results of follow-up audits to the corporate compliance officer
- Receives and investigates reports of HIM compliance violations and communicates this information to the corporate compliance officer
- Recommends disciplinary action for violation of the compliance program, the organization's standards of conduct, or coding policies and procedures to the corporate compliance officer
- Ensures the appropriate dissemination and communication of all regulation, policy, and guideline changes to affected personnel
- Serves as a resource for department managers, staff, physicians, and administration to obtain information or clarification on accurate and ethical coding and documentation standards, guidelines, and regulatory requirements
- Monitors adherence to the HIM compliance program
- Revises the HIM compliance program in response to changing organizational needs or new or revised regulations, policies, and guidelines
- Serves on the compliance committee
- Recommends revisions to the corporate compliance program to improve its effectiveness

Qualifications:
- Certification as a RHIA or RHIT
- CCS certification preferred (for ambulatory services, CCS-P certification preferred)
- Extensive knowledge of ICD-9-CM and CPT coding principles and guidelines
- Extensive knowledge of reimbursement systems
- Extensive knowledge of federal, state, and payer-specific regulations and policies pertaining to documentation, coding, and billing
- Five years of hospital coding experience (for ambulatory services, ambulatory coding experience)
- Strong managerial, leadership, and interpersonal skills
- Excellent written and oral communication skills
- Excellent analytical skills

Figure 2-7 *(Continued)*

Position Title: Inpatient Audit Consultants

Responsibilities: As an Inpatient Audit Consultant, you will travel to the client site and conduct coding assessments to help hospital clients stay on track with their inpatient compliance goals. You will be responsible for performing in-depth audits and for presenting your findings to our clients.

(Continues)

Figure 2-8 Inpatient Audit Consultants Sample Position Description

Physical Requirements: Consultants are expected to be able to lift or manage their own luggage, a laptop computer, portable printer, and a brief case.

Minimum Qualifications: Applicants for employment as Inpatient Audit Consultants are expected to possess the following qualifications:

- AHIMA-credentialed RHIA, RHIT, or CCS;
- Active member of AHIMA;
- Minimum 3 years recent ICD-9 CM coding experience in an acute care setting;
- Thorough working knowledge of ICD-9 CM, DRGs, CMS regulations, and QIO procedures;
- Able to travel as necessary;
- MS Windows, Word, and Excel experience;
- Able to handle/manage computer equipment;
- Well organized, detail-oriented, and able to work independently;
- Above-average verbal, written communication and personal interaction skills.

Figure 2-8 (*Continued*)

Position Title: Outpatient Consultants/Charge Master Audit Consultants

Position Responsibilities: As an Outpatient and Charge Master Audit Consultant, you will conduct coding assessments to help hospital clients stay on track with their outpatient compliance goals. You will be responsible for performing in-depth audits of hospital claims to support code assignments based on clinical documentation, and for presenting your findings to our clients. As a Charge Master Audit Consultant, you would be responsible for reviewing hospital charge masters to validate HCPCS and revenue coding and assisting the hospital clients in updating their charge description masters.

Physical Requirements: Consultants are expected to be able to lift or manage their own luggage, a laptop computer, portable printer, and a brief case.

Minimum Qualifications: Applicants for employment as Outpatient Audit Consultants are expected to possess the following qualifications:

- Credentialed, with your RHIA, RHIT, CCS, or CPC-H;
- Active member of AHIMA;
- At least 3 years recent CPT coding experience in an acute care setting;
- Thorough knowledge of APC outpatient reimbursement methodology;
- Familiar with CMS outpatient compliance guidelines;
- Able to travel nationwide, as necessary;
- MS Windows, Word, and Excel experience;
- Able to handle/manage computer equipment;
- Well organized, detail-oriented, and able to work independently;
- Above-average verbal, written communication, and personal interaction skills.

Figure 2-9 Outpatient Consultants Sample Position Description

Chapter 3

Components of an Effective Compliance Program

Learning Outcomes

- Identify the individual components of a compliance program
- Describe the importance of each component
- Explain the factors involved in designing an effective program
- Name the elements listed by the Federal Sentencing Guidelines relating to compliance programs
- Determine the actions involved in performing due diligence

Key Terms

allowances / from the FSG, a lessening of penalties or punishments assessed for finding an organization guilty of fraud

buy-in / a conscious agreement by all of those affected by the terms of the policy or procedure

disseminate / to disperse or spread information

due diligence / in criminal law, the proof that everything possible was done to prevent the act from happening with every reasonable precaution

Federal Register **/** the daily publication for rules, proposed rules, and notices of the federal government

fraud / using dishonest or inaccurate information with the intention of wrongly gaining money or other benefit

infraction / the failure to comply with a rule or policy

mitigating circumstance / an event that partially excuses a wrong or lessens the results

propensity / a tendency to demonstrate particular behavior

veracity / truthfulness

Chapter Case Study

"May 15, 2006: In Florida, Lincare Holdings, Inc. & Lincare, Inc. (Lincare) agreed to pay $10 million and to enter into a five-year integrity agreement to resolve its liability under the Anti-Kickback Statute provision of the CMPL and the Stark Law. The OIG alleged that Lincare offered and paid remuneration to potential and existing referral sources to induce referrals of patients to Lincare for the furnishing of durable medical equipment. The remuneration included sporting and entertainment event tickets, gift certificates, rounds of golf, golf equipment, fishing trips, meals, advertising expenses, office equipment, and medical equipment, as well as payments pursuant to purported consulting agreements." (http://www.oig.hhs.gov)

Introduction

Once the officers and the committee have been designated, the next step is to begin the project. Creating an official compliance program is a major undertaking. Policies and procedures that will be taken seriously by staff and be effective at curtailing illegal activity will need to be established.

Most professionals agree that the best way to begin a project of this magnitude is to create an outline first, then go back and fill in each individual component. This textbook is going to do just that. This chapter will identify all of the components of a strong compliance program, explaining the purpose of each. Then, the subsequent chapters will delve into the specific details of those components.

Essential Elements

When one is assessing a health care facility, legal compliance should be measured as critically as productivity, for if productivity is high, but illegal practices are being followed, the organization cannot be identified as one of excellence.

In chapter 1, you learned that the Federal Sentencing Guidelines (FSG) make certain **allowances** for those organizations with compliance programs designed to "detect and deter **fraud**, waste, and abuse." Specifically, the FSG Manual (§8A1.2, application note [k]) has identified steps that serve as the minimum requirement for the facility to be eligible for good corporate behavior credits.

Preliminarily, the compliance program must be:

- Rationally planned: At times, all organizations, regardless of their size, produce rules and regulations for staff and business associates that are not clear or logical. Some create policies that actually make doing the job more difficult. This then contributes to non-compliance because complying with the rules interferes with productivity. In other cases, some organizations establish policies that are so complex, no one really knows how to comply.

- Completely implemented: It is not sufficient to label a binder and put it on a shelf in the manager's office. The entire compliance program must be put into action and its policies integrated into all job descriptions and departmental day-to-day systems.

- Fully enforced: The organization, from president to part-time clerk, must take compliance seriously. This includes punishments when violations occur. There must be repercussions for non-compliance clearly spelled out in the program, and the administration needs to hand out disciplinary actions, as appropriate, for every **infraction**.

These preliminary standards make sense. If you are going to create a compliance program that is designed to avert illegal and unethical activities within your organization, it will have to be all three of these things: rationally planned; completely implemented; and fully enforced.

The Seven Steps of Due Diligence

The FSG look for evidence that the organization has consistently applied **due diligence** in its intention to prevent criminal conduct by its employees and other agents, or to discover violations as soon as is reasonable.

The FSG Manual provides an itemization of seven steps (Figure 3-1) that must have been taken by the facility to meet the minimum requirements of due diligence under the federal guidelines. Let's review each so we can clearly understand government expectations.

---

1. Establish compliance standards and procedures.
2. Assign overall responsibility to specific high-level individual(s).
3. Use due care to avoid delegation of authority to individuals with an inclination to get involved in illegal actions.
4. Effectively communicate standards and procedures to all staff.
5. Utilize monitoring and auditing system to detect non-compliant conduct.
6. Enforce adequate disciplinary sanctions when appropriate.
7. Respond to episodes of non-compliance by modifying program, if necessary.

Figure 3-1   The Seven Steps of Due Diligence

Step 1

(k)(1) The organization must have established compliance standards and procedures to be followed by its employees and other agents that are reasonably capable of reducing the prospect of criminal conduct.

This requirement has two parts. First, the facility provides its staff and business associates with standards of behavior and organizational processes so each member knows what is expected of her. Second, it is anticipated that these standards are designed to actually prevent activities that are against the law.

For example, the HIM department may establish a rule regarding the "incident to" regulation by stating that the physician on the premises must sign and date the documentation of the procedure performed, in addition to including the signature of the non-physician practitioner that provided the service. The paperwork should have the appropriate sign/date lines to reinforce the policy.

As you can see, this policy is straightforward regarding the behaviors expected of the non-physician practitioner, as well as the supervising physician. This policy also lays out what the coder should be looking for in the documentation, so that these procedures are not reported improperly, thereby complying with the regulations regarding "incident-to" billing.

Step 2

(k)(2) Specific individual(s) within high-level personnel of the organization must have been assigned overall responsibility to oversee compliance with such standards and procedures.

This requirement embeds the responsibility for compliance at the top, in the hierarchy of the organization. As discussed in chapter 2, the compliance director must be a top-tier executive in the facility with the authority to be proactive in the implementation and enforcement of the program's policies and procedures. In addition, you will remember that this compliance director, along with the compliance officer from each department, sits on the compliance committee that should include members of the board of directors, or at the very least, have access to them.

It all has to be about more than just following the rules, but also having an attitude of integrity and honesty. The best way for this to properly filter through the entire company is from the top down. The executives and administration must maintain these beliefs in their own words and actions. This means that compliance may be the job of the compliance director and officers, but it is the responsibility of everyone.

Step 3

(k)(3) The organization must have used due care not to delegate substantial discretionary authority to individuals whom the organization knew, or should have known through the exercise of due diligence, had a propensity to engage in illegal activities.

Compliance is all about the behavior of the people who work with and for the organization. Essentially, you should know your staff and be able to identify those who may have a **propensity** for breaking the rules.

Nationwide background checks should be done to look for any history of criminal activity. Licensure and/or certification compliance reviews should be performed annually and as needed, based on circumstances. In addition, the organization should perform a confirmation of status with the appropriate organizations or agencies. For example, while being a certified coder may not be a legal requirement, discovering that someone lied about having a certification is a strong indication of his or her **veracity**. In addition to the fact that lying on a job application can be considered illegal, an individual who lies on an application has demonstrated a propensity for avoiding the truth; it is reasonable to believe that this behavior may be carried over to actions with an insurance carrier or the federal government.

The old saying "Trust but verify" should be an important rule before hiring anyone for any position in the facility.

Step 4

(k)(4) The organization must have taken steps to communicate effectively its standards and procedures to all employees and other agents, e.g., by publications that explain, in a practical manner, what is required.

It is not enough to write this program clearly, you must distribute the policies and procedures to your staff. However, when you read this step carefully, it goes considerably further than just distributing the rules. The language used in this step indicates that responsibility must be taken for assuring that the information is appreciated and that everyone on your staff understands how to incorporate these policies into their daily job functions.

Notice the phrase "in a practical manner" used in this step. There are going to be members of your staff who will resist change, and others that will be overwhelmed by the new rules and how these adjustments to their daily work actually apply. You need to take this into consideration when sharing the program with your staff and embrace these feelings in order to work around them. Mandating attendance at a seminar and ordering compliance will not necessarily gain the very important **buy-in** that you really need to get everyone on the same page with the right attitude.

Step 5

(k)(5) The organization must have taken reasonable steps to achieve compliance with its standards, e.g., by utilizing monitoring and auditing systems reasonably designed to detect criminal conduct by its employees and other agents and by having in place and publicizing a reporting system whereby employees and other agents could report criminal conduct by others within the organization without fear of retribution.

Once you have carefully explained to all your staff and business associates how the laws and regulations provide direction regarding their behaviors in various situations, and written them all out for reference, you will have to reinforce the atmosphere of honest attitudes and actions. Establishing monitoring systems with built-in checks and balances, regularly performing internal and external audits, and establishing reporting systems for all members of the facility to identify suspected violations for further investigation are necessary to stay aware of how well the established policies and procedures are working. In addition, these follow-up systems will help the facility find and correct violations before the government finds them.

Step 6

(k)(6) The standards must have been consistently enforced through appropriate disciplinary mechanisms, including, as appropriate, discipline of individuals responsible for the failure to detect an offense. Adequate discipline of individuals responsible for an offense is a necessary component of enforcement; however, the form of discipline that will be appropriate will be case-specific.

Our society's justice system is based on the application of discipline, as are most parental theories for raising well-behaved children. Most humans adapt their behaviors based upon the results or consequences of those behaviors. For example, James touches a hot stove and gets burned. The pain he feels from the burn will help him remember not to do that again.

While some people do the right thing because it is consistent with their conscience, the key to stopping others from doing something wrong involves instilling fear of what might happen if they get caught breaking the law. For example, Rebecca tried to shoplift an expensive handbag and got caught. The horrors of a night in jail will stop her from ever trying that again. But what if she had not been caught? She might have kept stealing items because there were no negative penalties for her behavior.

This does not translate to the need to fire anyone who steps out of line. As this directive states, the punishment should fit the crime, so to speak. In addition, you can design levels of punishments: first violation gets a warning, second violation requires further education, third violation suspension, etc. Later on in this textbook, we will go into this in more detail. The point is that the compliance program must not only specify what will happen should someone fail to comply, the action must then be taken.

Step 7

(k)(7) After an offense has been detected, the organization must have taken all reasonable steps to respond appropriately to the offense and to prevent further similar offenses—including any necessary modifications to its program to prevent and detect violations of law.

There are those that believe a compliance program is a solid line that demands no one cross it. Others believe that spending thousands of dollars on the development of a compliance program will magically eliminate the danger that anyone within their organization will commit fraud or abuse the system. Everyone will know the right thing to do and always do it. There are no guarantees, especially when you are dealing with human behavior, that the organization can become perfect.

It is important that the compliance officers, directors, and committees continually monitor the actions of everyone in the organization and constantly look for ways to make the legal policies and procedures user-friendly so that compliance unites smoothly with daily operations, encouraging proper conduct. When necessary, policies should be adjusted to close unforeseen loopholes or to accommodate new regulations.

Planning the Compliance Project

Beginning with an outline can help to formulate a structure for the program upon which you can then build the details. Effective compliance programs that are designed to guide staff to perform legally and ethically should include:

1. Identification of all applicable laws, regulations, and standards
2. Creation of reasonable policies and procedures for compliance
3. Effective education of staff

4. Establishment of methods for reporting alleged violations without fear of reprisal

5. Institution of monitoring methodologies

6. Performance of regularly scheduled audits

7. Investigation of all circumstances of non-compliance

8. Enforcement of consequences for non-compliance

9. Application of corrective actions to policies when necessary

As indicated by this list, an effective program is a project that may be difficult for a small physician's practice or clinic to create and enforce. However, each of these elements can be pared down to an appropriate size for any facility.

The steps involved can be made simpler for a small office so the creation and implementation of the compliance program does not become a financial or operational burden. However, as discussed in earlier chapters of this book, the fact that a health care facility is small does not waive its liability under the law.

The *Federal Register* (Vol. 65, No. 194) is careful to assure physicians that individual and small group physician practices are simply encouraged to develop voluntary programs.

The strategic philosophy to create and implement a compliance program is a wise one. As noted in previous chapters, it is no more than a methodical path designed to encourage everyone in the organization to work within the law and ethical standards as accepted by the industry and our society.

Certainly, it takes time to do all this work and document all of the plan's components. It takes time to figure out how the processes and systems in this office should be adjusted or adapted so that day-to-day work can be done efficiently and still comply. It takes effort to **disseminate** all this information in a way that all staff members can understand. It takes motivation to work with all staff to lead them past their resistance to change and help them develop new, legal habits of getting their jobs done.

The lack of a compliance program may result in an office filled with health care professionals who state, "I didn't know that was illegal. It's the way we have always done it." But this does not establish a **mitigating circumstance**. As you read in chapter 1, the opposite is true. The implementation of a compliance program is the action that will lessen the opportunities for, and the repercussions of, illegal or unethical activity.

The Inspector General, June Gibbs Brown, wrote into the *Federal Register* on February 11, 1998, "*Ultimately, it is the OIG's hope that a voluntarily created compliance program will enable hospitals to meet their goals, improve the quality of patient care, and substantially reduce fraud, waste and abuse, as well as the cost of health care to Federal, State, and private health insurers*" [FR Doc. 98-4399 Filed 2-20-98; 8:45 a.m.].

Project Management

You may be the individual designated to spearhead this project alone or with a team. Depending upon the size of your facility, this may be your only responsibility, or it may be included with other day-to-day tasks. In any case, you will need to apply project management skills to keep the development of this program on schedule, to maintain quality, and to help manage the scope of the project (Figure 3-2).

1. Determine the Extent of the Project
   A. Subdivide project into sections
   B. Construct project path for each section
2. Identify Required Resources
   A. Distinguish types of resources necessary:
      i. People
      ii. Supplies
      iii. Money
   B. Recognize
      i. Available resources
      ii. Those yet to be obtained/accessed
3. Establish Timeline
   A. Document specific stages within the project and deadlines by which to complete those stages

Figure 3-2   Elements of Project Management

The Individual Steps to Success

The outline shown earlier in this chapter gives you the outside structure for this program. The next step is to break this outline into a specific to-do list of tasks. As you do this, you will notice that each duty involved in the entire program is actually made up of small, medium, and large jobs.

For example, you or your team will have to do some research to identify the laws, regulations, and official policies to which your facility must adhere. This research may involve searching government and organizational websites. The first job here is to make a list of those organizations and agencies and their website addresses (see chapter 12). Accomplish little steps toward the completion of the project, such as this one, in smaller snippets of time found between other, larger everyday tasks.

Creating a bulleted sub-listing of individual tasks will help you gain a sense of accomplishment as you work through this project.

Setting Deadlines

A reasonable amount of time must be identified for each task to be completed. The critical nature of this step of project management will help to reduce the stress created by unrealistic timelines. All managers know that rushing work under impossible time-frames increases the opportunity for errors and incompleteness. Neither of these characteristics would be acceptable in any measure as part of a successful compliance plan!

Deadlines and the overall timeline of the project should create a harmonious flow of work coming in and moving through to the completion of the program—especially if you, or another individual, are acting as the coordinator of the team effort. If all members of the team have the same deadline to submit first drafts, for example, this will create a tremendous bottleneck as you attempt to go through everyone's work at one time. Plus, your team members will be sitting around doing nothing until you get back to them. Staggering the deadlines, with due dates a couple of days to a week apart, will give you the opportunity to keep the activity on the project moving forward smoothly.

Each stage should be given its own deadline to be accomplished within the larger component. This will help the team members have a clear sense of productivity. In addition, you will have the data you need for progress reports and be able to identify potential trouble spots that may interfere with the project as a whole.

Each deadline should be expressed as specifically as possible. "Monday, June 12, 2008, no later than 5:00 p.m. eastern time" is much better than "within three weeks" or "the week of June 12, 2008." The coordinator or project chairperson can always grant an extension, under certain circumstances. Without specific deadlines, there is no control over the flow of work, and this can be a real problem when there are so many elements involved in a big project.

Delegation of Tasks

If you are working with a team, the list and sub-list will help you determine the assignment of tasks for each participant as you delegate the work. Make certain to not only hand out assignments in an orderly manner, but in an appropriate way. When working with a team, you must first get to know individuals' strengths and weaknesses. This will enable you to assign tasks to people based on their strengths, increasing the opportunity for quality and success. This will lessen the number of times you are disappointed, and put into a jam, by others failing to meet deadlines or doing such a poor job you feel obligated to do it over yourself. Duplication of efforts is another problem that can be avoided by orderly delegation.

> **EXAMPLE** Madeline, Frank, and Erlene will be working on the compliance plan committee. Erlene is very good at doing research, Frank is an excellent writer, and Madeline is great at dealing with small details. Therefore, Erlene is assigned to make a list of all of the applicable laws, with information on those laws. Frank will begin drafting the policies after the team meets and discusses the data Erlene found, and Madeline will organize all the information to ensure everything is included.

Creating a logbook or using project management software can help you keep close track of who is doing what. Writing this all down will help you monitor the different activities and their status throughout the project. Even if you are a team of one, this type of organizational tool can assist you with details of progress (for your supervisors) as well as keep your mind clear for work. Just like to-do lists, this methodology will avert constant thoughts of what needs to done next. That type of focused, repetitive thinking actual impedes your ability to produce other work.

There are two types of charts used commonly by project managers in various industries.

The PERT Chart

Program Evaluation and Review Technique (PERT) is a type of organizational chart. The United States Navy created this method of managing complex projects during

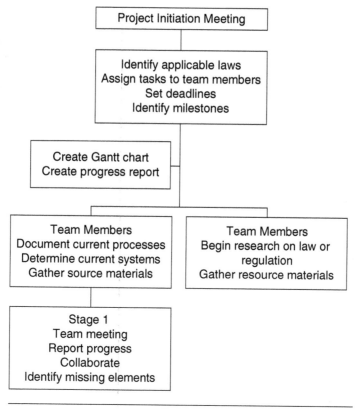

Figure 3-3 Compliance Project PERT Chart

the 1950s, and it can be very helpful in tracking a network of plan components, team members, and assigned tasks. Figure 3-3 is an example of a PERT chart that can be used for developing a health care compliance plan.

The Gantt Chart

Using a spreadsheet-based format, the Gantt chart assigns each required task to a line (row on a spreadsheet). The measures across the columns to the right identify the time spread allotted for this particular step.

Charles Gantt created this chart in 1917, and many project managers find it an effective tool for providing a snapshot of the big picture. Figure 3-4 shows an example of a Gantt project chart.

Specify Quality Measures

The very nature of a compliance program is essential accuracy. Guidelines for the creation of each portion of this program should include the qualifications of the elements

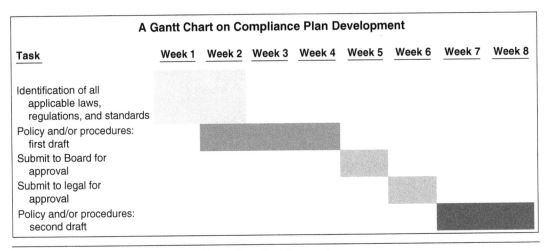

Figure 3-4   A Gantt Chart on Compliance Plan Development

and how to determine the quality of each piece. Unreliable data will not result in a policy that will effectively protect the organization or the individuals who work with it.

Make certain that all guidelines are in writing. Even if you are a team of one, the written guidelines will serve as an excellent reference while moving through all of the tasks. These must be solid, substantial measures that are explained clearly so everyone understands what is expected. For example, all resources for foundational data should be accurately cited with the name of the author, specific website address, and the organizational source. The date of acquisition of the information, as well as the date the information was created and posted on the website, are also important so that it can be confirmed that this is the most up-to-date material. All of these elements of quality verification must be itemized up front, before any work is done.

A review of these quality measurements with each participating member of the team is also necessary. Be certain that everyone understands not only the elements required and your definitions of quality, but why these criteria are important. This helps your team clearly identify their importance to the program, and that will motivate them to do a better job.

Be specific in your definitions of these quality determinants. Avoid generalizations. Don't assume that just because someone has a degree or experience means they know these parameters. It must be assured that those doing research, for example, understand that Google is not a legitimate reference, and neither is Wikipedia. They may have to be educated on how to evaluate the credibility of a source, how to use only governmental or official organizational websites, and how to use other credible sources.

Open Communications

Whenever you are working on a large project over a long period of time, open communication pathways are significant to the option of success. Members of the team will need motivation and encouragement throughout the length of their service. They must be kept involved in their part and be reminded of how their portion fits into the project as a whole, and is a valuable contribution. They must know, and be reminded, that what they are doing matters.

Clear and regularly scheduled communications will also help with the coordination of the project and its parts. You will be able to monitor the progress or lack thereof. If someone is having a problem completing their tasks, they may not confess this until you ask. Knowing about the snags will enable you to offer assistance or suggestions to overcome the obstacle. You can gain insights into potential pitfalls for team members who might be attempting to work outside of their capabilities. All of these issues are better known sooner rather than later, so you can institute corrective measures.

Content Reviews

Periodic checks on the work-in-progress should be made so time is not wasted on misdirection or misunderstandings of assignments. Whoever performs the review should be someone who can be objective, yet who is still conversant in the goals and objectives of the project. This may be the coordinator of the project, the compliance director, or an outside source. The reviews should be done in a timely fashion so they don't interfere with the project, or component, timelines. Actually, it is smart to include time for these reviews in those timeframes.

Feedback after the review should be provided to the individual in writing. Many people fail to hear enough details after the words, "You did a great job, but. . . ." The written input can create a template for improvement, making it easier for the team member to follow the suggestions. The reviewer can also edit the response to make certain that words are chosen carefully and are not too harsh. This should not be an opportunity to denigrate, but a reason to build up this person's efforts and help them improve.

Create a schedule for these checks and reviews in advance, so that they do not occur too frequently or too infrequently. When done too often, team members can feel as if they have someone looking over their shoulder and there is no trust in their ability to do the job effectively. This will typically demotivate, lower self-esteem, and interfere with the quality of the results. Reviews that are done too rarely lose their effectiveness and reduce the opportunity for redirecting someone who has veered off track.

Plan for the Unexpected

There is an old saying called "Murphy's Law" that states that anything that can go wrong, will go wrong. Everyone has experienced unexpected delays. The closer you are to a deadline, the more likely it is that a power surge will crash your computer. The more of a rush you are in, the slower your printer prints out your report.

First, when you are working on the timeline for the entire project, be certain to pad each segment. An extra few hours or days will not likely affect the program deadline as a whole. If all goes well, you can complete the project early. However, if little occurrences cause delays along the way, you can protect the project.

Second, always have a contingency plan for every part of the project. Be certain to write down and store the names and contact information of individuals who wanted to be on the team but missed the cut. This second-tier group of participants can provide critical reinforcement if someone on the team gets ill or must take time off. If the structure of this project depends upon a team, know who the potential alternates might be. This way you won't have to scramble to find a last-minute replacement. Even if you are a team of one, you might have a list of people who can pitch in and help you out in a jam.

Prepare a contingency plan for other aspects of the project, as well. For example, if the completed program is going to be printed and distributed, get bids from at least three different printers. Even if your office always uses the same shop, this might be important if lightening strikes and their store loses power and can't do the job on time.

Third, back up everything often. Don't depend on the office computer back-up system. Burn a CD every time a phase of the project is completed. Have team members burn CD-ROMs of each of their portions as they complete a segment. Keep a set of CD-ROMs off-site, whether it is at your home or the home of your supervisor, in a fireproof safe, if possible.

Work Smarter not Harder

There may be other health care facilities with existing compliance programs from which you may borrow a great deal of guidance and work. The directions on developing a compliance program from the *Federal Register,* the Office of the Inspector General, and the Centers for Medicare and Medicaid Services, as well as several private insurance carriers, can give your office's program a big boost. It makes sense to not waste time duplicating what has already been done. However, you must be careful. Take the proper precautions to assure that the content is relevant and worthwhile. Double-check the validity of their sources and confirm that the elements are up-to-date. Permit your team to read through the document and share their opinions as to how the systems in that program may or may not integrate well with the style of your facility. Not all offices are run the same way or with the same organizational processes. An existing program may require more work to get it to fit than writing one from scratch.

Plagiarism is against the law. How ironic would that be to break the law creating a document that helps staff members learn how to work without breaking the law? If the information comes from federal government sources, it most probably falls in the public domain. Again, you must know and cite all of your sources. (Note: This list of citations will make annual updates of the plan much easier!)

Managing this project is very much like coding: never assume, always double-check, and follow the law.

Chapter Summary

The *Federal Register,* the Office of the Inspector General, and the Centers for Medicare and Medicaid Services, along with other health care authorities, provide guidelines for health care organizations in their creation of effective compliance programs. Every health care organization, from the single physician's office to the largest multifacility system, must obey the laws. Creating and implementing a compliance program serves to protect every staff member as well as every patient for whom the organization cares.

This textbook will thoroughly review each of these components and serve as a guidebook for the creation of an operational program.

CHAPTER REVIEW

Multiple Choice Questions

1. All of these are components of a compliance program except
    a. methods for reporting alleged violations.
    b. mitigating circumstances for department managers.
    c. repercussions for non-compliance.
    d. plans for corrective actions.

2. An allowance is
    a. an amount of money given to a health care facility from the government.
    b. a waiver of total liability.
    c. the performance of due diligence.
    d. the lessening of penalties for a company found guilty of fraud.

3. Preliminarily, a compliance program should include all except
    a. protective systems.
    b. logically written policies and procedures.
    c. total implementation integrated in day-to-day systems.
    d. consistent enforcement of punishment for non-compliance.

4. The FSG Manual contains
    a. functional standards of government.
    b. federal sentencing guidelines.
    c. financial and structural guidelines.
    d. federal steps to guidance.

5. The Seven Steps of Due Diligence include
    a. standards of behavior that will foster criminal conduct.
    b. identification of those staff members with veracity.
    c. established monitoring systems.
    d. optional punishments for non-compliance.

6. The first step in creating a compliance program is
    a. investigation of all circumstances of non-compliance.
    b. performance of regularly scheduled audits.
    c. effective education of staff.
    d. identification of all applicable laws.

7. Education of staff means
    a. optional training sessions.
    b. explanations and encouragement of compliance.

    c. distribution of a manual.

    d. maintaining a binder in the HR department.

8. Creation of a compliance program for individual physicians' offices is
    a. mandatory.
    b. optional.
    c. voluntary.
    d. irrelevant.

9. The *Federal Register* lists
    a. all rules, proposed rules, and notices from the federal government.
    b. all licensed health care facilities.
    c. all licensed health care providers.
    d. all third-party payers approved to offer health care insurance.

10. Deadlines should be set
    a. to create a harmonized flow of work.
    b. to have all components finished by the same date.
    c. for each stage of the project.
    d. a and c only

11. When delegating tasks, assign work according to team members'
    a. availability.
    b. strengths.
    c. convenience.
    d. requests.

12. Project management software can help keep track of
    a. the status of activities.
    b. assignments for individuals.
    c. deadlines.
    d. all of the above

13. Every project assignment should include
    a. the general deadline.
    b. specific definitions of quality measures.
    c. open and nondescript guidelines.
    d. a complete list of approved resources.

14. Periodically, the project coordinator should perform
    a. content reviews.
    b. reassignment of components to second-tier participants.
    c. adjustments to timelines.
    d. verbal feedback.

15. Proper planning for a large project such as this includes all except
    a. a contingency plan.
    b. regular back-ups.
    c. random rotation of assignments.
    d. cushion time built into deadlines.

Research and Discussion Projects

1. Discuss the essential elements of a compliance program.
    a. How can each be used to help the program be more effective?

    _____

    _____

    _____

    _____

    b. What ethical and legal danger zones might be created in any of these areas?

    _____

    _____

    _____

    _____

2. Review the Seven Steps to Due Diligence.
    a. Provide an example of how you might suggest fulfillment of each step.

    _____

    _____

    _____

    _____

    b. Should each department complete these steps separately or on a facility-wide basis? Explain your answer.

    _____

    _____

    _____

    _____

    _____

    c. How would you handle a staff member found to have lied on his or her job application about being certified?

    _____

    _____

    _____

    _____

    _____

3. What actions would you take to get the buy-in from everyone in your department to take the compliance plan seriously?

_____

_____

_____

_____

4. What procedures would you institute to enforce punishments for non-compliance? Provide examples.

_____

_____

_____

_____

_____

5. Search on the Internet for various project management software programs. Compare and contrast the features. Write a proposal to recommend the purchase of one specific program.

_____

_____

_____

_____

_____

_____

Chapter 4

Legal and Ethical Considerations

Learning Outcomes

- Discern between a law, a regulation, and a policy
- Evaluate the effective rules of participation for third-party payers
- Identify the enforcement agencies that oversee HIM compliance
- Determine applicable laws, acts, and programs
- Enumerate the key areas of compliance concern

Key Terms

administrative laws / rules created by authorized agencies
civil laws / laws that deal with the rights of individuals
criminal laws / laws that protect individuals' health, safety, and welfare
electronic health records (EHR) / the creation and maintenance of patient charts in a computerized system
oversight / the responsibility to supervise
perpetuate / to continue, spread, disseminate
private laws / regulations dealing with interactions between individuals and each other and/or private businesses
public laws / laws regarding matters between the government and its people
rules of participation / the structure of the agreement between third-party payer and health care provider for reimbursement
statutes / laws established by a legislative body of the government

Chapter Case Study

"Calls to Blue Cross Blue Shield Michigan's (BCBSM) Anti-Fraud Hotline led to an investigation that resulted in the indictment of a crooked provider and his conspirators and stopped payment on nearly $500,000 in fraudulent claims.

Zack Brown, M.D., could not be paid directly by BCBSM because of previous fraud convictions, but that did not stop him from finding other ways to profit from health care fraud. This time, Brown needed help and was willing to share the money. Brown recruited BCBSM members, convincing them to share the profits of checks sent to them as reimbursement for injections and physical therapy services for which Brown billed BCBSM but never rendered. The scam worked like this:

- *Brown's batch billing alleged three treatments per week over periods ranging from six to 12 months.*
- *Members participating in the billing scam received checks from BCBSM, intended to be reimbursement for services for which Brown claimed they paid him, in amounts ranging from $3,000 to $5,000.*
- *The members split the profits from these fraudulent reimbursement checks with Brown and other conspirators.*
- *Many of these members also recruited their friends, relatives, and co-workers to participate in the billing scam.*

In a short period of time, Brown billed BCBSM for over $1,000,000 in fraudulent claims. BCBSM's fraud investigation unit was able to prevent payment of nearly half of these claims.

A cooperative investigation by BCBSM's fraud investigation unit, the FBI, and the Office of the Inspector General resulted in the following:

- *Brown, his biller, and seven others were indicted by a federal grand jury on charges including conspiracy, mail fraud and health care fraud.*
- *Seven individuals have agreed to plead guilty to federal health care fraud charges.*
- *Nineteen more individuals entered into pretrial diversion agreements.*

Pending further investigation, additional charges for other participants are anticipated."
(http://www.bcbsm.com)

Introduction

The watchwords for a compliance program are the same words used in many areas of health care including coding: *never assume*. The staff often does not know what the real obligations are under the different laws. For example, the Health Insurance Portability and Accountability Act (HIPAA) went into effect in April 2003. Yet there are still many who are incorrectly informed about the Privacy Rule and its impact on day-to-day health care. This is a law that many health care employees say they understand, and yet they continue to **perpetuate** misinformation. Imagine, then, how many are not up-to-date on federal and state anti-kickback laws or the False Claims Act.

In addition, ethical guidelines can get blurred because most organizations do not plainly communicate these critical beliefs. This leaves the decision about what to do in certain circumstances to the interpretation of each person as they attempt to compare written policies with observed behaviors.

Types of Legal Considerations

There are actually different types of laws, rules, and regulations with which a health care organization must comply.

Statutory laws, also called **statutes**, are laws created and enacted by either federal or state legislatures (Congress). HIPAA and the federal False Claims Act are both examples of statutory law.

Administrative laws are created by agencies that are given authority by the legislature to oversee particular areas. Under the Administrative Procedures Act (a federal statute), implementation and administration of specific complex laws are delegated to administrative agencies. These agencies are thereby empowered to create rules and regulations to ensure compliance and to make these available to the public. The *Federal Register* is used for this purpose. The Centers for Medicare and Medicaid Services (CMS) and the Department of Health and Human Services (HHS) are two examples of administrative agencies.

> **EXAMPLE** A statute established the Medicare program (health insurance coverage for the elderly, those permanently disabled, and those with end-stage renal disease). Then, Congress created CMS to determine and implement necessary rules and regulations to assure the proper administration of this program.

Both statutes and administrative rules and regulations are classified as **public laws**. This means that they involve matters between the government and its people. Legal issues between individuals, or between an individual and a private organization, are regulated by **private laws**. Therefore, aspects of health care that relate to a health care professional sending claims to Medicaid (a government-sponsored program) would need to be compliant with public laws, while that same health care professional would be covered by private laws when billing a privately-owned insurance company.

Civil laws deal with the relationships between individuals, private organizations, and/or the government. Accusations of fraud and failure to comply with the terms of a contract are examples of violations of civil law. **Criminal laws** govern acceptable behaviors of both individuals and organizations in regard to actions that are contrary to the health, safety, and welfare of another. A crime is also considered an action that is prohibited by a law.

> **EXAMPLE** An invasion of an individual's privacy is considered a violation of a civil law. If a health care professional sells a patient's private health care information, however, that is a criminal act. This explains why a violation of HIPAA's Privacy Rule may have both civil and criminal penalties.

Other regulations with which health information management professionals must comply are third-party payer policies and procedures. These are the **rules of participation** that health care facilities and practitioners must abide by in order to qualify to be reimbursed for services provided to the beneficiaries, or insureds.

Often, when a health care professional is interested in becoming a part of an insurance company's network, also known as a participating provider, the itemization of these conditions is presented in writing. As a part of the application, the professional must sign an affidavit attesting to the fact that he or she understands that receiving money in exchange for services to the patients is contingent upon following these rules.

CMS outlines their rules of participation in their *Conditions of Participation* (CoP). The CoP identifies the minimum health and safety standards that this agency considers to be mandatory for protecting beneficiaries and improving the quality of their health. Blue Cross Blue Shield's *Participation Programs and Responsibilities* is a section within their manual for participating health care professions.

In addition to the rules set out for the providers, third-party payers also publish written directives for elements related to coding and billing. Each organization communicates its own definition of medical necessity, identifies the claim form to be used when billing it, as well as acceptable methods of transmittal for claims, and more. These manuals give you the information you need to create the compliance program's foundation.

Health Care Enforcement Agencies and Programs

There are many state and federal agencies charged with the **oversight** of various aspects of health care. In addition, state governments have their own task forces or initiatives for investigating and combating health care fraud and abuse. Private companies that are involved in health care, such as insurance carriers, also maintain health care fraud hotlines for reporting suspected fraud.

Some of these agencies, and their role in health care, are:

Agency for Health Care Administration (AHCA) http://ahca.myflorida.com

The organization was created to oversee accessible, affordable, quality health care within the state of Florida, including investigations of long-term care facilities. This is an example of the individual agencies that operate within each state to watch over the health care industry within the state, act as a resource for providers, facilities, and patients, and help oversee anti-fraudulent activities. What is the organization or agency in your state?

Agency for Health Care Research and Quality (AHRQ) http://www.ahrq.gov

Part of the United States Public Health Service, this agency supports, collects, and disperses research findings, treatment guidelines, and other qualified data with the intention of contributing to the quality and effectiveness of health care decision-making and services.

Center for Medicare and Medicaid Services (CMS) http://www.cms.hhs.gov

CMS is an agency within the Department of Health and Human Services (DHHS) charged with overseeing the processes of the Medicare and Medicaid programs, as well as the State Children's Health Insurance Program (SCHIP) for the federal government.

Comprehensive Error Rate Testing (CERT)

CMS created the Comprehensive Error Rate Testing (CERT) program to measure the error rate for claims that were mistakenly paid to providers after being submitted to Carriers, Durable Medical Equipment Regional Carriers (DMERCs), and Fiscal Intermediaries (FIs).

Durable Medical Equipment Regional Carriers (DMERC)

While each state has its own fiscal intermediary to process claims for health care services provided to Medicare beneficiaries, claims for reimbursement for durable medical equipment (DME) are delegated to four regional organizations based on the geographical location of the service provision.

Federal Bureau of Investigation (FBI) http://www.fbi.gov

The FBI maintains their own initiatives to support health care fraud investigations focused on organizations and individuals suspected of defrauding health care systems, whether public or private.

Fiscal Intermediaries (FI)

Medicare and Medicaid are both federal programs that are state administered. Each state contracts with an FI to handle the evaluation, processing, and payment (or denial) of claims from health care providers in that particular state.

Hospital Payment Monitoring Program (HPMP)

The Hospital Payment Monitoring Program (HPMP) was established by CMS to calculate the error rate for claims submitted and approved by the Quality Improvement Organizations (QIOs) which should not have been paid. This group, just like CERT, is designated to uncover mistakes made by QIOs on behalf of Medicare.

Joint Commission http://www.jointcommission.org

Formerly known as the Joint Commission for the Accreditation of Healthcare Organizations (JCAHO), the Joint Commission is an independent, not-for-profit organization that sets standards and accredits those health care organizations that meet or exceed those standards. While participation is voluntary, many states use Joint Commission accreditation as an indicator that a health care facility provides quality and safety of care and to qualify the facility to participate in programs such as Medicare and Medicaid.

Medicaid Fraud Control Units (MFCU) http://oig.hhs.gov/publications/mfcu.html and State Medicaid Fraud Control Units (SMFCU)

At this time, 47 states and the District of Columbia receive federal grant monies through the Medicare and Medicaid Anti-Fraud and Abuse Amendments of 1997 to establish SMFCU, delegated to investigate and take legal action against Medicaid providers suspected of fraud, as well as to evaluate occurrences of patient abuse and neglect. The OIG certifies each SMFCU to ensure compliance with federal regulations regarding the function and operations of these units.

Office of the Inspector General (OIG) http://oig.hhs.gov

The Partnership Plan was established by the OIG to work jointly with state auditors in an effort to more effectively use limited state and federal resources and perform broader coverage of the reviews of Medicare and Medicaid program participants. The Office of Counsel to the Inspector General (OCIG) represents the OIG in the settlement of cases filed under the False Claims Act, develops compliance program directives, enforces program exclusions, adjudicates civil money penalties to health care providers, and litigates actions within DHHS.

Office of Civil Rights (OCR)

The OCR is the sector within the Department of Health and Human Services charged with overseeing compliance with HIPAA as well as the investigation and prosecution of violations.

Program Safeguard Contractors (PSC)

A PSC is a specialty contractor who works to support the Medicare Integrity Program (MIP) that was created as a part of HIPAA. They perform medical reviews, execute cost report audits, complete data analysis, conduct provider education, and work to prevent, and, when necessary, detect fraudulent activity.

It's The Law

"In 1999, CMS developed the PSC program to support the Medicare Integrity Program (MIP). MIP was created as part of the Health Insurance Portability and Accountability Act (HIPAA) of 1996. Part of MIP's purpose is to strengthen CMS' ability to deter fraud and abuse in the Medicare Program by giving CMS specific contracting authority, consistent with Federal Acquisition Regulations, to enter into contracts with entities to promote the integrity of the Medicare program. A PSC can take on some, all, or any subset of the work associated with the following payment safeguard functions:

- Medical review
- Cost report audit
- Data analysis
- Provider education and fraud detection
- Prevention"

(http://www.cms.hhs.gov)

Recovery Audit Contractors (RAC)

A RAC also functions under the MIP to perform audits with the intention of identifying any underpayments and overpayments made in response to claims filed for Medicare beneficiaries of both Part A and Part B. In addition, this group has the authority to reclaim any overpayments discovered during their reviews. By 2010, CMS plans to have four RACs in place, each responsible for identifying improper payments in about 25 percent of the country.

It's The Law

"Section 306 of the Medicare Prescription Drug, Improvement and Modernization Act of 2003 (MMA) required CMS to complete a demonstration project to demonstrate the use of recovery audit contractors (RAC) in identifying underpayments and overpayments and recouping overpayments under the Medicare program for services for which payment is made under part A or B of title XVIII of the Social Security Act."

(http://www.cms.hhs.gov)

State Attorneys General (SAG)

Each state has its own set of laws and regulations that govern its residents, in addition to those enacted by the federal government. The state attorney general is the chief legal officer of the state and oversees enforcement of the laws. The SAG works with the OIG and other federal law enforcement agencies to investigate and prosecute suspected violations of applicable state and federal laws within its borders.

U.S. Department of Justice (DOJ) http://www.usdoj.gov

The DOJ created the National Procurement Fraud Task Force in October 2006 to endorse the prevention, early detection, and prosecution of procurement fraud, including false claims, ethics and conflict of interest violations.

Applicable Laws and Regulations

Your compliance program must begin with the identification of all applicable laws, regulations, and guidelines that affect your facility and your patient population. For example, if you work for a pediatrician you may need to become familiar with the State Children's Health Insurance Program (SCHIP) and its policies in your state. It may seem like an overwhelming task, but if you break it down into areas of focus, tackling this big project will be easier.

There are some laws that do not apply to every facility. For example, the new rule about reporting Present on Admission (POA) indicators does not affect physicians' offices. Typically, Medicare billing guidelines are of no concern to a neonatology office, and the Joint Commission standards are not requirements for family practitioners. On the other hand, there are laws and regulations in effect that may not relate to your facility now, but will in the future. For example, your office may not be utilizing **electronic health records** (EHR) and, therefore, may believe there is no reason to address these factors now. However, the law directs all health care facilities to be using EHR by 2010, so the sooner you implement policies, the easier it will be for staff to comply when the time comes.

Once you identify the laws and regulations, you will need to read the specifications and create a summary of the details. Most often, this is best done as bullet points because these can get the details across more easily and quickly.

Acts and Programs

Some of the guidance health information management professionals need can be found in specific acts passed by Congress or programs developed to care for particular segments of the population. Some of these are:

Beneficiary Complaint Response Program

This program assists Medicare beneficiaries or their representatives, following through the process of investigation initiated by a written or telephoned complaint.

Children's Health Insurance Program (CHIP) and State Children's Health Insurance Program (SCHIP)

Implemented under the Balanced Budget Act of 1997, this is a federal program administered separately by each state, expanding the inclusion of Medicaid to provide health insurance for children that are not covered by a parent's policy.

Comprehensive Error Rate Testing (CERT)

Mandated by Congress, a CERT Review Contractor is designated to measure the accuracy of Medicare claims payment processes and provider billing practices. They examine paid claims by reviewing the associated documentation to ensure that the claim was paid correctly.

Emergency Medical Treatment and Active Labor Act (EMTALA)

Passed in 1986, EMTALA directs a specific obligation to Medicare-participating hospitals that provide emergency services to perform a medical screening examination and/or emergency medical treatment to stabilize a patient requiring such service, including a woman in active labor, without regard to the patient's ability to pay.

It's The Law

"In 1986, Congress enacted the Emergency Medical Treatment & Labor Act (EMTALA) to ensure public access to emergency services regardless of ability to pay. Section 1867 of the Social Security Act imposes specific obligations on Medicare-participating hospitals that offer emergency services to provide a medical screening examination (MSE) when a request is made for examination or treatment for an emergency medical condition (EMC), including active labor, regardless of an individual's ability to pay. Hospitals are then required to provide stabilizing treatment for patients with EMCs. If a hospital is unable to stabilize a patient within its capability, or if the patient requests, an appropriate transfer should be implemented."

(http://www.cms.hhs.gov/emtala)

Federal False Claims Act

This law specifically forbids the transmission of claims with the intention of gaining reimbursement under false conditions. The government has the power to seek restitution from everyone who has, or should have, the knowledge of the falsehood.

It's The Law

"31 U.S.C. § 3729. While the False Claims Act imposes liability only when the claimant acts 'knowingly,' it does not require that the person submitting the claim have actual knowledge that the claim is false. A person who acts in reckless disregard or in deliberate ignorance of the truth or falsity of the information, also can be found liable under the Act. 31 U.S.C. 3729(b)."

(http://thomas.loc.gov)

CASE STUDY

"According to the Justice Department, the United States recovered the largest amount ever recorded in a single year in the fiscal year ending September 30 [2006]. Since 1986 the government has recovered $18 billion under the False Claims Act.

"In fiscal year 2006, whistleblower lawsuits were responsible for $1.3 billion of the total $3.1 billion recovered. The whistleblowers received $190 million for their efforts, with the remaining funds restored to the government for the benefit of the taxpayers. Health care recoveries comprised 72 percent and defense industry recoveries comprised 20 percent of the total recovery. Settlements against Tenet Healthcare Corporation and the Boeing Company accounted for almost half of the $3.1 billion total. Of the $2.2 billion in settlements and judgments in health care fraud, Tenet's settlement accounted for $920 million. Of the $609 million in settlements and judgments in defense procurement fraud, Boeing's settlement accounted for $565 million."

(http://www.usdoj.gov)

Health Care Fraud and Abuse Control Program (HCFACP)

The OIG, along with the Department of Justice, oversees activities under the Health Care Fraud and Abuse Control Program (HCFACP), created under the provisions of HIPAA. This program has the power to enforce federal, state, and local laws with regard to the provisions of services and payments received under Medicare, Medicaid, and private health care, and to conduct investigations including audits.

It's The Law

"HIPAA established the Health Care Fraud and Abuse Control (HCFAC) program to consolidate and strengthen ongoing efforts to combat fraud and abuse in health care programs and expand resources for fighting health care fraud. The Attorney General and the Secretary of HHS through the HHS Office of Inspector General (HHS/OIG) administer HCFAC. The HCFAC program goals are to:

- Coordinate federal, state, and local law enforcement efforts to control fraud and abuse associated with health plans;
- Conduct investigations, audits, and other studies of delivery and payment for health care for the United States;
- Facilitate the enforcement of the civil, criminal, and administrative statutes applicable to health care;
- Provide guidance to the health care industry, including the issuance of advisory opinions, safe harbor notices, and special fraud alerts; and
- Establish a national database of adverse actions against health care providers."

(http://thomas.loc.gov)

Health Care Quality Improvement Program (HCQIP)

Administered by peer-review organizations, the HCQIP identifies and implements health care improvement opportunities based on scientific quality indicators.

It's The Law

"The definition of a Quality Improvement Project (QIP) evolves from the definition of a quality review study contained in 42 CFR 480.101. The regulations define a quality review study as 'an assessment, conducted by or for a QIO of a patient care problem for the purpose of improving patient care through peer analysis, intervention, resolution of the problem, and follow-up.'"

(http://thomas.loc.gov)

Health Insurance Portability and Accountability Act (HIPAA) http://www.dhhs.gov

This federal law, passed in 1996, covers the legal responsibility of respecting a patient's privacy (the Privacy Rule), securing electronic transmissions of sensitive health care information (the Security Rule), and the Health Care Fraud and Abuse Control Program (HCFAC).

It's The Law

DEPARTMENT OF HEALTH AND HUMAN SERVICES

Centers for Medicare & Medicaid Services [CMS–0014–N]
  Procedures for Non-Privacy Administrative Simplification Complaints Under the Health Insurance Portability and Accountability Act of 1996
  AGENCY: Centers for Medicare & Medicaid Services (CMS), HHS.
  ACTION: Notice.
  SUMMARY: This notice sets forth the procedures for filing with the Secretary of the Department of Health and Human Services a complaint of non-compliance by a covered entity with certain provisions of the administrative simplification rules under 45 CFR parts 160, 162, and 164. It also describes the procedures the Department employs to review the complaints. These procedures are intended to facilitate the investigation and resolution of these complaints.

Federal Register/Vol. 70, No. 57/Friday, March 25, 2005/Notices (http://www.gpoaccess.gov/fr)

The Physician Self-Referral Act—Stark I, II, and III

The Stark law (42 CFR Parts 411 and 424), named for U.S. Congressman Pete Stark who sponsored the original legislation, identifies specific circumstances under which a physician may not, legally, send a patient to another facility. These restrictions apply to those cases when the referring physician actually owns, in whole or part, the facility or organization to which the patient is being sent.

> **EXAMPLE** Dr. Rogers refers Colleen Madison to Fairview Imaging Center for an MRI. The concern is that Dr. Rogers invested in Fairview Imaging Center last year.

The question: is Dr. Rogers sending Colleen for the MRI because she needs the test and it is the best facility in the area *OR* is he referring her there because he owns the company and her test will increase his own profits? It is like he is referring the patient to himself, which is why this law is commonly known as the Physician Self-Referral Act.

Stark II seeks to avoid any situations where questions might arise about the motives of the physician—was the referral made because this was what is best for the patient or because the physician wanted to make more money?

It's The Law

(1) In general.—Except as provided in subsection (b), if a physician (or an immediate family member of such physician) has a financial relationship with an entity specified in paragraph (2), then—

  (A) the physician may not make a referral to the entity for the furnishing of designated health services for which payment otherwise may be made under this title, and

  (B) the entity may not present or cause to be presented a claim under this title or bill to any individual, third party payor, or other entity for designated health services furnished pursuant to a referral prohibited under subparagraph (A).

(Continues)

(2) Financial relationship specified.—For purposes of this section, a financial relationship of a physician (or an immediate family member of such physician) with an entity specified in this paragraph is—
   (A) except as provided in subsections (c) and (d), an ownership or investment interest in the entity, or
   (B) except as provided in subsection (e), a compensation arrangement (as defined in subsection [h][1]) between the physician (or an immediate family member of such physician) and the entity.

An ownership or investment interest described in subparagraph (A) may be through equity, debt, or other means and includes an interest in an entity that holds an ownership or investment interest in any entity providing the designated health service.

Sec. 1877. [42 U.S.C. 1395] (a) Prohibition of Certain Referrals (http://www.ssa.gov)

While Stark is a federal law governing only those referrals involving Medicare and Medicaid patients, virtually all states have enacted their own versions of this law, prohibiting physician referrals to services and facilities that may result in the financial benefit of that physician.

A separate but related law, the Anti-Kickback Law, prohibits a facility from paying a physician for a referral. Again, this law seeks to avoid the question regarding the physician's motives for referring the patient.

It's The Law

"This notice extends the timeline for publication of the Phase III final rule through March 26, 2008. In accordance with section 1871(a)(3)(C) of the Act, the March 26, 2004 interim final rule shall remain in effect through March 26, 2008 (unless Phase III is published and becomes effective before March 26, 2008)."

Federal Register/Vol. 72, No. 56/Friday, March 23, 2007

Penalties for non-compliance with Stark can include lifetime exclusion from Medicare participation as well as repayment of all reimbursement received from Medicare for any referral that violates the statute (usually along with penalties). Additionally, prosecutors have found success in charging those guilty of a Stark violation under the False Claims Act at the same time.

Your compliance plan must include awareness for hospitals and facilities because health care organizations are responsible, under this law, in addition to the referring physician. Stark III actually includes a proposal that hospitals be mandated to perform thorough investigations to clearly identify all investments, ownership interests, rental agreements, and compensation contracts with physicians.

CASE STUDY

FLORIDA RADIOLOGIST TO PAY U.S. $7 MILLION TO RESOLVE FRAUD CLAIMS

WASHINGTON—April 14, 2008—A board-certified radiologist, Fred Steinberg, M.D., his imaging centers and related entities in Palm Beach County, Fla., have reached a settlement with the United States to resolve allegations of health care fraud, the Justice Department announced today. Under the terms of the settlement, the U.S. recovered $7 million.

"The settlement also resolves allegations that financial inducements were paid to physicians for patient referrals, which are prohibited under the Stark law and the Anti-Kickback statute. These inducements took the form of medical directorship, clinical research, employment, facility use and equipment lease agreements that exceeded fair market value or otherwise failed to comply with federal law.

"This settlement confirms our vigorous pursuit of allegations of fraud and abuse in federal health care programs, against both companies and individuals," said Jeffrey S. Bucholtz, acting Assistant Attorney General for the Department of Justice's Civil Division.

U.S. Department of Justice (http://www.usdoj.gov)

Risk Areas

Of course, your facility and your staff should follow all of the laws all of the time. However, it is understandable that as you look through all of the agencies and laws that focus on the honorable practice of health care, there are certain items that are targeted for investigation and therefore can provide help with prioritizing issues that must be covered. The following are some of the "hot button issues" of investigative agencies, some of which will be covered in more detail in the upcoming chapters of this textbook. Following is a brief overview to provide you with a sense of what types of concerns should be addressed in the compliance program.

Physician Services

Advance beneficiary notice (ABN): Proper use of the ABN involves having Medicare beneficiaries sign a document agreeing to pay a specified amount for a health care provision that is not expected to be covered.

Beneficiary billing: Participating providers with Medicare are not permitted to invoice the beneficiary for any monies over and above the CMS' agreed amount.

CASE STUDY

NOTE: In each CMP case resolved through a settlement agreement, the settling party has contested the OIG's allegations and denied any liability. No CMP judgment or finding of liability has been made against the settling party.

(Continues)

CASE STUDY (*Continued*)

May 15, 2007

Lee R. Rocamora, M.D., North Carolina, agreed to pay $106,600 to resolve his liability for allegedly violating the Civil Monetary Penalties Law.

The OIG alleged that the practitioner requested payments from Medicare beneficiaries in violation of his assignment agreement. Specifically, the practitioner allegedly asked his patients to enter into a membership agreement for his patient care program, under which the patients paid an annual fee. In exchange for the fee, the membership agreement specified that the practitioner would provide members with:

1. An annual comprehensive physical examination;
2. Same day or next day appointments;
3. Support personnel dedicated exclusively to members;
4. 24 hours a day and 7 days a week physician availability;
5. Prescription facilitation;
6. Coordination of referrals and expedited referrals, if medically necessary; and
7. Other service amenities as determined by the practitioner.

Office of the Inspector General (http://www.oig.hhs.gov)

Coding for coverage: This practice is one of changing a diagnosis or procedure code from that which is accurate to one that is known to be *covered* (paid for) by the patient's insurance policy. This fraudulent behavior includes coders directing physicians to document one diagnosis or procedure over the actual circumstance to support coding for coverage.

Credit balances: When a health care organization receives an overpayment, it must, by law, refund the monies to the payer, whether the insurance carrier or the patient. It is illegal to keep the money and apply it to another date of service, or another service, even when this is for the same patient.

False claims: It is considered fraud when a claim is sent for reimbursement of services that are excluded from a policy; for example, sending a claim for an experimental procedure when the policy specifically states the treatment is not covered. Also illegal is the transmittal of claims for services that are not medically necessary, as well as those provided by a physician not licensed or credentialed to perform the treatments reported, such as the removal of a cyst located on the patient's hand by a podiatrist.

Additional References

The Joint Commission

Most health care professionals are aware that the Joint Commission (formerly called the Joint Commission for Accreditation of Healthcare Organizations—JCAHO) oversees the activities of hospitals and determines accreditation worthiness. This accreditation is often used to determine a facility's eligibility for programs such as

Medicare. However, you should be aware that this highly regarded organization also accredits:

- Ambulatory care centers
- Assisted living facilities
- Behavioral health centers
- Critical access hospitals
- Home care agencies
- Laboratory services
- Long-term care facilities
- Office-based surgeries

Their list of standards, as well as patient safety goals, can be found at their website: http://www.jointcommission.org.

OIG Work Plan

Each year, on October 1, the OIG releases its work plan for the following fiscal year, identifying specific areas of concern and upcoming investigation for all types of health care facilities. The document can be downloaded from the OIG website: http://oig.hhs.gov.

Chapter Summary

There are many levels of laws, rules, and regulations that a health information management department within a health care facility must follow. Researching the federal and state governments as well as the agencies involved in overseeing health care is important to establish those factors involved in maintaining a legally compliant organization.

CHAPTER REVIEW

Multiple Choice Questions

1. Laws that are created and enacted by the legislature are called
   a. policies.
   b. administrative laws.
   c. statutes.
   d. regulations.

2. When an agency of the government creates rules, these are also called
   a. policies.
   b. administrative laws.
   c. statutes.
   d. regulations.

3. HIPAA is an example of a
   a. policy.
   b. administrative law.
   c. statute.
   d. regulation.

4. Blue Cross Blue Shield's *Participation Programs and Responsibilities* is an example of
   a. policies.
   b. administrative laws.
   c. statutes.
   d. regulations.

5. Violation of HIPAA can result in
   a. civil penalties.
   b. criminal penalties.
   c. exclusion.
   d. a and b only

6. A state's fiscal intermediary is in charge of processing claims for
   a. malpractice.
   b. Medicare.
   c. the Partnership Plan.
   d. the state's attorney general.

7. The Joint Commission does not accredit
   a. physicians' offices.
   b. hospitals.
   c. ambulatory care centers.
   d. long-term care centers.

8. The agency that oversees HIPAA and investigates violations is the
   a. RAC.
   b. OCR.
   c. OIG.
   d. DOJ.

9. CLIA certifies
   a. laboratory facilities.
   b. lab tests performed in a physician's office.
   c. lab tests performed in a hospital.
   d. all of the above

10. The law that prohibits the exchange of money or benefits for referrals of health care services is the
    a. federal False Claims Act.
    b. EMTALA.
    c. Federal Anti-Kickback Statue.
    d. Stark.

11. The National Practitioner Data Bank was created to provide easier
    a. licensure check.
    b. medical malpractice history.
    c. clinical privileges.
    d. all of the above

12. *Qui Tam* is also known as
    a. HCFAC.
    b. the Whistleblower statute.
    c. the Patient Self-Determination Act.
    d. the Health Care Quality Improvement Program.

13. The act that ensures that a patient will receive written notice of their right to refuse medical treatment is the
    a. HCFAC.
    b. Whistleblower statute.
    c. Patient Self-Determination Act.
    d. Health Care Quality Improvement Program.

14. Balance billing may be illegal when done by a
    a. participating provider.
    b. hospital.
    c. billing service.
    d. free-standing diagnostic laboratory.

15. Claims can be fraudulent when they are
    a. reported with too many modifiers.
    b. submitted for inpatient services.
    c. unsupported by documentation.
    d. sent by paper.

Research and Discussion Projects

1. Go to http://www.cms.hhs.gov and find the Conditions of Participation (CoP). Read them and discuss the standards listed.
    a. Why do you think each was included?

    _____

    _____

    _____

    _____

    b. Are there any specific actions or elements that you think are missing?

    _____

    _____

    _____

    _____

c. Compare and contrast Medicare's CoP with the rules of participation for providers to join Blue Cross Blue Shield's network and/or other private insurance carriers' networks.

_____

_____

_____

_____

_____

2. Locate and review the Comprehensive Error Rate Testing results in your state. Look through the list of elements that are studied by this evaluation of claims payments.
   a. What surprises you most?

_____

_____

_____

_____

   b. Are there any additional areas that you believe should be measured?

_____

_____

_____

_____

   c. Had your facility been evaluated by a CERT, what would you do to improve performance?

_____

_____

_____

_____

3. Identify the fiscal intermediary in your state and go to their website.
   a. What information is there that would help you with writing a compliance program?

_____

_____

_____

_____

   b. What details can you find relating to:
      i. Medicare claims processing

_____

_____

    ii. Medicaid claims processing

_____

_____

    iii. SCHIP claims processing

_____

_____

4. Research the details of the federal False Claims Act.
    a. What aspects of this law do you believe to be most important?

_____

_____

_____

_____

    b. Compare and contrast the segments of the law that affect
      i. Physician's offices

_____

_____

_____

_____

      ii. Hospitals

_____

_____

_____

_____

      iii. Long-term care facilities

_____

_____

_____

_____

Chapter 5

Compliance: Patient Consent

Learning Outcomes

- Identify the various situations in which consent is required
- Determine the components of each type of written consent form
- Explain the types of advance directives
- Establish internal policies for acquiring patient consent
- Design a process to handle release of information

Key Terms

advance directive / a document in which an individual states his agreement and/or refusal for future health care services

consent for treatment / a written authorization, signed by the patient or guardian, for the physician or health care facility to provide services and treatments

Do Not Resuscitate (DNR) order / a form expressing that, should the patient go into cardiac arrest, he does not wish to be resuscitated, or have any heroic measures taken to save his life

express consent / written consent that is specific and signed by the individual

health care surrogacy / an individual named to speak for a patient regarding procedures and treatments when that patient is unable to communicate their wishes

informed consent / a regulation mandating the sharing of information with a patient by a health care provider to assist the patient in deciding to agree or refuse treatment

implied consent / a situation where agreement can be reasonably assumed based on an individual's actions or behavior

living will / a legal document specifying life-saving procedures and treatments to which the individual agrees or refuses

superconfidentiality / PHI that may not be disclosed without written permission of the patient, except to a governmental agency as prescribed by law

74

Chapter Case Study

"July 28, 2003: A physician from Minneapolis, Minnesota, agreed to pay $53,400 to resolve his liability under the CMP [Civil Monetary Penalties] provision applicable to violations of a provider's assignment agreement. By accepting assignment for all covered services, a participating provider agrees that he or she will not collect from a Medicare beneficiary more than the applicable deductible and coinsurance for covered services.

"The OIG alleged that the physician created a program whereby the physician's patients were asked to sign a yearly contract and pay a yearly fee for services that the physician characterized as 'not covered' by Medicare. The OIG further alleged that because at least some of the services described in the contract were actually covered and reimbursable by Medicare, each contract presented to the Medicare patients constituted a request for payment other than the coinsurance and applicable deductible for covered services in violation of the terms of the physician's assignment agreement. In addition to payment of the settlement amount, the physician agreed not to request similar payments from beneficiaries in the future." (http://www.oig.hhs.gov)

Introduction

Knowledge is power. You have heard that said, read it on bumper stickers, and probably believe it in part. Patients in the 21st century have the ability to gain knowledge and participate in their health care process as never before.

In the last decade or so, the Internet has enabled virtually everyone to become better educated about health, disease, diagnoses, and treatments. One does not have to go to medical school to be able to investigate interactions of medications, research signs and symptoms; one can even watch a video of actual surgery at some websites. Those patients who actively get involved in their health care with their physicians and health care providers often have better outcomes.

The laws see this as an important part of the process, as well. Therefore, your facility must be knowledgeable about issues regarding patient consent.

Patient Consent

The Patient Self-Determination Act (PSDA) 42 U.S.C. 1395 cc (a), part of the Omnibus Budget Reconciliation Act, was created to increase interactivity between patients and their health care professionals when making decisions that affect them and their health.

It's The Law

"(a) to provide written information to each such individual concerning

    (i) an individual's rights under State law to make decisions concerning such medical care, including the right to accept or refuse medical or surgical treatment and the right to formulate advance directives; and

    (ii) the provider's or organization's written policies respecting the implementation of such rights;

(b) to document in the individual's medical record whether or not the individual has executed an advance directive;

(c) not to condition the provision of care or otherwise discriminate against an individual based on whether or not the individual has executed an advance directive;

(d) to ensure compliance with requirements of State law respecting advance directives; and

(e) to provide for education for staff and the community on issues concerning advance directives."

(http://www.thomas.loc.gov)

Initially, this law referred only to life-sustaining aspects of health care. However, over the years, it has evolved to a wider aspect of treatments, including surgery and clinical trials.

Originally, there was objection by the clinical community to the opportunity for a patient to consent or refuse medical treatment. The feelings were held that only a health care professional, generally the attending physician, was qualified and educated enough to determine what the best course of treatment should be. However, it was soon realized that individual patients, while not having the medical training, did have their own perception of potential outcomes and should have a say in these important decisions that resulted in such a tremendous impact on their lives. The issues of quality of life became a point of discussion and consideration, especially because it is the patient, and not the physician, who must enjoy or suffer the consequences of any procedure.

The next step was to take the concept of consent further. If a patient is to participate in the decision-making process, he or she will need to be given details by the physician regarding the recommendation. This is the foundation of **informed consent**; the stated responsibility of health care professionals to provide the appropriate specifics so the patient can make an informed decision.

The principle of informed consent, and the right to refuse medical treatment, is evident in the Fourteenth Amendment, section 1, of the U.S. Constitution (see below).

It's The Law

Section 1. All persons born or naturalized in the United States, and subject to the jurisdiction thereof, are citizens of the United States and of the State wherein they reside. No State shall make or enforce any law which shall abridge the privileges or immunities of citizens of the United States; nor shall any State deprive any person of life, liberty, or property, without due process of law; nor deny to any person within its jurisdiction the equal protection of the laws.

When lawsuits were filed seeking to defend an individual's right to be free of undesired medical intervention, the right was readily recognized and clearly affirmed. As a matter of fact, the Supreme Court ruled that the Fourteenth Amendment protected a right to refuse medical treatment in Cruzan v. Director, Missouri Department of Health (1990).

Consent to Treat

The courts ruled that patients with the mental capacity for decision-making have the right to refuse medical interventions even when those procedures and services are life-sustaining. These rulings have given way to what you know as informed consent for treatment. The American Medical Association (AMA) states on its website, *"Providing the patient relevant information has long been a physician's ethical obligation, but the legal concept of informed consent itself is recent"* (http://www.ama-assn.org, Legal Issues, Informed consent).

For decisions that are so important to the patient and may have a tremendous legal impact on your health care organization, it is always best to get the patient's consent, or refusal, in writing. Actual written documentation, a **Consent for Treatment** form, provides evidence that rules were followed and patients' rights were protected. You never want to depend on someone's memory, especially when it comes to health care decisions that are often wrapped up with emotions and interpersonal relationships.

If a health care professional treats a patient without consent, it can be construed as nonconsensual touching, also known as battery—a felony in some states.

Types of Consent

Consent means the same thing in health care as it does in everyday life—agreement. Patient consent can take two formats: **implied consent** and **express consent**.

Implied consent indicates that the patient did not specifically write down an agreement to be treated by a health care professional; however, their actions indirectly indicated this agreement.

EXAMPLE Drew Endicott called and made an appointment to see Dr. Keiths. He then came to Dr. Keiths' office and willingly walked into the examination room to meet with this physician. Drew's actions indicate that he has agreed to see this physician and have this physician care for him.

Express consent is a more formal process of consent that, most often, includes the signing of a consent form by the patient.

To create a thorough and compliant informed consent document, there are several components that should be included. The United States Code of Federal Regulations (CFR) identified eight elements that must be included in an agreement for people to participate in a health-related research study. While surgery or other therapies provided in your facility most probably do not typically fall into the category of research, this list can be adapted to support all of the factors that would go into the process of making the best decision for oneself or a family member.

Let's review each of these components, as adapted from the AMA and the CFR, to ensure the definition of informed consent is met:

• *The patient's diagnosis or reason underlying the recommendation for this procedure or protocol.* It is important to clearly state the condition or illness that the procedure is designed to address. Some patients may have more than one health concern, so the focus of the decision should be pinpointed.

- *A description of the procedure or therapy protocol.* This should be as complete as possible without getting into technical details. Included in this section should be the type of anesthesia that is expected to be used and any mid-procedure changes or extensions that may be deemed necessary.

  EXAMPLE The consent form for Catherine DeMarco's upcoming hysterectomy surgery might include that the procedure will take an abdominal approach under general anesthesia, and there is a possibility that her ovaries and fallopian tubes will be removed, as well as her uterus. However, this will not be known until Dr. Harrison can visualize the organs during the surgery.

- *The expected benefits.* The primary intention of recommending the procedure or protocol should be described with as few absolute terms as possible. There are few guarantees in health care, so it is important that the language of this portion of the document does not promise something that cannot absolutely be accomplished.

  EXAMPLE This radiation protocol is expected to prevent the malignant cells from spreading to any other organs.

- *The potential risks of having the procedure or therapy, including side effects.* This listing of potential risks and side effects must be complete. It is advisable to include the risks of the procedure and anesthesia, as well as any medications expected to be routinely provided immediately before and after the event.

- *The potential risks of* not *having the procedure or therapy.* This should not be used to scare the patient into agreeing to the procedure, but enable them to understand the repercussions of refusing. There are cases when there is little downside to refusing a medical treatment. At other times, it can be fatal.

- *Alternative treatments.* The health care industry has become much more open to alternative methods such as acupuncture, physical therapy, and herbal remedies. These options should be presented without opinions of their ability to help the patient. However, if credible statistics are available, they can be included. In certain cases, a timeline may be integrated for realistic measurement of success. This way, a patient can decide to try an alternative, yet know when to come back and move forward with this physician's recommendation for a more traditional approach.

  EXAMPLE A landmark study has shown that acupuncture provides pain relief and improves function for people with osteoarthritis of the knee and serves as an effective complement to standard care. The study, the largest Phase III clinical trial of acupuncture for knee osteoarthritis, was funded by NCCAM and the National Institute of Arthritis and Musculoskeletal and Skin Diseases, both components of the National Institutes of Health.

  (National Center for Complementary and Alternative Medicine (NCCAM), National Institutes of Health, http://nccam.nih.gov/research/results/acuosteo.htm)

- *Length of time for recovery.* Very often patients want, and need, to know when they will be able to resume certain activities, such as returning to work or caring for a child. Depending upon the case, you might want to include estimates for a partial recovery, and then complete recovery.

Consent forms should be certain the time frames for the patient's recovery after the procedure are stated as estimates. Different patients heal at different rates. It is recommended to include a phrase that identifies that the time frame is based on there being no complications or other health conditions that may slow healing.

- *Necessary aftercare.* Some procedures and therapies will require the patient to have assistance after they are discharged from the facility. This may relate to a physician's orders not to drive or for complete bed rest. Even one day of complete bed rest for someone who lives alone will require the patient to make special arrangements for a relative, a friend, or a home-health agency. Include any potential special equipment that might be necessary, such as crutches or a bedpan.

- *Patient costs.* Regardless of the terms of their insurance policy, the patient deserves the right to know, in advance, what the insurance company will most likely cover and how much the patient may be expected to pay. The financial obligation may be an important component in the patient's decision-making process to consent. The patient may need some time to save up or make alternate financial arrangements. When someone is recuperating from a procedure, he or she should be able to focus on getting better, not worrying about paying a surprise medical bill. In addition, when the patient understands his or her financial obligation and agrees, in writing, the chances of your facility being paid without a collection agency increase dramatically.

This may seem like a great deal of work. However, keep in mind that your office or facility will most likely perform the same procedure over and over. Create a file on your computer so you can print out the applicable consent form any time a patient is preparing for a procedure. Figure 5-1 is an example of a consent form used in a physician's office.

Advance Directives

In cases where patients have lost their ability to decide for themselves but have an **advance directive**, the courts have ruled that these advance wishes should be honored.

Essentially, an advance directive is a written, or oral, statement made by a patient detailing what health care treatments they consent to and which they refuse. This is a way for the individual to consent or refuse treatment even when they are unable to evaluate the circumstances and communicate these wishes at the time. The patient is directing their care before, or in advance of, needing to make these decisions.

The most common type of advance directive is a **living will**. Each state has its own variation of the language for these forms, but they are very similar. Figure 5-2 is a sample living will from the state of Florida. Notice that the individual completing the will has the option to request or refuse various types of procedures to patients in life-threatening circumstances.

Health Care Center
123 Healthy Way
Methods, FL 01234

PATIENT INFO

AUTHORIZATIONS & AGREEMENTS

CONSENT TO TREATMENT AND RELEASE OF INFORMATION

Consent to Treatment: I/we voluntary authorize the rendering of such care, including diagnostic procedures and medical treatment, by authorized agents and employees of the Health Care Center (HCC), and the medical staff, or their designees, as may in their professional judgement be deemed necessary or beneficial, and may include testing for HIV (the virus that causes AIDS) and other blood borne diseases. I/we acknowledge that no guarantees have been made as to the effect of such examination of treatment on my condition or the condition of the person for whom I am duly authorized to sign. I/we understand that I/we have the right to make decisions concerning my health care or the health care of the person for whom I am duly authorized to make such decisions, including the right to refuse medical and surgical procedures.

☐ I have formulated Advance Directives (living will, health care surrogate declaration, durable power of attorney) and request that these directives govern my course of care, in as much as is possible under state or federal law. I understand that it is my responsibility to provide the HCC with a copy of my Advance Directives and that those directives will not govern my course of care until they have been filed in my medical record.
☐ Advance Directives attached   ☐ Advance Directives not attached

☐ I have not formulated Advance Directives (living will, health care surrogate declaration, durable power of attorney), but I understand that it is my right to make decisions regarding my course of treatment, including the executing of advanced directives.

Release of Information: I authorize the release from my medical records or the records of the person for whom I am duly authorized to do so, of such medical and/or psychiatric information as may be required by;
1. Any health, sickness, and accident insurance carrier, workman's compensation or agency (social welfare, governmental) which is legally responsible, or which the HCC has good cause to believe is legally responsible for all or any part of HCC's charges and/or professional fees.
2. Physicians or health care facilities rendering professional care to the patient.
3. The Peer Review Organization responsible for reviewing medical care under Public Law.
The signed authorization complies with rules governing the release of PRIVILEGED information, it assures confidentiality of information and permits the HCC to correspond with those agencies/persons having legitimate interest in the course of care rendered.

Procurement of Information: I/we authorize the release of any medical records of other physicians, hospitals or health care facilities that the Hospital needs for my present medical care or the present medical care of the person for whom I am duly authorized to sign.
This consent may be revoked at any time, except is the extent that action has already been taken, by the patient/duly authorized agent and will expire automatically one year from the date below.

_____   _____   _____
Signature of Patient or Next of Kin, Legal Agent/Guardian   Signature of Witness   Date
and Relationship to Patient

FINANCIAL RESPONSIBILITY

Guarantee of Payment: I/we agree to be responsible to the Health Care Center (HCC) for charges resulting from services rendered at their prevailing rates. I/we agree all bills are due in full upon demand. Should I/we fail to honor this agreement, I/we agree to pay any collection cost or attorney fees resulting from the collection of my accounts.

No granting of extensions, indulgences or forbearances to the patient or any responsible party and no delays or lack of diligence on the part of the HCC in enforcing any rights shall in any manner release the undersigned liability. If the undersigned is more that one person this obligation shall be joint and several. I/we agree the HCC is not party to any disputed claim or peer-review decision which affects payment of any claim filed on my behalf and that upon request for payment from the HCC, I/we agree to pay any outstanding balance.

Assignment of Benefits: I/we hereby assign all rights and privileges and authorize payment directly to the HCC for any claim filed on my behalf or on the behalf of the person for whom I am duly authorized to sign for insurance benefits. I/we agree this assignment is primary to any assignment given after this date including any cost relative to attorney fees. I/we also understand that I/we am financially responsible to the Hospital for charges not covered by this assignment or not paid on a timely basis by the insurance company.

Certification: I certify that I have read and understand the authorizations given above and I am the patient, or I am duly authorized by the patient to execute the above and accept its terms.

_____
Date
If patient is unable to sign, secure consent of
Next of Kin or Legal Agent and Indicate reason below:
☐ Minor   ☐ Disoriented

☐ Medically Unstable   ☐ Incompetent

_____
Signature of Patient or Next of Kin, Legal Agent/Guardian or Relationship to Patient

_____
Signature of Witness

Figure 5-1   Consent to Treatment and Release of Information

Living Will

Declaration made this _____ day of _____, 2____, I, _____,
willfully and voluntarily make known my desire that my dying not be artificially prolonged under the
circumstances set forth below, and I do hereby declare that, if at any time I am mentally or physically
incapacitated and

_____(initial) I have a terminal condition,

or _____(initial) I have an end-stage condition,

or _____(initial) I am in a persistent vegetative state,

and if my attending or treating physician and another consulting physician have determined that there is
no reasonable medical probability of my recovery from such condition, I direct that life-prolonging
procedures be withheld or withdrawn when the application of such procedures would serve only to
prolong artificially the process of dying, and that I be permitted to die naturally with only the
administration of medication or the performance of any medical procedure deemed necessary to provide
me with comfort, care, or to alleviate pain.

I do ___, I do not ___ desire that nutrition and hydration (food and water) be withheld or withdrawn when
the application of such procedures would serve only to prolong artificially the process of dying.

It is my intention that this declaration be honored by my family and physician as the final expression of
my legal right to refuse medical or surgical treatment and to accept the consequences for such refusal.

In the event I have been determined to be unable to provide express and informed consent regarding the
withholding, withdrawal, or continuation of life-prolonging procedures, I wish to designate, as my
surrogate, to carry out the provisions of this declaration:

Name _____

Street Address _____

City _____ State _____ Phone _____

I understand the full import of this declaration, and I am emotionally and mentally competent to make this
declaration.

Additional Instructions (optional): _____

_____

_____

_____

_____

(Signed) _____

Witness _____   Witness _____

Street Address _____   Street Address _____

City _____ State _____   City _____ State _____

Phone _____   Phone _____

At least one witness must not be a husband or wife or a blood relative of the principal.

Figure 5-2 Sample living will

> An attorney is not required to create an advance directive. Be aware, however, that each state has its own variations of these documents. It is important to follow the laws of the state in which the patient is being treated.

In most states, by law, hospitals, nursing homes, home health agencies, assisted living facilities, and hospices are required to present written information to patients at admission educating them about their rights to complete a living will and/or appoint a health care surrogate. It is good practice for physicians' offices to provide this information to their patients, as well as to most particularly primary care physicians, and those whose specialties may involve working with patients diagnosed with life-threatening conditions, such as oncologists, neurologists, and cardiologists. The health information management department in all health care facilities should keep a copy of the patient's signed living will in their chart so it is available whenever necessary.

Living wills are valid from the date they are signed and must be witnessed, but are not usually notarized. An attorney is not required to create a legally binding living will. A patient can change his or her mind at any time and either issue a new living will or communicate his or her new desires in some other manner. The most recently dated living will, if the patient has more than one, is considered the current document.

Another type of advance directive is known as a DNR, the acronym for **Do Not Resuscitate (DNR) order**. This is a form signed by a patient, most often one who is in terminal or end-of-life stages, who decides that if cardiac arrest occurs, he or she does not wish any measures to restore life, such as cardiopulmonary resuscitation (CPR) or being placed on a respirator.

Health Care Surrogates

When there is no written living will, and the patient is currently unable to make informed decisions due to physical or mental dysfunction, the courts have determined standards for proxy decision-making. This means that an individual other than the patient is designated to assist with making decisions for the patient. The courts have concluded that the loss of the ability to exercise the right to refuse treatment does not necessitate the loss of the right itself. The courts also decided that, in order to prevent this right from being overshadowed, that another person must exercise the right on the patient's behalf.

The official naming of another person who is given the authority to make decisions for the patient, when the patient is unable to do this for himself or herself, is another type of advance directive, called a **health care surrogacy**. While the patient is still capable of making a decision, he or she can document the designation of a health care surrogate. This should be someone who can carry out the patient's wishes, knowing the patient well enough to be able to decide what the patient would consent to if able. A health care surrogate does not have to be a relative. Actually, under certain circumstances, it may be advisable that the next-of-kin be avoided for this responsibility. Some life-and-death decisions may have to be made, such as withholding food and water. This is not a decision that should be made, under usual conditions, by the patient's young child, for example.

Some states call this document "Designation of Health Care Surrogate," as shown in Figure 5-3, while others might title this a "Durable Power of Attorney

Designation of Health Care Surrogate

Name: _____

In the event that I have been determined to be incapacitated to provide informed consent for medical treatment and surgical and diagnostic procedures, I wish to designate as my surrogate for health care decisions:

     Name _____
     Street Address _____
     City _____ State _____ Phone _____
     Phone: _____

If my surrogate is unwilling or unable to perform his or her duties, I wish to designate as my alternate surrogate:

     Name _____
     Street Address _____
     City _____ State _____ Phone _____

I fully understand that this designation will permit my designee to make health care decisions and to provide, withhold, or withdraw consent on my behalf; or apply for public benefits to defray the cost of health care; and to authorize my admission to or transfer from a health care facility.
Additional instructions (optional):

_____
_____
_____
_____

I further affirm that this designation is not being made as a condition of treatment or admission to a health care facility. I will notify and send a copy of this document to the following persons other than my surrogate, so they may know who my surrogate is.

Name _____
Name _____

Signed _____

Date _____

Witnesses   1. _____

                2. _____

At least one witness must not be a husband or wife or a blood relative of the principal.

Figure 5-3   Sample of a designation of health care surrogate form

for Health Care" or "Health Care Proxy." Regardless of the title, patients should be helped to understand that the scope of the authority is limited to health care decisions alone and does not involve access to bank accounts or other personal assets.

Advance Beneficiary Notice

The Advance Beneficiary Notice (ABN) is another form used in the process of obtaining consent to treat. This form is mandated for consent to treat a Medicare beneficiary whose procedure or service is known, or expected, to be denied Medicare coverage, resulting in the patient having to pay all charges, or a portion of the charges beyond their co-payment and co-insurance. This should also be executed whenever the cost falls under the patient's obligation to pay because he or she has not yet met this year's annual deductible, or the co-insurance payment is substantial.

EXAMPLE

SPECIFIC CRITERIA FOR THE ADVANCE BENEFICIARY NOTICE (ABN)

An acceptable ABN for the denial or reduction of payment must meet the following criteria:

- The notice must be given in writing and in advance of providing the service/item (where a standard form is mandatory, notice must be given using the standard form).
- The notice must include the patient's name, description of service/item, and reason(s) the service/item may not be paid for by Medicare.
- The patient or authorized representative must sign and date the ABN before a service is rendered, indicating that the patient assumes financial liability for the service/item if payment is denied or reduced for the reasons indicated on the ABN.
- The original ABN should be filed with the patient's medical records. Providers are also encouraged to provide the beneficiary with a copy of the signed notice.

ABN forms are already designed by CMS (see Figure 5-4), and it is recommended that your facility use its official form to assure that all information is covered. Make certain that every blank line is completed and, if this is done by hand, confirm that the handwriting is very legible. Ambiguity will not protect your office.

Exhibit 1
Advance Beneficiary Notice (CMS-R-131-G) For General Use

Patient's Name:_____Medicare # (HICN):_____

ADVANCE BENEFICIARY NOTICE (ABN)

NOTE: You need to make a choice about receiving these health care items or services.

We expect that Medicare will not pay for the item(s) or service(s) that are described below. Medicare does not pay for all of your health care costs. Medicare only pays for covered items and services when Medicare rules are met. The fact that Medicare may not pay for a particular item or service does not mean that you should not receive it. There may be a good reason your doctor recommended it. Right now, in your case, **Medicare probably will not pay for –**

Items or Services:

Because:

The purpose of this form is to help you make an informed choice about whether or not you want to receive these items or services, knowing that you might have to pay for them yourself. Before you make a decision about your options, you should **read this entire notice carefully.**

- Ask us to explain, if you don't understand why Medicare probably won't pay.
- Ask us how much these items or services will cost you (**Estimated Cost: $_____**), in case you have to pay for them yourself or through other insurance.

PLEASE CHOOSE **ONE** OPTION. CHECK **ONE** BOX. SIGN & **DATE YOUR** CHOICE.

☐ **Option 1. YES.** **I want to receive these items or services.**
I understand that Medicare will not decide whether to pay unless I receive these items or services. Please submit my claim to Medicare. I understand that you may bill me for items or services and that I may have to pay the bill while Medicare is making its decision. If Medicare does pay, you will refund to me any payments I made to you that are due to me. If Medicare denies payment, I agree to be personally and fully responsible for payment. That is, I will pay personally, either out of pocket or through any other insurance that I have. I understand I can appeal Medicare's decision.

☐ **Option 2. NO.** **I have decided not to receive these items or services.**
I will not receive these items or services. I understand that you will not be able to submit a claim to Medicare and that I will not be able to appeal your opinion that Medicare won't pay.

Date **Signature of patient or person acting on patient's behalf**

NOTE: Your health information will be kept confidential. Any information that we collect about you on this form will be kept confidential in our offices. If a claim is submitted to Medicare, your health information on this form may be shared with Medicare. Your health information which Medicare sees will be kept confidential by Medicare.

OMB Approval No. 0938-0566   Form No. CMS-R-131-G   (June 2002)
Exhibit 2
Advance Beneficiary Notice (CMS-R-131-L) For Laboratory Tests.

Patient's Name: Medicare # (HICN):

Figure 5-4 Advance Beneficiary Notice

Protected Health Information

The Privacy Rule portion of the Health Insurance Portability and Accountability Act (HIPAA) directs every health care organization to protect patients' confidential health information. There are several requirements for patient consent with regard to protected health information (PHI).

Privacy Notices

The Office of Civil Rights (OCR), within the U.S. Department of Health and Human Services (HHS), oversees compliance with HIPAA.

It's The Law

"Privacy Practices Notice. Each covered entity, with certain exceptions, must provide a notice of its privacy practices. The Privacy Rule requires that the notice contain certain elements. The notice must describe the ways in which the covered entity may use and disclose protected health information. The notice must state the covered entity's duties to protect privacy, provide a notice of privacy practices, and abide by the terms of the current notice. The notice must describe individuals' rights, including the right to complain to HHS and to the covered entity if they believe their privacy rights have been violated. The notice must include a point of contact for further information and for making complaints to the covered entity. Covered entities must act in accordance with their notices."

(http://www.hhs.gov/hipaa)

HIPAA requires that the first time a patient makes contact with a health care facility, he or she must be presented with a copy of the organization's privacy practices notice. To confirm that this is done, this law goes on to mandate a written acknowledgement, signed by the patient, confirming that the patient did receive the notice and has been made aware of their rights under this law.

It's The Law

"Acknowledgement of Notice Receipt. A covered health care provider with a direct treatment relationship with individuals must make a good faith effort to obtain written acknowledgement from patients of receipt of the privacy practices notice. The Privacy Rule does not prescribe any particular content for the acknowledgement. The provider must document the reason for any failure to obtain the patient's written acknowledgement. The provider is relieved of the need to request acknowledgement in an emergency treatment situation."

(http://www.hhs.gov/hipaa)

The signed acknowledgement should be placed in the patient's chart so it can be available should an audit occur. Figure 5-5 is a sample of a privacy practices notice acknowledgement.

Health Care Center

NOTICE OF PRIVACY PRACTICES

ACKNOWLEDGEMENT

I have received a copy of the HCC *Notice of Privacy Practices.* I understand that HCC has the right to change its *Notice of Privacy Practices* from time to time and that I may contact HCC at any time to obtain a current copy of the *Notice of Privacy Practices.*

Patient Name (print) _____

Signature of Patient/
Legal Representative _____

Relationship to Patient _____

Date _____

FOR OFFICE USE ONLY	
PRINT PLEASE	
I have attempted to obtain the patient's signature on this form, but was not able to for the following reason:	
Date:	*Please document the reasons you were unable to obtain the signature.*
Initials:	

Figure 5-5 Notice of Privacy Practices Acknowledgment

Release of Information

The Privacy Rule (45 CFR §164.530) covers the conditions with which you must protect PHI, as well as those circumstances that permit you to disclose the confidential details of a patient's health status.

> **It's The Law**
>
> "Disclosures and Requests for Disclosures. Covered entities must establish and implement policies and procedures (which may be standard protocols) for routine, recurring disclosures, or requests for disclosures, that limit the protected health information disclosed to that which is the minimum amount reasonably necessary to achieve the purpose of the disclosure. Individual review of each disclosure is not required. For non-routine, non-recurring disclosures, or requests for disclosures that it makes, covered entities must develop criteria designed to limit disclosures to the information reasonably necessary to accomplish the purpose of the disclosure and review each of these requests individually in accordance with the established criteria."
>
> (http://www.hhs.gov/ocr/hipaa)

As you have read in this chapter already, the documentation, whether paper or electronic, must be in place before any PHI is disclosed outside of those permitted uses and disclosures listed in the HIPAA Privacy Rule. Note that it is advisable, whenever possible, to obtain written permission in all circumstances, even those when it is not required. You may have had this experience when requesting a copy of your own health care records from one of your health care professionals. They should have had you complete a Release of Information form indicating:

- *The patient identification:* This should include the name and identifying information, such as birth date, of the individual whose PHI is being requested to be disclosed.

- *To whom the PHI is permitted to be disclosed:* The name of the person or entity that is being given permission to receive this information. For example, if the copies of the PHI are of the patient's own personal records, this would show that individual's information as the recipient. If the patient is requesting records be copied to a new physician, for example, the name of the new physician and practice would be shown in this section.

- *Precisely who will be releasing the PHI:* Here, the patient should identify the facility that is in current possession of the records containing the PHI. This is the entity to whom permission is being given to release the information.

- *Specifically what information is to be disclosed:* The exact scope of the PHI to be disclosed. The patient may indicate "all records" or "from May 5 through July 2" or "all records pertaining to the diagnosis and treatment of the fractured ulna."

- *An expiration date or event for this release:* Releases are not permitted to be open-ended, and must have a specific time frame assigned to them.

- *A statement notifying the signer that he or she may revoke this permission at any time.* The patient or signer of the release may revoke, or take back this permission, at any time.

The facility at which you work, regardless of size or structure, should already have a form. It will look similar to the sample shown in Figure 5-6.

Release of information (ROI) has actually become a business of its own. Many independent companies, specializing in the processing of disclosure requests from patients, have opened.

HCC
Health Care Centre

AUTHORIZATION TO PERMIT DISCLOSURE OF PROTECTED HEALTH INFORMATION
PLEASE COMPLETE ALL APPROPRIATE GRAY AREAS ON THIS FORM. SEE PAGE TWO (2) FOR INSTRUCTIONS.

Your Name: _____   Your Birth Date: ____ / ____ / ____
                                                              MONTH   DAY   YEAR

Your Address: _____

Insurance Policyholder's Name: _____

Customer Number: _____   Telephone: _____

SECTION 1. Please provide the name of the persons or organizations that you are authorizing to receive your Protected Health Information from HCC.

_____   Relationship to you (check one)
                                          ☐ Spouse   ☐ Parent
Name   DateofBirth   ☐ Child
                                          ☐ Other _____
Note-If a person listed is a Power of Attorney (POA) or other legal representatives, see reverse side for further instructions.

SECTION 2a. Please check a box to indicate the INFORMATION to be disclosed.

☐ ALL - Check this box if you wish to have all information disclosed to the individual identified in SECTION 1 above.
OR
☐ SPECIFIC – Check if you wish to have only the following specific health information about you disclosed (must fill in):

_____
_____

SECTION 2b. Please check this box to indicate the PURPOSE of the disclosure of your health information.

☐ Check if the disclosure is "at the request of the individual" (or the individual's personal representative).
OR
☐ Check if the disclosure is only for the following SPECIFIC purpose listed below (must write in the specific purposes):

_____
_____

SECTION 3. I understand that I have the right to revoke this authorization at any time by providing a written statement of revocation to HCC. I am aware that my revocation will not be effective until received by HCC and will not be effective regarding the uses and/or disclosures of my health information that HCC has made prior to receipt of my revocation. If the authorization was obtained as a condition of obtaining insurance coverage, other law provides HCC with the right to contest a claim under the policy or the policy itself. A copy of this form shall be as valid as the original.

I understand that I am under no obligation to sign this form and that HCC may not condition payment, health plan enrollment or benefits eligibility on my decision to sign this authorization unless this authorization is being sought for determinations of health plan enrollment, eligibility, underwriting,and/or risk rating. I understand that once information is disclosed pursuant to this authorization, it may no longer be protected by federal privacy regulations and could be re-disclosed by the person or entity that receives it. I am entitled to keep a copy of this form for my records.

SECTION 4. This authorization will expire 30 MONTHS from the date signed. If you want this authorization to expire prior to the 30-month limit, please indicate an expiration dateor an event that relates to you (the customer), or the purpose of this authorization:

_____
_____

Signature of You or Your Personal Representative: _____

Please print name: _____   Date: _____
(If signed by Your Personal Representative, please see page two (2) for additional instructions.)

(Continues)

Figure 5-6 Authorization to disclose protected health information sample form

---

About this form and who fills it out:

This Authorization Form is to be used when an individual wishes to give another person access to his or her health information. When completed, it will allow HCC to disclose your health information to the person(s) stated on the form. Your health information is protected by the Health Insurance Portability and Accountability Act of 1996 ("HIPAA"), State Laws, and the privacy policies and procedures at HCC.

SECTION 1.

The information completed in this section tells us to whom you want the information released. If the person identified is a Power of Attorney (POA) or other legal representative who has paperwork identifying their health care decision-making abilities on your behalf, please submit a copy of that paperwork, along with this completed form to HCC for review.

SECTION 2a & 2b.

In this section, you tell us what information you wish to be released (2a) and the purpose of the disclosure (2b). You may choose to have **all** of your protected health information released to the person named in Section 1, or if you choose not to release all information, then you must **specify** with a written description the information to be disclosed to the designated individual.

SECTION 3.

This section outlines your rights regarding this form. Please read thoroughly.

SECTION 4.

This authorization form will expire in 30 months from the date signed. If you want this form to naturally expire, please skip to the signature portion of this form. If you want this authorization to expire prior to the 30-month limit, please indicate date, or an event that relates to you, the customer, or the purpose of this authorization.

After completing this form, please send it back to us.

Fax the form to us at: **500-555-3626**

Or mail the form to us at: **HCC MEMBER SERVICES**
PO BOX 5555
Anytown, FL 33333

Figure 5-6   *(Continued)*

Consent to Contact

In a facility's efforts to assure the protection of a patient's PHI from any and all unauthorized disclosure, it is a good idea to include, in the patient's records, the individual's preferred and approved method of contact. This should cover all contact between the facility and the patient, including, but not limited to, reminders for upcoming appointments, notification of test results, or anything else that one might think was not a violation of confidentiality, and yet . . . is.

> **EXAMPLE** Mary Gatson made an appointment with an oncologist because her physician suspected that the lump she felt might be malignant. Terry, the nurse, called and left a voice mail reminding her of the appointment and to bring certain documents with her. Mary did not want anyone to know, but her gossipy roommate picked up the voice mail, and the next thing Mary knew, her whole apartment building knew she might have cancer.

As a part of the new patient or admissions packet, it is a good idea to include a form permitting the patient to choose their acceptable methods of contact. Examples include: voice mail, e-mail, regular mail, etc.

Superconfidential Information

There are certain conditions that are considered **superconfidential**. This means that you are not permitted to release this information without written patient permission, unless mandated by law. There are five health conditions covered by this layer of extra protection:

- HIV/AIDS
- Pregnant minors
- Sexually Transmitted Diseases (reportable transmittable diseases)
- Alcohol and drug addiction (substance abuse)
- Mental health conditions

State laws vary; however, in most cases, diagnoses of HIV and most STDs must be reported to the state department of health. Beyond reporting these to the appropriate state health officials, your facility is not permitted to use or disclose information about these circumstances without the patient's written permission. Your personal feelings as to whether a patient's parents should know about the child's pregnancy or the spouse should know about the diagnosis of an STD are irrelevant. You are entitled to your opinions, but you are not permitted to voice them, write them down, or communicate them in any other way. It is not your PHI and, therefore, you have no say in the use or disclosure of this very delicate information. It is not your job to interfere in the personal relationships of your patients.

> Remember that identifying a procedure or treatment may be as revealing as disclosing the actual diagnosis. So, your policy should be to disclose NOTHING to ANYONE.

Chapter Summary

Documentation is critical to your compliance with laws and regulations. Whether paper or electronic, these forms provide definite evidence that your facility is following the rules. This chapter has covered the circumstances in which you will need to document consent from the patient, or his or her guardian, to care for the patient, to disclose information, and other particular issues.

CHAPTER REVIEW

Multiple Choice Questions

1. The Fourteenth Amendment of the U.S. Constitution supports the right to
   a. free medical care.
   b. refuse medical treatment.
   c. home health care.
   d. know all diagnoses of one's spouse.

2. One type of patient consent is
   a. obligatory consent.
   b. statutory consent.
   c. implied consent.
   d. inferred consent.

3. Express consent means consent was given
   a. quickly.
   b. in a same-day surgery center.
   c. by a legal guardian.
   d. in writing.

4. Without a signed consent to treat, a health care professional might be charged with
   a. battery.
   b. an extra fee.
   c. penalties.
   d. failure to approve.

5. Informed consent forms should include the
   a. patient's diagnosis.
   b. patient's address.
   c. patient's insurance policy identification.
   d. patient's next-of-kin.

6. An example of an advance directive is a
   a. living will.
   b. DNR.
   c. health care surrogacy.
   d. all of the above

7. The acronym PHI stands for
   a. patient hotline identification.
   b. protected health information.
   c. primary health insurance.
   d. protective health inservices.

8. Under HIPAA, all covered entities must get a signed
   a. registration form.
   b. insurance policy waiver.
   c. acknowledgement of notice receipt.
   d. benefits approval.

9. To disclose PHI, it is often required to get the patient to sign a
   a. release of information form.
   b. credit card approval notice.
   c. consent for treatment form.
   d. ABN.

10. Superconfidential information includes diagnoses of:
    a. pregnancy (in minors).
    b. sexually transmitted disease.
    c. alcohol addiction.
    d. all of the above

11. Informed consent is a principle that has been taken from
    a. the Patient Budget Law.
    b. the Patient Self-Determination Act.
    c. HIPAA.
    d. the Law of Demand.

12. Before agreeing to a procedure, a patient should be told the
    a. length of time for recovery.
    b. length of time for the procedure.
    c. potential risks of having the procedure.
    d. a and c only

13. When a patient signs a DNR, it means they refuse
    a. medications.
    b. transfer to a nursing home.
    c. CPR.
    d. a second opinion.

14. The acronym ABN stands for
    a. authorized benefit notary.
    b. anterior bilateral neofusion.
    c. advance beneficiary notice.
    d. alternate beneficiary notation.

15. A health care surrogate must be
    a. anyone.
    b. a blood relative.
    c. a spouse or child.
    d. a member of the facility staff.

Research and Discussion Projects

1. Go to your state's website and retrieve information on advance directives.
   a. Compare and contrast your state's form with that shown in figure 5-2, sample living will.

   _____

   _____

   _____

   _____

b. Do you believe the differences ensure more rights to residents in one state over another?

_____

_____

_____

_____

c. Discuss the importance of the idea that everyone should complete an advance directive.

_____

_____

_____

_____

2. Discuss the issue of superconfidentiality.
   a. Why do you think these specific conditions are listed?

_____

_____

_____

_____

   b. Do you think there are any other conditions that should be added to the list?

_____

_____

_____

_____

3. Choose a procedure, such as brain surgery or an organ transplant. Do some research on the procedure and create an informed consent form. Compare your form with the others in your class.

_____

_____

_____

_____

Chapter 6

Compliance: Documentation

Learning Outcomes

- Identify the various uses for health care documentation
- Explain the essential components of quality documentation
- Categorize the documentation guidelines under the federal False Claims Act
- Determine the documentation required for compliance under the Federal Stark law
- Enumerate the aspects of documentation compliance with regard to electronic health records

Key Terms

acronym / a word or term formed by the grouping of initials or parts of the words in a phrase

age of majority / when a person is no longer considered a minor; the age of 18

allocation / assignment of equipment, supplies, manpower, and/or money to various tasks, departments, or other sectors of an organization

coding for coverage / reporting a code based on what the third-party will pay for, rather than accurately reporting what occurred with the patient

documentation / the process of providing tangible, written (hand-written, typed, or computerized) details

query / to ask

random sampling / the choosing of a specific item or organization solely by chance, using no other determining factors

Chapter Case Study

"On March 8, 2007, in Tyler, TX, Artis Anderson was sentenced to 24 months in federal prison and ordered to pay $828,092 in restitution for federal health care fraud violations and engaging in monetary transactions with property derived from specified unlawful activity. Anderson pleaded guilty to the charges on December 8, 2005.

"According to information presented in court, Anderson helped durable medical equipment providers in Houston, TX to submit fraudulent Medicare claims for motorized wheelchair and scooter reimbursement. He later opened a medical equipment business in Gregg County, TX and submitted fraudulent claims for motorized wheelchairs to Medicare." (http://www.irs.gov)

Introduction

Physicians, and other clinicians, are not taught about **documentation** thoroughly in medical school. In addition, laws and regulations change on a regular basis with regard to documentation requirements.

There are many important reasons for the physicians to learn and maintain proper documentation habits. Most of them include protecting these clinicians as well as the organization from breaking laws that can result in fines, loss of license to practice, and at times, jail or prison.

Uses for Health Care Documentation

Many clinicians feel that doing paperwork interferes with their ability to care for their patients. Help them understand that this is not a competition, and that documentation and patient care work together to improve service. There are several important uses for these records.

- *Support of medical decision making:* Physicians and other health care professionals cannot make the best decisions for their patients in an informational vacuum. The October 2006 issue of the *Annals of Internal Medicine* reported that 48% of physician errors are made due to "too little knowledge." In order to make quality decisions, physicians need to know a complete history, vital signs, allergies, test results, etc. This data will lead to their determination of diagnoses and recommended treatment plans.

  > **EXAMPLE** Without documentation, Dr. Weiss cannot know that Evan Percell's blood pressure has been continuously high for the last three months rather than this occurrence being a single event. It is the tracking of Evan's B/P in his chart that will direct Dr. Weiss to determine the best course of treatment to avert any long-lasting effects of his hypertension.

- *Continuity of patient care:* The team involved in patient care, including physician specialists, radiologists, pathologists, nurses, and others must know what the others have observed and done for the patient so time is not wasted by duplicating efforts.

- *Patient safety:* Being an extension of the factors in continuity of care, incomplete information can create a dangerous situation for the patient. Without the documentation, how will the nurse on the next shift know when to give the patient the next dose of medication? Without documentation, how will the physician know this patient is allergic to penicillin?

> **EXAMPLE** Lorraine Sennac has severe pain in her abdomen. Dr. Louis, the gastroenterologist, read in her record that Lorraine's cardiologist, Dr. Jewel, has her on medication for a heart murmur. Knowing this will effect what treatments Dr. Louis prescribes so he can avoid an adverse reaction from a drug interaction.

- *Public safety:* The local, state, and federal governments collect health care data to ensure that effective measures are taken to keep the community safe. Without documentation, and the reporting of that information, there would be no way to know that prenatal care has a positive impact on the health of both mother and child. This data is also used to identify key concerns needing funding for research.

> **EXAMPLE** The Centers for Disease Control (CDC) identified that 7% of children ages 1–2 years have an iron deficiency. This research can then support a program to educate parents of young children.

- *Evidence of compliance:* Proper documentation provides evidence that your facility has complied with many laws and regulations. One of the first things that an investigator will do is come into your facility and pull the documentation for the case(s) in question.

It's the Law

"We will review the appropriateness of Medicare Part B payments for selected physician services. Section 1861(q) of the Social Security Act describes physician services as professional services performed by physicians, including surgery; consultation; and home, office, and institutional calls. Medicare reimbursement for physician services is made on the basis of a fee schedule, which is a predetermined payment amount set forth by law. Section 1833(e) of the Social Security Act precludes payments to any provider of services unless the provider has furnished the information necessary to determine the amounts due such provider. We will review the appropriateness of Medicare payments for various types of physician services to determine whether these services were paid in accordance with Medicare requirements."

From the 2008 OIG Work Plan: Medicare Payments for Selected Physician Services (http://www.oig.hhs.gov)

- *Resource allocation:* From documentation, statistics can be pulled and used to support the operations and management of the health care facility, regardless of how large or small. Administration can then distribute budgets, equipment, and staff more effectively and efficiently. If your department has a budget that will increase next year, how will you spend that money? Raises for current staff, hiring of additional staff, upgrading the computer system…there are so many needs, and the tracking of work flow through your department will help direct you.

EXAMPLE Waterford Medical Center has seen an increase in orthopedic injuries over the last two years since there has been more construction in the area. Therefore, they recently added an orthopedic specialist to the staff, and coders were sent to a special training for coding complex orthopedic cases.

- *Research and education:* Scientists must begin with some kind of indication of a problem or health concern so they know which gene to search for or which disease to investigate to find better diagnostic tools or, perhaps, a cure. These indicators come from the documentation of signs, symptoms, and diagnoses. From this, scientists work toward improved methodology of diagnosis and care. Then, health care professionals are educated on the new policies and procedures so they can be implemented and benefit the population.

- *Quality improvement programs:* Reviewing documentation can illuminate opportunities for additional training or adjustments to existing processes or office systems. A compliance program is a part of an improvement process implemented by an organization as long as the information is evaluated and then acted upon. In 1999, the Agency for Healthcare Research and Quality (AHRQ) was mandated by the U.S. Congress to report to the country about health care quality on an annual basis. This information can help the nation improve the entire health care system.

- *Reimbursement:* Claims cannot be created and submitted without proper documentation. Without claims being submitted, the facility's revenue may be severely reduced, causing financial problems for patients and staff alike. Health information professionals must remember that if it is not documented, it didn't happen! Health information professionals cannot assume, surmise, guess, calculate, or figure out. That is against the law.

The teen birth rate was at an all-time low, according to a study comparing 2005 to 1991. This indicates that education programs are working.

The Institute of Medicine reported in *To Err Is Human* that "When patients see multiple providers in different settings, none of whom has access to complete information, it becomes easier for things to go wrong."

ICD-9-CM Coding Guidelines state, "The importance of consistent, complete documentation in the medical record cannot be overemphasized. Without such documentation accurate coding cannot be achieved. The entire record should be reviewed to determine the specific reason for the encounter and the conditions treated."

Documentation Essentials

All health care professionals must develop the habit of creating documentation that is:

- *Complete:* All factors and issues that relate to this patient must be documented so the information is available for continuity of care, reimbursement, and evidence of performance. This documentation will prove that the physician did ask all the right questions and will identify the patient's responses. Everything must be included because one never knows what will be important at a later date. Some hospitals have specified "record completion" areas. Others use incentives or threats to get physicians to complete their documentation. Whatever the system used, it is important to help clinical staff understand the critical aspect of this task.

- *Accurate:* This may clearly be unnecessary to list; however, attention to accurate details is critical. When errors are discovered, corrections must be made in the approved manner as quickly as possible. The error should be identified by one single line drawn through the incorrect information, initialed, and dated by the individual making the correction. The correct information should then be added, initialed, and dated by the person adding the data. Correction fluids and erasures are never permitted in a health record.

- *Timely:* The attending professional should complete their documentation as soon as possible. With certain health situations, time can be a deadly factor. For example, Marlon is seen in the hospital during a vacation in another city. By the time he gets home and sees his regular physician, he forgets much of what the physician at the hospital said about his condition. The encounter notes were requested and it took two months for the physician to dictate his visit with Marlon. By this time, the small spot on his lung metastasized. Some agencies have published timeline requirements for certain types of notes, and many third-party payers have limitations on how long a facility can take to file a claim. You should check out the deadlines that affect your facility and create processes to enforce them.

  EXAMPLE The Joint Commission's Management of Information Standard, Elements of Performance for IM.6.30 (M) C 3. *An operative progress note is entered in the medical record immediately after the procedure.*

- *Accessible:* The documentation must be available to those authorized to see it at any time. What good can a patient chart do a physician when it is locked up in a file cabinet? HIPAA demands that a health care facility keep patient records secure; however, not from health care professionals engaged in caring for the patient. EHR is beneficial to complying with both of these requirements: security and accessibility.

  EXAMPLE The development of regional health information organizations (RHIO), a sub-structure of the National Healthcare Information Network (NHIN), is working toward connectivity of EHR throughout an entire geographic region. This means that at some point in the future, a physician seeing an unconscious patient in the emergency room on a Saturday night will be able to access that patient's record and have the important data required for better medical decision making.

- *Signed/Confirmed:* The individual who creates the notes must sign and confirm the entry in the record. If the health care professional is entering information into the patient's record by hand, then he must sign his entry. When a physician dictates the details of an encounter or procedure, another person (the transcriptionist) must listen to that tape (or digital file) and type it up. These notes cannot be added to the official patient file until the provider has read the transcription and confirms that it is an accurate report. This is important because accents and regional pronunciations can cause misunderstandings.

EXAMPLES

The physician dictated: a nervous stomach

The transcriptionist typed: a nerve of stomach

The physician dictated: post-operative cast shoe

The transcriptionist typed: post-operative cashew

Abbreviations and Terminology

Health care, like so many other industries, uses a large number of abbreviations, rather than having to say or write long, complex terms. As if learning all these acronyms and terms were not complicated enough, different facilities interpret the same abbreviation or acronym differently, or use a different abbreviation for the same term.

EXAMPLE

ext can be interpreted as meaning: extremities *or* external *or* extract *or* extension

Chief complaint can be abbreviated CC *or* C/C *or* cc

Every facility should publish an approved abbreviations list for use by its staff that assigns one meaning to each abbreviation. This way, when new employees are hired, they can be provided with a clear understanding of all elements in the documentation.

The Joint Commission has published a list of abbreviations, seen in Figure 6-1, which may not be used in their member facilities. You can see that these abbreviations can be easily misunderstood and result in an error.

CERT Investigation Results

Earlier in chapter 4 you learned about CERT programs and their responsibility to investigate possible occasions of an inaccurate or inappropriate payment made to a provider of services of a Medicare beneficiary. These contractors have the authority to review a random sampling of approximately 120,000 claims submitted to a particular FI, obtain the medical records that support these claims from the providers who submitted the claims, and audit the claims and documentation for compliance with Medicare coverage, coding, and billing rules.

OFFICIAL "DO NOT USE" LIST[1]

DO NOT USE	POTENTIAL PROBLEM	USE INSTEAD
U (unit)	Mistaken for "0" (zero), the number "4" (four) or "cc"	Write "unit"
IU (International Unit)	Mistaken for IV (intravenous) or the number 10 (ten)	Write "International Unit"
Q.D., QD, q.d., qd (daily)	Mistaken for each other	Write "daily"
Q.O.D., QOD, q.o.d, qod (every other day)	Period after the Q mistaken for "I" and the "O" mistaken for "I"	Write "every other day"
Trailing zero (X.0 mg)* Lack of leading zero (.X mg)	Decimal point is missed	Write X mg Write 0.X mg
MS	Can mean morphine sulfate or magnesium sulfate	Write "morphine sulfate" Write "magnesium sulfate"
MSO_4 and $MgSO_4$	Confused for one another	

[1]Applies to all orders and all medication-related documentation that is handwritten (including free-text computer entry) or on pre-printed forms.

*Exception: A "trailing zero" may be used only where required to demonstrate the level of precision of the value being reported, such as for laboratory results, imaging studies that report size of lesions, or catheter/tube sizes. It may not be used in medication orders or other medication-related documentation.

ADDITIONAL ABBREVIATIONS, ACRONYMS AND SYMBOLS
(For <u>possible</u> future inclusion in the Official "Do Not Use" List)

DO NOT USE	POTENTIAL PROBLEM	USE INSTEAD
> (greater than) < (less than)	Misinterpreted as the number "7" (seven) or the letter "L" Confused for one another	Write "greater than" Write "less than"
Abbreviations for drug names	Misinterpreted due to similar abbreviations for multiple drugs	Write drug names in full
Apothecary units	Unfamiliar to many practitioners Confused with metric units	Use metric units
@	Mistaken for the number "2" (two)	Write "at"
cc	Mistaken for U (units) when poorly written	Write "ml" or "milliliters"
g	Mistaken for mg (milligrams) resulting in one thousand-fold overdose	Write "mcg" or "micrograms"

Figure 6-1   Official "Do Not Use" list

These on-going investigations identify problems with supporting documentation, at times resulting in providers being required to return monies paid in error. Just because a claim was paid doesn't mean that your facility will get to keep the money.

It's the Law

Beginning in 2003, CMS elected to calculate a provider compliance error rate in addition to the paid claims error rate. The provider compliance error rate measures how well providers prepare Medicare FFS claims for submission. CERT reports identified:

No documentation: "No documentation" means the provider did not submit any medical record documentation to support the services provided.

Insufficient documentation: "Insufficient documentation" means that the provider did not include pertinent patient facts (e.g., the patient's overall condition, diagnosis, and extent of services performed) in the medical record documentation submitted.

Medically unnecessary services: "Medically Unnecessary Services" include situations where the CERT or HPMP claim review staff identifies enough documentation in the medical record to make an informed decision that the services billed to Medicare were not medically necessary.

Incorrect coding: Providers use standard coding systems to bill Medicare. For most of the coding errors, the medical reviewers determined that providers submitted documentation that supported a lower code than the code submitted (in these cases, providers are said to have "overcoded" claims). However, for some of the coding errors, the medical reviewers determined that the documentation supported a higher code than the code the provider submitted (in these cases, the providers are said to have "undercoded" claims).

Other errors: Under CERT, other errors include instances when provider claims did not meet billing requirements, such as those for not covered or unallowable services and for duplicate claim submissions.

False Claims Act

There are specific elements within the federal False Claims Act that require compliance with documentation guidelines. The patient records must be complete and specific with regard to:

- *Medical necessity:* There must be a legitimate medical reason, according to current accepted standards of health care, for whatever type of service, procedure, or DME provided to the patient. The reason or reasons must be documented in the patient record and signed by the physician. This documentation requirement covers prescriptions, as well. Documenting this foundation for the physician's medical decision making provides protection for the patient, the physician, and the facility.

- *Certification of Medical Necessity (CMN):* Before a third-party payer, like Medicare, will agree to pay for a patient to receive DME (e.g., a wheelchair, scooter, or cane) or certain other services, a physician must certify that the patient has a medical condition that requires the use of that equipment or service. There are many cases where individuals have been charged with fraud when investigations proved that physicians signed medical necessity certification for DME for patients they have never examined, and, in some cases, never seen. In addition, there have been DME companies charged with forgery of medical necessity certificates, and still others that bill the insurance company for more expensive equipment, then deliver a lesser unit to the patient.

It's The Law

Certificate of Medical Necessity (CMN)

CMNs are only required for providers that submit claims to Durable Medical Equipment Regional Carriers (DMERCs) for ambulance, cataract glasses, chiropractor, Durable Medical Equipment (DME), enteral/parenteral nutrition, oxygen, and certain types of podiatry. However, institutional providers may be asked by suppliers to furnish specific information necessary for the CMN forms that the supplier is required to submit.

Figure 6-2 shows an example of a CMS Certificate of Medical Necessity form that must be completed to support reimbursement for certain types of DME.

Section 5.3.3, Chapter 5, Medicare Program Integrity Manual

- *Refunding of overpayments:* Errors can be made and a health care facility may inadvertently be paid more than it should for a particular procedure or service. It may be that the insurance carrier paid more than expected, or the patient overpaid. However it happened, it is illegal for the facility to keep the extra funds. The law does not permit the facility to apply these monies to another date of service or another procedure, even if the patient is scheduled for regular, continuous treatments, such as with allergy shots or chiropractic services. The money must be returned to the party who overpaid and there must be documentation of this.

- *Contractual agreements with billing service companies: The 2007 OIG Work Plan* includes investigations of the relationship between a physician's office and its designated billing company. There is concern that there may be an improper impact when the billing service is paid based on a percentage of the physician's total claims. There is evidence that a payment arrangement of this nature may encourage the biller to inflate the claim amount by overcoding (or "upcoding") or other fraudulent activity with the intent of increasing their own revenues.

- *Release of information reimbursement:* HIPAA's Privacy Rule section 164.524(c) permits covered entities to charge reasonable fees, determined by the real costs, for providing a copy of the patient's medical record. The cost basis for calculating the fee may include the actual costs for supplies, the cost of labor for copying the information, as well as any postage (should the individual request delivery of the records). The facility may also charge for the time required to prepare a summary or explanation of the information, when requested by the individual. There are some investigations looking into facilities suspected of falsifying, or artificially inflating, their costs reports.

DEPARTMENT OF HEALTH AND HUMAN SERVICES
CENTERS FOR MEDICARE & MEDICAID SERVICES

Form Approved
OMB No. 0938-0534

CERTIFICATE OF MEDICAL NECESSITY
CMS-484 — OXYGEN

DME 484.03

SECTION A	Certification Type/Date: INITIAL __/__/__ REVISED __/__/__ RECERTIFICATION__/__/__

PATIENT NAME, ADDRESS, TELEPHONE and HIC NUMBER

(_ _ _) _ _ _ - _ _ _ _ HICN _____

SUPPLIER NAME, ADDRESS, TELEPHONE and NSC or applicable
NPI NUMBER/LEGACY NUMBER

(_ _ _) _ _ _ - _ _ _ _ NSC or NPI #_____

PLACE OF SERVICE_____ HCPCS CODE

PT DOB __/__/__ Sex ____ (M/F)

NAME and ADDRESS of FACILITY
If applicable (see reverse)

PHYSICIAN NAME, ADDRESS, TELEPHONE and applicable
NPI NUMBER or UPIN

(_ _ _) _ _ _ - _ _ _ _ UPIN or NPI #_____

SECTION B	Information in This Section May Not Be Completed by the Supplier of the Items/Supplies.

EST. LENGTH OF NEED (# OF MONTHS): _____ 1-99 *(99=LIFETIME)*   DIAGNOSIS CODES (ICD-9): _____ _____ _____ _____

ANSWERS	ANSWER QUESTIONS 1-9. (Circle Y for Yes, N for No, or D for Does Not Apply, unless otherwise noted.)
a)_____mm Hg b)_____% c)____/____/____	1. Enter the result of most recent test taken on or before the certification date listed in Section A. Enter (a) arterial blood gas PO2 and/or (b) oxygen saturation test; (c) date of test.
1 2 3	2. Was the test in Question 1 performed (1) with the patient in a chronic stable state as an outpatient, (2) within two days prior to discharge from an inpatient facility to home, or (3) under other circumstances?
1 2 3	3. Circle the one number for the condition of the test in Question 1: (1) At Rest; (2) During Exercise; (3) During Sleep
Y N D	4. If you are ordering portable oxygen, is the patient mobile within the home? If you are not ordering portable oxygen, circle D.
_____LPM	5. Enter the highest oxygen flow rate ordered for this patient in liters per minute. If less than 1 LPM, enter an "X."
a)_____mm Hg b)_____% c)____/____/____	6. If greater than 4 LPM is prescribed, enter results of most recent test taken on 4 LPM. This may be an (a) arterial blood gas PO2 and/or (b) oxygen saturation test with patient in a chronic stable state. Enter date of test (c).

ANSWER QUESTIONS 7-9 **ONLY** IF PO2 = 56–59 OR OXYGEN SATURATION = 89 IN QUESTION 1

Y N	7. Does the patient have dependent edema due to congestive heart failure?
Y N	8. Does the patient have cor pulmonale or pulmonary hypertension documented by P pulmonale on an EKG or by an echocardiogram, gated blood pool scan or direct pulmonary artery pressure measurement?
Y N	9. Does the patient have a hematocrit greater than 56%?

NAME OF PERSON ANSWERING SECTION B QUESTIONS, IF OTHER THAN PHYSICIAN (Please print):
NAME: _____TITLE: _____EMPLOYER:_____

SECTION C	Narrative Description of Equipment and Cost

(1) Narrative description of all items, accessories and options ordered; (2) Supplier's charge; and (3) Medicare Fee Schedule Allowance for each item, accessory and option. (See instructions on back.)

SECTION D	Physician Attestation and Signature/Date

I certify that I am the treating physician identified in Section A of this form. I have received Sections A, B and C of the Certificate of Medical Necessity (including charges for items ordered). Any statement on my letterhead attached hereto, has been reviewed and signed by me. I certify that the medical necessity information in Section B is true, accurate and complete, to the best of my knowledge, and I understand that any falsification, omission, or concealment of material fact in that section may subject me to civil or criminal liability.

PHYSICIAN'S SIGNATURE _____ DATE ____/____/____

Figure 6-2   Certificate of Medical Necessity

- *Diagnostic X-ray interpretation:* Auditors are investigating those cases in which a payment is made to a second professional for an additional reading of an X-ray for an emergency room patient (use of modifier 77). There must be documentation in the patient's file to explain the medical necessity of the second opinion.

- *Certification of compliance:* Medicare, along with other agencies and health care-related organizations, publish conditions of participation for patients as well as participating providers. Documentation of compliance with the stated conditions is required for one to gain the full benefits of the program. The issuance of a fake certification of compliance and/or the provision of substandard care to patients in any setting violates Medicare's conditions of participation. Copies of this documentation, along with supporting evidence of the individual components, should be retained by the facility in case an investigation ensues.

- *Dates of service:* As you read about earlier in this chapter, the documentation must confirm the date, and sometimes the time, that a service or procedure was provided. The date is a mandated entry in this legal document, and therefore cannot be changed for any reason. Falsifying dates of service is a serious offense.

    EXAMPLE Matthew's insurance coverage doesn't go into effect until Monday. However, the cut on his hand was so infected he just had to see the physician Thursday afternoon. He begged the nurse to post-date the encounter to Monday so his insurance would pay for the visit.

- *Unsupported claims:* Submitting a claim reporting diagnoses and/or procedures that are not documented is fraud. There must be evidence, signed by the attending health care professional, that the patient was seen, diagnosed, and treated. Health information management professionals involved in submitting claims without supporting records may be found guilty of violating the federal False Claims Act, as well as any applicable state versions of this law.

In addition to the federal False Claims Act, each state is encouraged to establish versions of this law. This means that, if found guilty, a facility can be charged and penalized at both the state and federal levels.

It's The Law

State False Claims Act Reviews

As enacted by section 6031 of the Deficit Reduction Act of 2005, section 1909 of the Social Security Act:

"(Act) provides a financial incentive for States to enact false claims acts that establish liability to the State for the submission of false or fraudulent claims to the State's Medicaid program. If a State false claims act is determined to meet certain enumerated requirements, the State is entitled to an increase of 10 percentage points in the State medical assistance percentage, as determined by section 1905(b) of the Social Security Act, with respect to any amounts recovered under a State action brought under such a law."

(Continues)

In order for a State to qualify for the incentive under section 1909 of the Act, the State must have in effect a law that meets the following requirements:

1. Establish liability to the State for false or fraudulent claims described in the False Claims Act (FCA) with respect to any expenditures related to State Medicaid plans described in section 1903(a) of the Act;

2. Contain provisions that are at least as effective in rewarding and facilitating *qui tam* actions for false or fraudulent claims as those described in the FCA;

3. Contain a requirement for filing an action under seal for 60 days with review by the State Attorney General;

4. Contain a civil penalty that is not less than the amount of the civil penalty authorized under the FCA.

42 U.S.C. § 1396h(b).

Under section 1909(b) of the Act, OIG is required to determine, in consultation with the Attorney General of the United States, whether a State has in effect a law relating to false or fraudulent claims submitted to a State Medicaid program that meets these enumerated requirements. The effective date of section 1909 of the Act is January 1, 2007.

On August 21, 2006, OIG published a notice in the Federal Register (71 FR 48552 PDF) that sets forth OIG's guidelines for reviewing State false claims acts. The guidelines invited States to request OIG's review of State laws to determine if the laws meet the requirements of section 1909(b) of the Act. The following is a list of State laws that have been reviewed by OIG.

Office of the Inspector General (http://www.oig.hhs.gov)

Federal Stark Law

This civil law prevents referrals made for Medicare and Medicaid beneficiaries for services when the referring physician gains financially. As in so many other cases, most states have their own law that expands upon Stark and applies this same restriction to beneficiaries of all third-party payers, whether governmental or private. Section 411.361 (a) states that all health care facilities, regardless of size, that provide services to Medicare beneficiaries must report their financial relationships with any other entities that may also provide services to these same patients.

The financial relationship referred to in this statute is far reaching. This can be part or complete ownership, a vendor relationship (the entity is a customer of other products or services), or a tenant or lessee of a building owned by the referring physician.

EXAMPLE Dr. Daniels decides that Gigi Myers, a Medicare patient, needs a CT scan to determine why she is having pain in her head. He sends her to Ransen Diagnostic Imaging Center because it is the closest facility. However, Dr. Daniels invested in this company last year and now is part owner. This is illegal because no one can know if he ordered Gigi's CT scan because she really needed it or because he wanted to make more money from his investment.

No additional evidence is required to be found guilty of violating this law becaı no intent must be proved. If the referral is made, the party is automatically guilty.

Of course, patients are going to ask for direction (a referral) when they are required to go to an outside facility. How can they know which imaging center, laboratory, etc. is any good? To enable the physician, or health care facility, to help the patient and comply with this law, the office should provide the patient with a list of several names of local organizations, permitting the patient to choose from the list.

Federal Anti-Kickback Statute

This is a criminal statute that prohibits the exchange of any type of benefit for a referral. This covers more than Stark because the violation is not limited to actions involving Medicare and Medicaid beneficiaries. The receipt of money, services, or product in exchange for any health care-related referral is illegal under the False Claims Act. This law includes benefits that might be received, such as vacations, free gifts, and deep discounts on products or services.

It's The Law

"On the books since 1972, the federal anti-kickback law's main purpose is to protect patients and the federal health care programs from fraud and abuse by curtailing the corrupting influence of money on health care decisions."

Complying with this federal statute and the variations that have been enacted in each state again relies on accurate documentation. As long as the patient record provides evidence that the physician was acting according to the standards of accepted medical practice by ordering a test or prescribing a drug, there should be no problem.

From the OIG (http://www.oig.hhs.gov)

Elements of Documentation

There are basic elements that a physician must document for every patient encounter. These rules should be in place whether the meeting is face-to-face or without the patient present, such as on the phone, in conference with another health care professional, online, or under some other circumstance.

All patient encounters must be documented with at least the following:

- *The specific date* the encounter occurred (time is not required, but recommended)
- *The identity of the patient*, or subject, of the encounter: This includes the patient's full name, address, phone number(s), date of birth, and emergency contact information
- *A unique identifier* for the patient: This may be a medical record number (MRN), patient number, or any other internal identification device
- *The identity of the health care professional or provider* of the service or treatment

- *The reason for the encounter* or provision of the service (diagnosis or signs and symptoms), also known as the "chief complaint"
- *Details of any discussions*, communications, or information exchanged between the provider and the patient. This includes, but is not limited to, the history of present illness; past, family, and social histories (PFSH); allergies; current medications; previous surgeries; and other pertinent information
- *Details of any physical examination* including vital signs, physical examination of body areas and organ systems, descriptions of specimens taken, tests performed, and all results available at the time the documentation was created [NOTE: Results of all tests and procedures should be documented (lab reports, radiology reports, etc.) and included in the patient chart.]
- *Objective findings* are the documentation of the physician's interpretations and observations of the patient, including descriptions of skin tone, gait, balance, level of alertness, etc.
- *A complete description of all services*, treatments, and/or procedures provided or performed
- *Follow-up orders* or recommendations, including prescriptions written
- *The professional or provider's signature* and any other authentification required

Hospital Documentation

In January 2007, CMS began mandating that hospitals report those conditions identified for each patient that were present at the time of admission. These codes are called Present On Admission (POA) indicators.

In order to correctly report those conditions, the coder must have complete documentation from the admitting physician. Those notes that may be used include:

- Emergency room notes
- History and physical (H&P)
- Progress notes
- Admitting notes

Physicians' notes must cover everything required for a complete legal and ethical record of the patient's care. When admitting a patient to an acute care facility (hospital) the documentation must include:

- Conditions present and diagnosed prior to admission
- Conditions diagnosed as existing during the admission process and therefore present before admission
- Any suspected, possible, probable, or to-be-ruled-out conditions
- Differential diagnoses
- Underlying causes of any sign or symptom present on admission
- Specific identification of the acute or chronic status of any condition
- External causes (the "how" and "where") of any injury or poisoning

When the documentation is complete, the facility's coding professionals can accurately determine which diagnoses listed on the discharge notes were POA and which were not.

The guidelines from CMS specifically state that nurses' notes cannot be used for assigning POA indicators. However, these notes, lab reports, and other data in the patient's chart can help coding professionals discover inconsistent, missing, conflicting, or unclear information.

The Querying Process

There are occasions when health information management professionals may realize that the documentation is incomplete, ambiguous, or contradictory. In these cases, the coder must **query** the physician who wrote the notes to amend the documentation.

Querying is a key factor in helping your clinical staff build better documentation habits. They can learn which elements are needed, because they get asked for the same adaptation to their notes over and over again.

You will need to establish an approved process for formatting the coders' requests for additional information from the physicians. This approach is to enable the coder to gain information that is already in the physician's head and have her write it into the chart.

1. *The physician must write the response into the patient's chart.* The query process cannot be answered verbally, on a separate slip of paper, or in an e-mail.* Therefore, the querying process should include the logistics of providing the patient's chart, along with the question(s), to the physician of record. [*Some believe that, as long as the e-mail can be authenticated as being from the physician and unedited, and can be either electronically appended to an EHR or printed out and placed in the patient chart, it can be a valid addition to the documentation. Each facility should have a written policy regarding this issue.]

2. *The question must not imply the answer.* This means that the question must be worded in a manner that does not tell the physician what to write. This might imply the fraudulent behavior called **coding for coverage**. It is not the coder's place to diagnose the patient or redefine the procedure.

    EXAMPLE Does the patient have acute bronchitis? [This question implies a desired answer.]

Some facilities design queries as a multiple-choice question. While this is on the edge, it does not rise to the level of illegal. The explanation for this format is to let the physician know what additional data you are seeking, rather than have him or her try to guess at what exactly it is you need clarified or included.

    EXAMPLE Would you categorize the patient's bronchitis as: acute, chronic, or with exacerbation, or some other qualifier?

3. *The question should be worded in a manner that will not insult the physician.* You must remember that you are not questioning the physician's capabilities. This is simply

a matter of the documentation being insufficient. Physicians do not write their notes for HIM purposes alone. They are not trained in the same areas as you and your staff are, so they do not know, off the top of their heads, which details are important to the reimbursement and statistical data processes and which are not. This is why you must help them understand. As any coder knows, some diagnosis codes differ as to whether the condition is acute or chronic, while others need other details, such as which bone and which section of the bone has been broken in a fracture. Physicians should not be expected to know this. It is the responsibility of the HIM department to educate the physicians as to what details you need to do your job with excellence.

Electronic Health Record Documentation

Every day more and more health care facilities are implementing electronic health record (EHR) systems. In 2004, President George W. Bush announced the goal that "within the next 10 years [by 2014], electronic health records will ensure that complete health care information is available for most Americans at the time and place of care, no matter where it originates" (http://www.whitehouse.gov). The President's Information Technology Advisory Committee provided evidence that EHR systems are expected to help health care become more effective and more cost efficient.

The requirements for proper health information documentation do not change when working with EHR. It is the methodology that is changing: instead of using a dictation machine or pen and paper, the clinician will enter the data into a computer.

This new technology enables the ultimate product—the patient's record—to be more complete and more accurate. The electronic template, provided in virtually all EHR programs, is designed to prompt the physician to include all required elements of the patient encounter. This reduces the opportunity for the physician to forget any components, due to electronic alerts that are triggered when something is missing. Built-in electronic monitors can guard against other common human errors involved in the documentation phase of care.

Test results from laboratories and imaging departments/centers, including digital images, can be linked directly to the EHR. Ultimately, this system will enhance continuity of care, as well as coding and billing efforts, because any physician, anywhere, who is treating the patient can access all the data without having to rely on the patient's memory.

Securing EHR

You will be working with your technology department to ensure that the EHR are kept secure and protected.

- *Identity confirmation:* Have an in-person meeting with each individual who will be interacting with EHR. During this meeting, verify that the individual is, in fact, who they say they are. Make a copy of some photo identification (such as a driver's license) to place in their file. [This will be the file that the HIM department maintains, not the individual's personnel file held by human resources.] Use the *Healthcare*

Integrity and Protection Data Bank (HIPDB) (http://www.npdb-hipdb.hrsa.gov) to check on a health care provider or supplier's past activities, as they relate to cases of fraud and abuse. Then, check the *National Practitioner Data Bank* (NPDB) (http://www.npdb-hipdb.hrsa.gov/). The NPDB is a unified informational source for all health care providers across the United States. This data is collected to make it easier to check specific areas of a physician's licensure, professional memberships, medical malpractice history, and details of clinical privileges. The NPDB data is to be used as a part of the credentials check. Also, check your state's website. Most now provide access to licensing and background information on any health care professional that is required to be licensed in the state, such as physicians, nurses, and therapists. Do not assume that the human resources department did this when they hired this individual, particularly if you work for a smaller organization.

CASE STUDY

NOTE: In each CMP (Civil Monetary Penalties) case resolved through a settlement agreement, the settling party has contested the OIG's allegations and denied any liability. No CMP judgment or finding of liability has been made against the settling party.

January 4, 2008

After it self-disclosed conduct to the OIG, Shands at Alachua General Hospital (Shands), Florida, agreed to pay $119,838 and to enter into a 3-year certification of compliance agreement for allegedly violating the Civil Monetary Penalties Law. The OIG alleged that Shands employed an individual that Shands knew or should have known had been excluded from participation in Federal health care programs.

Office of the Inspector General (http://www.oig.hhs.gov)

- *Assign a unique password:* Once the individual's identity has been verified, establish a password to be used only for access into the EHR and nothing else, such as the facility intranet or the e-mail system. Using an alphanumeric password (both letters and numbers) will provide more security. In addition, the formation of the password should not use a formula, such as first initial last name, but be more random. Again, this is another level of protection against access from unauthorized personnel.

- *Restrict access:* It is important to limit the actions of each individual with approved entry into the EHR, based on their role and responsibility. Work in conjunction with the IT department to establish levels of access such as read-only; the ability to enter data in limited areas (such as test results); and/or total access (for the attending physicians only).

EXAMPLE
Jasmine, the coder, needs access to read the complete EHR, but should not be able to change any information.

Dr. Morrison, the attending physician, created the EHR for Enrique Mendez, so he should be able to amend the record whenever necessary.

- *Authentification of records:* This will not be the same as the password, because only the attending physician who authored the notes is permitted to authenticate the document. This can be anything from a second password to an electronic signature to a fingerprint scanner for completion. This action virtually seals the record.
- *Audit trails:* Electronic trails must be imbedded so that a report can be generated showing every individual who accessed a particular patient chart. This is in compliance with both HIPAA's Security Rule and Privacy Rule.

> **EXAMPLE** October 11, 2007, twenty-seven staff members at a New Jersey hospital were suspended for reportedly viewing George Clooney's confidential patient chart after the actor was treated following a motorcycle accident. This hospital discovered the violation of HIPAA's Privacy Rule by checking the electronic audit trail in their system.

Clinical Laboratory Improvement Amendments (CLIA)

Under the oversight of CMS, these regulations seek to ensure the quality of laboratory testing wherever they are performed: a clinical laboratory, a hospital, or a physician's office. CLIA certifications (outlined in Figure 6-3) are required for all locations and are based on the types of testing performed.

Pathology testing performed in physicians' offices are regulated under CLIA and are reimbursed at a national rate of approximately $1 billion a year. The 2007 OIG

TYPES OF CLIA CERTIFICATES

Certificate of Waiver
This certificate is issued to a laboratory to perform only waived tests.

Certificate for Provider-Performed Microscopy Procedures (PPMP)
This certificate is issued to a laboratory in which a physician, midlevel practitioner, or dentist performs no tests other than the microscopy procedures. This certificate permits the laboratory to also perform waived tests.

Certificate of Registration
This certificate is issued to a laboratory that enables the entity to conduct moderate or high-complexity laboratory testing or both until the entity is determined by survey to be in compliance with the CLIA regulations.

Certificate of Compliance
This certificate is issued to a laboratory after an inspection that finds the laboratory to be in compliance with all applicable CLIA requirements.

Certificate of Accreditation
This is a certificate that is issued to a laboratory on the basis of the laboratory's accreditation by an accreditation organization approved by HCFA.

Figure 6-3   Types of CLIA Certificates

work plan includes an investigation of these services, as well as the relationships between physicians' offices and outside labs.

Required Notifications

Hospitals are also required to document compliance with a CMS regulation requiring all inpatient Medicare beneficiaries to receive written notification of their rights involving their discharge.

The form, titled "An Important Message From Medicare About Your Rights," seen in Figure 6-4, explains the right that a Medicare beneficiary has to challenge their discharge from the hospital if the patient feels it is too soon and that leaving the facility at the time suggested might endanger their health.

Many individuals believe that the physician is the only one who can decide when a patient can be discharged. News reports carry stories of people whose well-being has been in peril because the physician's decision to discharge was influenced by insurers insisting upon rapid release from an acute care facility to lessen the cost of the treatment. These underlying concerns have led to an effort to educate patients about their ability to speak up on their own behalf.

The form requires that the appropriate phone numbers are included so the patient has easy access to asking for help. The patient retains a copy, and the hospital must keep a copy with the patient's signature acknowledging receipt of the information.

Patient Name: _____

Patient ID Number: _____

Physician: _____

DEPARTMENT OF HEALTH AND HUMAN SERVICES
CENTERS FOR MEDICARE & MEDICAID SERVICES
OMB Approval No. 0938-0692

AN IMPORTANT MESSAGE FROM MEDICARE ABOUT YOUR RIGHTS

AS A HOSPITAL INPATIENT YOU HAVE THE RIGHT TO:

- *Receive Medicare covered services. This includes medically necessary hospital services and services you may need after you are discharged, if ordered by your doctor. You have a right to know about these services, who will pay for them, and where you can get them.*

- *Be involved in any decisions about your hospital stay, and know who will pay for it.*

- *Report any concerns you have about the quality of care you receive to the Quality Improvement Organization (QIO) listed here:*

_____

Name of QIO

_____

Telephone Number of QIO

_____

YOUR MEDICARE DISCHARGE RIGHTS

Planning For Your Discharge: *During your hospital stay, the hospital staff will be working with you to prepare for your safe discharge and arrange for services you may need after you leave the hospital. When you no longer need inpatient hospital care, your doctor or the hospital staff will inform you of your planned discharge date.*

If you think you are being discharged too soon:

- *You can talk to the hospital staff, your doctor and your managed care plan (if you belong to one) about your concerns.*

- *You also have the right to an appeal, that is, a review of your case by a Quality Improvement Organization (QIO). The QIO is an outside reviewer hired by Medicare to look at your case to decide whether you are ready to leave the hospital.*

    ○ **If you want to appeal, you must contact the QIO no later than your planned discharge date and before you leave the hospital.**

    ○ *If you do this, you will not have to pay for the services you receive during the appeal (except for charges like copays and deductibles).*

- *If you do not appeal, but decide to stay in the hospital past your planned discharge date, you may have to pay for any services you receive after that date.*

- **Step by step instructions for calling the QIO and filing an appeal are on page 2.**

To speak with someone at the hospital about this notice, call _____.

Please sign and date here to show you received this notice and understand your rights.

Signature of Patient or Representative	Date

Form CMS-R-193 (approved 05/07)

Figure 6-4 An Important Message from Medicare About Your Rights form

discharge. Similarly, MA organizations are required to provide enrollees with a notice of non-coverage, known as the Notice of Discharge and Medicare Appeal Rights (NODMAR), when a beneficiary disagrees with a discharge decision (or when the individual is not being discharged, but the organization no longer intends to cover the inpatient stay).

"Beginning July 1, 2007, hospitals must deliver a revised version of the Important Message from Medicare (IM), CMS-R-193, which is an existing statutorily required notice, to explain discharge appeal rights. Hospitals must issue the IM within 2 calendar days of the day of admission, and obtain the signature of the beneficiary or his or her representative to indicate that he or she received and understood the notice."

CMS Pub. 100-04 Transmittal: 1257 Date: May 25, 2007

Retention

The U.S. federal government requires health care facilities to retain patient records for ten years, in most cases. Individual agencies and individual states have varying requirements. The directive may come from:

- The state in which the facility is located
- Third-party payers, including CMS
- Accreditation organizations, such as the Joint Commission
- The current statutes of limitation for any type of health care-related lawsuit, such as medical malpractice

Each facility is responsible for identifying the federal, state, and individual third-party payer documentation retention mandates that apply to their specific patient population. As you can tell from the above, one facility may be required to follow several different rulings in order to stay compliant. This is why the American Hospital Association (AHA) and the American Health Information Management Association (AHIMA) both advise retaining patient records for a minimum of ten years after the last date of treatment.

It's The Law

HIPAA's Privacy Rule:

"Documentation and Record Retention. A covered entity must maintain, until six years after the later of the date of their creation or last effective date, its privacy policies and procedures, its privacy practices notices, disposition of complaints, and other actions, activities, and designations that the Privacy Rule requires to be documented."

Some of the specific regulations include:

- Medicare-participating acute care centers (hospitals) must retain all documentation for radiology services, nuclear medicine, and all services involving radiopharmaceuticals for a minimum of five years for both inpatient and outpatient provisions. (42 CFR 482.24, 482.26, and 482.53)

(Continues)

- Psychiatric hospitals must retain documentation for diagnostic services, assessments, treatment plans, progress logs, and discharge records (planning and summaries) for a minimum of five years.
- Comprehensive outpatient rehabilitation facilities (CORF) are required to retain clinical documentation for Medicare beneficiaries receiving diagnostic and treatment services for a minimum of five years after discharge. (452 CFR 485.60)
- Rural health clinics receiving reimbursement for treatments to both Medicare and Medicaid beneficiaries are required to retain all health care documentation for a minimum of six years from the last treatment date or clinical notation.
- Nursing facilities are required to retain clinical documentation for a minimum of five years after the date of discharge unless there is a state requirement for longer retention.
- Pediatric patient records must be kept for a minimum of three years after the age of majority. In the U.S., the **age of majority** is 18 years. (42 CFR 483.75)

With the conversion to electronic records, the storage of these charts will be easier and require less space. Most agencies permit the storage of these records to be retained on paper, electronically, or on microfilm. As long as the records are accessible when needed, it shouldn't matter.

When the time comes to destroy old records, there are processes that must be followed.

1. Document a sincere attempt to contact the patient to offer them the opportunity to come and pick up their records. This should be done in person so a member of your staff can confirm the identity of the person taking the records, to ensure protection of the individual's confidentiality. You, or your administration, may feel that records that are ten years old are irrelevant, but that is not true. Regardless, this is someone else's PHI and, therefore, it is not your decision to make. For those patients who have moved out of the area, you might consider requiring the release of information to be notarized.

2. If the patient cannot be found, or the patient turns down the opportunity to take possession of their old records, the files must be destroyed in the proper manner. Some states may differ in their requirements regarding the destruction of these documents; however, most support using crosscut shredders.

3. Whether the record has been taken by the patient or destroyed in an approved manner, there should be notations of time, date, place, and a complete list of patient names, dates of birth, and identification or medical record number. It is recommended that at least two staff members sign as witnesses of the destruction. A copy of the patient's current identification for those who picked up their records should also be included in this file. Make certain that documentation is kept for evidence of compliance.

Chapter Summary

Do not get into a tug of war with physicians comparing the importance of documentation to the importance of patient care. That is a losing battle. Of course, if you were the patient, you would probably agree. Promoting proper documentation is not asking the physicians to do more work, it is asking them to do the same amount of work with slight modifications.

Documentation is an important factor in the continuity of care for the patient and it is the evidence of compliance.

CHAPTER REVIEW

Multiple Choice Questions

1. Health documentation is used for
   a. continuity of care.
   b. patient safety.
   c. public safety.
   d. all of the above.

2. Statistics culled from patient records may be used to
   a. allot facility resources.
   b. support research proposals for funding.
   c. a & b
   d. none of the above

3. Details in patient records help
   a. get publicity for the facility.
   b. get reimbursement for treatment plans.
   c. advertise new services at your facility.
   d. liven up the office holiday party.

4. Clinicians must ensure that patient documentation is all except
   a. complete.
   b. timely.
   c. accurate.
   d. collated with lab reports.

5. Abbreviations may be used in the patient record as long as
   a. they are on the approved list.
   b. the entire word is also written every time.
   c. every workstation has a medical dictionary.
   d. the physician wrote it.

6. A Certificate of Medical Necessity is used to justify payment for
   a. in-patient surgical events.
   b. outpatient surgical events.
   c. durable medical equipment.
   d. prescription medications.

7. Should a health care facility receive an overpayment from a third-party payer, they must
   a. apply the funds to a future service.
   b. return the funds.
   c. give the money to the patient.
   d. give the money to the facility general fund.

8. Charging for the release of information is
   a. based on whatever the facility wishes to charge.
   b. forbidden by HIPAA.
   c. calculated from actual cost.
   d. only permitted by authorized vendors.

9. Referring a patient to a specific imaging center might be a violation of
   a. Stark.
   b. False Claims Act.
   c. HIPAA.
   d. CERT.

10. The local laboratory sent Dr. Frune two tickets to the basketball game as a thank you for referring patients to its testing center. This is a violation of
    a. the False Claims Act.
    b. Anti-Kickback.
    c. medical necessity.
    d. the Langdon Act.

11. PFSH should be included in encounter notes. This acronym stands for
    a. Patient Friendly Strategic Healthcare.
    b. Present Filing System Holograms.
    c. Past, Family, and Social History.
    d. Portable Financial Strata Healthcare.

12. When admitting a patient into the hospital, the physician must document all
    a. patient next-of-kin.
    b. potential tests and procedures.
    c. health insurance policies.
    d. present-on-admission signs, symptoms, and diagnoses.

13. Whenever physician's notes are _____, HIM must query the physician.
    a. incomplete
    b. ambiguous
    c. contradictory
    d. all of the above

14. Keeping EHR secure will require that all individuals with access have
    a. a thorough background check.
    b. high-speed internet.
    c. a password based on a formula.
    d. computer certification.

15. Lab tests performed in any health care facility most probably will need a certificate under
    a. HIPAA.
    b. CMS.
    c. CLIA.
    d. HCFA.

Research and Discussion Projects

1. Review the various uses for health care documentation and discuss how each has an impact on the health care delivery system.

_____
_____
_____
_____
_____
_____
_____
_____
_____

2. One of the uses for health care documentation is resource allocation.
    a. Explain how you would use statistics taken from a group of patient records to manage existing resources in a health care facility.

_____
_____
_____
_____
_____

    b. How would you use these statistics to support the purchase of new resources or hiring additional personnel?

_____

_____

_____

_____

_____

3. Look at the section on developing a querying process. Working on your own or with another student, design a form that would comply with the law about querying and still get the necessary information. The form should not be more than one page in length.

Chapter 7

Compliance Reporting

Learning Outcomes

- Identify the important issues regarding ethical coding practices
- Explain the most common illegal practices for HIM reporting
- Name the key concerns under the federal False Claims Act that relate to reporting
- Determine the impact of the Physician Quality Reporting Initiative (PQRI) on HIM processes in physicians' offices
- Distinguish the circumstances under which a health care professional is mandated to report a patient's diagnosis

Key Terms

contagious / transferred from one individual to another

epidemic / a disease that spreads more quickly and more extensively within a population than is statistically reasonable

evaluation and management (E/M) code / a procedure code that reports physician services for assessing a patient's condition, determining a treatment plan, and continued supervision of care

pandemic / a widespread epidemic, typically international in scope

relators / individuals who relate or tell

superbills / preprinted forms used in health care facilities that contain the diagnosis and procedure codes most often used in that facility

unbundled / to engage in the fraudulent coding practice of reporting separate codes rather than one code that identifies all of the components

Chapter Case Study

"May 2006, in North Carolina, an ambulance company and its owner were sentenced related to billing Medicare and Medicaid for dialysis patient transports that were not medically necessary. The owner was sentenced to 120 months in jail for health care fraud and to an additional 31 months in jail (to be run consecutively) for obstruction. The company and the owner were also ordered to pay $604,000 in joint and several restitution. Investigation revealed that emergency medical technicians were instructed to enter false information on ambulance reports falsely indicating patients required an ambulance when, in fact, they did not and could have been transported by other means. The owner also instructed billing personnel to submit claims indicating that patients were bed-confined when, in fact, they were not bed-confined. In addition, prior to an audit, the owner and the billing manager changed records to indicate medical necessity. The owner also intentionally withheld subpoenaed documents. The billing manager was previously sentenced and was ordered to pay $30,000, a portion of the joint and several restitution amount." (http://www.oig.hhs.gov)

Introduction

Interpreting and reporting data are two of the primary reasons for the existence of the health information management (HIM) department. Reporting requirements exist for reimbursement processes as well as the delivery of important statistics to government agencies.

The statistics collected and reported establish the basis for allotment of research directives and funding. For example, how else could the health care science community know that our population needs a treatment for Alzheimer's disease? HIM departments of all types and sizes submit codes reporting every patient's signs, symptoms, and diagnoses. These codes can then be analyzed by computer programs designed to identify trends and indicators that, with research, can lead to understanding the etiology of disease-causing elements. Remember the movie, *Erin Brockovich*? Based on a true story, that movie provided an excellent example of what can be discovered, and ultimately corrected, when health record statistics are collated. Individually, each case was just another ill child. However, it was only when the reports were put together that the investigators realized that one county had an extraordinarily frequent occurrence of a specific diagnosis. This revelation led to further investigation to find the underlying cause.

Reporting health care statistics is important and, in many cases, mandated by law.

Health Care Coding

Coding is the translation of diagnoses and procedures performed from medical terminology into numbers and letters. The purpose is to create a standardized format for these interpretations so the data can be more easily analyzed.

The process of coding has been part of the organization of health information prior to the implementation of computer technology. However, the integration of technology has made the use of codes more widespread. This also makes the codes more important and the necessity for them to be accurate even more imperative.

The American Health Information Management Association (AHIMA) has developed and published their Standards for Ethical Coding, shown in Figure 7-1. These standards identify some important guidelines for the reporting of diagnoses and procedures using approved code sets: International Classification of Diseases—9th revision—Clinical Modification (ICD-9-CM) and Current Procedural Terminology (CPT).

Health information management professionals must ensure that only valid, accurate data is passed through them to the agencies and third-party payers who rely on this information.

Coding professionals should:

1. Apply accurate, complete, and consistent coding practices for the production of high-quality healthcare data.

2. Report all healthcare data elements (e.g. diagnosis and procedure codes, present on admission indicator, discharge status) required for external reporting purposes (e.g. reimbursement and other administrative uses, population health, quality and patient safety measurement, and research) completely and accurately, in accordance with regulatory and documentation standards and requirements and applicable official coding conventions, rules, and guidelines.

3. Assign and report only the codes and data that are clearly and consistently supported by health record documentation in accordance with applicable code set and abstraction conventions, rules, and guidelines.

4. Query provider (physician or other qualified healthcare practitioner) for clarification and additional documentation prior to code assignment when there is conflicting, incomplete, or ambiguous information in the health record regarding a significant reportable condition or procedure or other reportable data element dependent on health record documentation (e.g. present on admission indicator).

5. Refuse to change reported codes or the narratives of codes so that meanings are misrepresented.

6. Refuse to participate in or support coding or documentation practices intended to inappropriately increase payment, qualify for insurance policy coverage, or skew data by means that do not comply with federal and state statutes, regulations and official rules and guidelines.

7. Facilitate interdisciplinary collaboration in situations supporting proper coding practices.

8. Advance coding knowledge and practice through continuing education.

9. Refuse to participate in or conceal unethical coding or abstraction practices or procedures.

10. Protect the confidentiality of the health record at all times and refuse to access protected health information not required for coding-related activities (examples of coding-related activities include completion of code assignment, other health record data abstraction, coding audits, and educational purposes).

11. Demonstrate behavior that reflects integrity, shows a commitment to ethical and legal coding practices, and fosters trust in professional activities.

Figure 7-1 AHIMA Standards of Ethical Coding

Let's begin looking over the most common areas of concern when it comes to reporting accuracies and complying with these regulations.

Place of Service Codes

Reporting inaccurate place of service (POS) codes on a claim form is fraud.

You can find the complete listing of POS codes in Figure 7-2, and their complete definitions on the first page inside some Current Procedural Terminology (CPT) books. These two-digit codes, ranging from 01 through 99, identify the category or type of facility in which the procedure, service, or treatment was provided to the patient. The code is entered in box 24B on the CMS-1500 claim form.

It's The Law

"We will review physician coding of place of service on claims for services performed in ambulatory surgical centers (ASC) and hospital outpatient departments. Federal regulations at 42 CFR § 414.22(b)(5)(i)(B) provide for different levels of payments to physicians depending on where the services are performed. Medicare pays a physician a higher amount when a service is performed in a non-facility setting, such as a physician's office, than it does when the service is performed in a hospital outpatient department or, with certain exceptions, in an ASC. We will determine whether physicians properly coded the places of service on claims for services provided in ASCs and hospital outpatient departments."

From the 2008 OIG Work Plan: Place of Service Errors (http://www.oig.hhs.gov)

There are many different components that go into the calculation of the cost and ultimate reimbursement for a specific service. As you can see in the example, Medicare will pay more for a procedure when it is provided in a physician's office than in a hospital outpatient department. Similar differences apply to fee-for-service pricing paid by other third-party payers. Certainly, you can see that reporting an inaccurate location will increase or decrease payment to the physician or facility. In addition, this is considered fraud. You must make certain that the correct location is identified when you report the provision of a procedure.

Duplicate Billing

Mistakes happen, and it is possible that you, or one of your staff, might accidentally submit a claim for the same procedure, same patient, on the same date of service. Most claims processing software programs, as well as national health care clearinghouses, are designed to prevent this from happening.

It is fraudulent to send two invoices for the same services to the same patient on the same date. Computers can easily spot this on two different claims from the same facility, or from two different facilities. For example, both the physician's office and the outside lab send claims reporting the provision of the same diagnostic test.

When this happens once or twice, it is considered human error. Often, the third-party payer's computer will notice this and reject or deny the claim as being previously reimbursed. However, again, mistakes can happen and the third-party payer might accidentally pay your facility a second time for the same services.

01	Pharmacy	42	Ambulance—Air or Water
02	Unassigned	43–48	Unassigned
03	School	49	Independent Clinic
04	Homeless Shelter	50	Federally Qualified Health Center
05	Indian Health Service Free-standing Facility	51	Inpatient Psychiatric Facility
06	Indian Health Service Provider-based Facility	52	Psychiatric Facility-Partial Hospitalization
07	Tribal 638 Free-standing Facility	53	Community Mental Health Center
08	Tribal 638 Provider-based Facility	54	Intermediate Care Facility/Mentally Retarded
09	Prison-Correctional Facility	55	Residential Substance Abuse Treatment Facility
10	Unassigned	56	Psychiatric Residential Treatment Center
11	Office	57	Non-residential Substance Abuse Treatment Facility
12	Home	58–59	Unassigned
13	Assisted Living Facility	60	Mass Immunization Center
14	Group Home	61	Comprehensive Inpatient Rehabilitation Facility
15	Mobile Unit	62	Comprehensive Outpatient Rehabilitation Facility
16–19	Unassigned	63–64	Unassigned
20	Urgent Care Facility	65	End-Stage Renal Disease Treatment Facility
21	Inpatient Hospital	66–70	Unassigned
22	Outpatient Hospital	71	Public Health Clinic
23	Emergency Room—Hospital	72	Rural Health Clinic
24	Ambulatory Surgical Center	73–80	Unassigned
25	Birthing Center	81	Independent Laboratory
26	Military Treatment Facility	82–98	Unassigned
27–30	Unassigned	99	Other Place of Service
31	Skilled Nursing Facility		
32	Nursing Facility		
33	Custodial Care Facility		
34	Hospice		
35–40	Unassigned		
41	Ambulance—Land		

Figure 7-2 Place of Service Codes for Professional Claims

It's The Law

"We will determine whether States have effective controls in place to preclude duplicate payments. Under the Medicaid program, FFP is available for design, development, installation, and operation of State mechanized Medicaid claims-processing and information retrieval systems. Federal regulations require that States conduct prepayment claims reviews to prevent duplicate claims. A prior OIG review disclosed that duplicate payments were made as a result of ineffective claims resolution."

From the 2008 OIG Work Plan: Claims-Processing Controls To Prevent Duplicate Payments for Medicaid Services (http://www.oig.hhs.gov)

The law states that should you receive a duplicate payment or any other payment in error, you are required to return the funds immediately. You are *not permitted* to keep it, give it to the patient, or apply it to another service or date of service. Make certain you contact the party that sent the duplicate payment as soon as you identify the error. Each organization has its own policies with regard to returning the monies. You cannot just send back the check or issue one of your own. This could create an opportunity for that money to get lost or inaccurately credited, and you will still be held legally responsible for those funds.

Unbundling

The standards of care, as set forth by national health care organizations such as the American Medical Association, determine that a specified sequence of procedures or services is probable to occur under certain circumstances.

EXAMPLE

90704 Mumps virus vaccine

90705 Measles virus vaccine

90706 Rubella virus vaccine

90707 Measles, mumps, rubella virus vaccine (MMR)

Take a look at our example. One might justify the reporting of 90704, 90705, and 90706 as being the truth, because all three vaccines were actually provided to the patient. However, using code 90707 is more accurate, and therefore the only code that is honest to report. Reporting the three individual codes is called unbundling, because you are taking apart the combination code (90707).

You may ask why this is such a big deal. Let's look at an analogy from the meal deal at a local restaurant. If purchased individually, the hamburger is $2.85, the fries are $1.99, and the drink is $1.50: a total cost of $6.34. However, this restaurant is offering a meal deal for all three items for only $4.99—a savings of $1.35. How would you feel if you ordered the meal deal and paid $6.34? Cheated? Exactly. This is the agreement with the third-party payers, as well. Code 90707 represents the meal deal, and because it is bundled, it gets one price. It is wrong; it is fraud to **unbundle**.

Phantom Patients

In some cases, the health information management professional may need to confirm that the physician and/or the patient was actually in the office on the stated date and time of service. Some organizations term this practice "billing for ghost patients." Needless to say, this is illegal.

This may seem to be ridiculous to state that it is illegal to charge for services, procedures, and treatments that were never done. However, unfortunately, this is something that does go on all over the country.

Even though this behavior is criminal, there are some who view it as justified. These individuals claim that they are "forced" to do this as a result of unreasonably low payments from third-party payers, with which they cannot make an honest living. Therefore, they rationalize billing for services not provided in conjunction with services that were provided to total an amount that they consider fair.

Illegal is illegal. There are legal and ethical ways to increase a business's revenue.

CASE STUDY

TWO CHARGED IN FALSE CLAIMS TO MEDICAID

"Two Orlando Medicaid providers were arrested Friday and an arrest warrant was issued for a third amid allegations the trio took more than $110,000 in 888 bogus claims..."

"The three submitted claims for services not rendered and falsified medical records, officials said."

The Orlando Sentinel, Saturday, July 31, 2004

"Incident to" Services

Generally, if a nurse provides a health care service, rather than a physician, the reimbursement rate is 80 percent that of the physician fee-for-service. However, the "incident to" rule permits full payment for a service or treatment provided by a nurse or other non-physician professional as long as the physician is on the premises, supervising the treatment, and is available just in case something goes awry.

It's The Law

"We will review Medicare claims for services furnished 'incident to' the professional services of selected physicians. Medicare Part B generally pays for services 'incident to' a physician's professional service; such services are typically performed by a non-physician staff member in the physician's office. Federal regulations at 42 CFR § 410.26(b) specify criteria for 'incident to' services. We will examine the Medicare services that selected physicians bill 'incident to' their professional services and the qualifications and appropriateness of the staff who perform them. This study will review medical necessity, documentation, and quality of care for 'incident to' services."

From the 2008 OIG Work Plan: Medicare "Incident to" Services (http://www.oig.hhs.gov)

If the physician is not present, and the claim indicates that he or she has the intention of gaining the additional payment—it is fraud. In addition, "incident to" billing is not permitted if the patient has a new problem or complaint. Whatever the diagnosis or concern that is being attended to, it must be an issue for which this patient has already seen this physician.

One might ask how the auditors could know if the physician was there or not when Nurse Franken gave those flu shots. They will know by looking at every patient record for those seen that day in that office. If Dr. Trainer had been in the office, he would have seen patients, made phone calls, and/or worked on his computer. They might go so far as to look at his credit card statements to identify charges made on that date from a distant location. There are so many methods that investigators can use.

Ensure that your office is reporting the truth on all documentation, including the identification of the providers of each service.

Services Not Performed

It may be hard to believe, but health care professionals and their billing and coding staff members have been found guilty of submitting claims for procedures and treatments that were actually never provided. Of course, this can be a difficult situation for a reimbursement specialist because we are not in the treatment room. However, this occurrence does underscore the importance of making certain no claims are created without written documentation that has been authorized (signed) by the providing professional.

CASE STUDY

"WASHINGTON—April 14, 2008—A board-certified radiologist, Fred Steinberg, M.D., his imaging centers and related entities in Palm Beach County, Fla., have reached a settlement with the United States to resolve allegations of health care fraud, the Justice Department announced today. Under the terms of the settlement, the U.S. recovered $7 million.

"The settlement resolves allegations that portions of CT scans were not performed, even though the procedures were billed and reported to patients' physicians as if they were done. CT scans, which take detailed pictures of structures inside the body, are often taken using a dye (or contrast material) to highlight certain conditions. In addition to performing CT scans with contrast, scans may also be done without contrast. The bills submitted by Steinberg and his entities to federal health care programs, including Medicare, reflected that thousands of CT scans were carried out both with and without contrast, when in reality the CT scans without contrast were not performed. In addition, the government alleged that the Steinberg entities did CT scans and ultrasound exams that were not ordered by physicians and were not medically necessary."

U.S. Department of Justice (http://www.usdoj.gov).

Balance Billing

Medicare and other health care third-party payers have specific policies regarding the physician's right to invoice the patient for the difference between the carrier's allowed amount and the physician's charge. This is also known as a violation of the assignment rules for Medicare-participating providers. Virtually every third-party payer has a rule regarding "*balance billing*" by participating providers. Balance billing means that the health care facility sends an invoice to the patient for the difference between the amount charged for a procedure and the amount paid by the insurance carrier.

EXAMPLE

Cystoscopy	Amount charged	$300.00
Medicare	Allowed amount	$203.42
Patient	Co-payment	$ 20.00
Patient	Co-insurance	$ 40.68
Patient	Deductible	0
Balance		$157.26

Take a look at this example. After the patient paid $60.68 to the health care facility, and Medicare paid $203.42, there is a balance on this account of $157.26. Medicare says that because this facility is a participating provider, it is not permitted to now send an invoice to the patient for the $157.26. This amount must be written off, or adjusted to bring the account to zero—paid in full. Sending the patient a bill is illegal.

UPIN/NPI

The Unique Physician Identification Number (UPIN) is required for each individual health care professional to submit claims to third-party payers.

"The National Provider Identifier (NPI) is a requirement of the Health Insurance Portability and Accountability Act of 1996 (HIPAA), and the NPI will replace the use of UPINs and other existing legacy identifiers." (www.hhs.gov/hipaa)

On January 23, 2004, the Secretary of the Department of Health and Human Services officially enacted the creation of a program to assign one standard unique health identifier, known as the National Provider Identifier (NPI), for each health care provider. The NPI is designed to replace all previous provider identifiers, including the UPIN, to identify health care providers. There is no cost at all to apply for an NPI.

Claims forms, including the CMS-1500 used for billing physician and outpatient services, and the UB-04, used for inpatient (acute care) hospital claims, have been redesigned to provide space for the NPI.

The compliance concern is with using the *correct* NPI for each individual physician or health care facility, determined by *who provided* the service or treatment at the encounter being reported, and not any other health care professional. For example, Dr. Smith and Dr. Jones are married and in practice together. They each have their own patient list. It is fraud to use Dr. Smith's NPI on a claim form for a patient seen by Dr. Jones. You must remember that the claim form is a legal document. Completing a form using Dr. Smith's NPI is legally testifying that Dr. Smith cared for that patient and provided that service. Even if Dr. Smith is the physician of record and Dr. Jones saw the patient this one time, there is no justifiable reason to report this fraudulently.

Federal False Claims Act

There are aspects of the federal False Claims Act (FCA), in addition to what was covered in previous chapters, that place responsibility on any individual involved with submitting a claim to the federal government that she knows, or should know,

> **It's The Law**
>
> "The False Claims Act ('FCA') pertains to:
>
> (a) Any person who
> Knowingly presents, or causes to be presented, to an officer or employee of the United States Government or a member of the Armed Forces of the United States a false or fraudulent claim for payment or approval;
> Knowingly makes, uses, or causes to be made or used, a false record or statement to get a false or fraudulent claim paid or approved by the Government;
> Conspires to defraud the Government by getting a false or fraudulent claim paid or approved by the Government; . . . or
> (7) Knowingly makes, uses, or causes to be made or used, a false record or statement to conceal, avoid, or decrease an obligation to pay or transmit money or property to the Government.
>
> (b) For purposes of this section, the terms "knowing" and "knowingly" mean that a person, with respect to information
> Has actual knowledge of the information;
> Acts in deliberate ignorance of the truth or falsity of the information; or
> Acts in reckless disregard of the truth or falsity of the information..."
>
> 31 U.S.C. § 3729 False Claims Act (http://www.cms.hhs.gov/smdl/downloadsSMD032207Att2.pdf)

is false. As an extension of this law, virtually all of the states have enacted their own laws, making filing a false claim illegal in any case, not just those involving the federal government, and extending the application of this law to state agencies and private organizations, such as the insurance companies.

Look carefully at the phrase that is found in this and most other laws: " . . . knows or should know." This means that if you work in a health care facility as a biller and you are told that you must blindly create claims from **superbills** only, it is still your legal obligation to assure the accuracy of the data on the superbill and not turn a blind eye. When you are involved with any portion of the process to create and submit claims, you are equally responsible under the law.

> **EXAMPLE** Robin works in a small physician's office. Part of her job includes entering the information from patients' visits into the computer so the claims can be created and electronically submitted. The superbill used in this office includes the code 99000 Handling Fee. When she asked, Robin was told by the office manager that this code was used in order to receive payment for the nurse's labeling a specimen for the lab to come and pick up.

Every time Robin, in our example, participates in placing this code on a claim form for a patient who is a Medicare beneficiary, she is guilty of a federal crime—and she may not know it. But she should know! All Robin has to do is look in a procedure coding book to discover that code 99000 is for the transfer of the specimen from the physician's office to the laboratory...something the lab does. Therefore, each time 99000 is placed on a claim form from this office, it is a request for payment for a service that is being provided by another company. Robin can be found guilty of violating the federal False Claims Act and she cannot use ignorance as a defense because she is "supposed to" know.

Compliance with the federal False Claims Act and its state counterparts begins with never assuming that, just because a superbill is printed and has been used for a long time, it is correct and legal. All codes on any type of check-off list used by physicians should be reviewed carefully for accuracy. This should be done at a minimum each September, to check for upcoming changes to diagnosis codes and inpatient procedure codes, and November, to check for upcoming changes to procedure codes.

The second, very important step to comply with this law is to assure that coders review the physician's documentation (encounter [SOAP] notes, operative reports, lab reports, etc.) in addition to any coding shortcuts such as superbills.

Auditors will look for incidents of:

- *Upcoding:* Upcoding is the practice of using a code whose description reports a more intense condition or more complex procedure than what really occurred.

CASE STUDY

"July 2007: In Florida, a doctor was sentenced to 78 months in prison and ordered to pay $504,000 in restitution and forfeit an additional $705,000 after a jury found her guilty on all counts of an 89-count indictment including 44 charges of health care fraud. The female physician, who practiced dermatology, billed Medicare as if she performed highly complex surgical closure procedures when she actually only performed simple surgical stitches or no procedure at all."

(http://www.oig.hhs.gov)

- *Clustering:* There are cases when the coders do not fully understand how to assign an accurate **evaluation and management (E/M) code,** so they simply report all cases with the middle levels available for that location. [NOTE: Evaluation and management codes are determined by the location of the encounter. For example: office, hospital, emergency room, nursing home, etc.] This happens frequently in physicians'offices when the E/M code is chosen from a checklist (superbill) and not determined by the documentation required to identify the levels of history, physical exam, and medical decision-making.
- *Billing for a discharge instead of a transfer:* When a patient is moved from an acute care facility to a rehabilitation center or assisted living facility, this is called a "transfer." The hospital is transferring the patient to another facility. The patient is not discharged from the hospital and admitted into the nursing center. Billing for a discharge under these circumstances is fraud.

It's The Law

"We will review coding of claims submitted by hospitals for erroneously coded discharges that should have been coded as transfers. Pursuant to Federal regulations at 42 CFR § 412.4 (e), a hospital discharging a beneficiary is paid the full DRG payment. In contrast, under 42 CFR § 412.4(f), a hospital that transfers a beneficiary to another facility is paid a graduated per diem rate, not to exceed the full DRG payment that would have been made if the beneficiary had been discharged without being transferred. We will determine whether claims were appropriately coded."

From the 2008 OIG Work Plan: Compliance With Medicare's Transfer Policy (http://www.oig.hhs.gov)

- *Incorrectly using time to determine E/M levels:* This is another issue with the documentation to support E/M codes. The guidelines state that when counseling takes more than 51 percent of the encounter, time may be used as the determining factor for choosing the most accurate code. However, there are cases where physicians indicate the level of E/M based on the time spent in the exam room with the patient, even though the counseling rule does not apply. This most often results in fraudulent billing when superbill check sheets are used to create claims rather than the physician's documentation of history, exam, and medical decision-making that actually occurred.

- *Miscoding of global surgery E/M services:* Global surgery packages already include, and therefore already pay for, the provision of certain E/M services. Billing separately for the E/M service is a form of unbundling and constitutes fraud. However, there must be documentation that a follow-up appointment did occur. Therefore, when a patient is seen for a visit that is already included in the surgery code reimbursement, code 99024 Postoperative Follow-up Visit should be used on the claim form rather than any code from the 99212–99215 range.

It's The Law

"We will review industry practices related to the number of evaluation and management (E&M) services provided by physicians and reimbursed as part of the global surgery fee. CMS's 'Medicare Claims Processing Manual,' Chapter 12, section 40, contains the criteria for the global surgery policy. Under the global surgery fee concept, physicians bill a single fee for all of their services usually associated with a surgical procedure and related E&M services provided during the global surgery period. The global surgery fee includes payment for a certain number of E&M services provided during the global surgery period. We will determine whether industry practices related to the number of E&M services provided during the global surgery period have changed since the global surgery fee concept was developed in 1992."

From the 2008 OIG Work Plan: Evaluation and Management Services During Global Surgery Periods (http://www.oig.hhs.gov)

- *DRG creep:* This is the hospital version of upcoding, where the coders report diagnoses inaccurately, causing the classification of a diagnosis-related group (DRG) to be inflated. For in-patient services provided to Medicare beneficiaries, the amount of reimbursement is calculated based on the DRG. An inflated DRG may get the

facility more money than it has legally earned. A higher level of DRG can be falsified by upcoding or merely designating a secondary diagnosis as the principle. In
any regard, this is a fraudulent practice.

CASE STUDY

In a report from the Office of the Inspector General, with recommendations regarding the evidence of upcoding DRGs by hospitals:

- The agency could use a variety of analytical approaches, such as examining claims data for
  patterns, trends, change pairs, and spikes in DRG billing volume. This analysis also could
  include examination of coding validation data for trends in miscoding as a way to detect
  problem DRGs, providers, or coding situations.

- The agency could establish criteria, policies, and procedures to make referrals for collection to
  the Office of Inspector General or to fiscal intermediaries, as appropriate, from providers who
  are deliberately exploiting and abusing the system through upcoding claims for payment.

Monitoring the Accuracy of Hospital Coding
Office of the Inspector General (http://www.oig.hhs.gov)

- *Observation versus inpatient status:* There is evidence that some patients admitted for dialysis treatments were reported as inpatient admissions resulting in
  higher payments than had they been reported under observation status.

It's The Law

"We will review Medicare payments to hospitals for admissions for observation status versus an
inpatient stay for dialysis services. CMS's 'Medicare Benefit Policy Manual,' Pub. No. 100-02, Chapter 1, section 10, states that renal dialysis treatments are usually covered only as outpatient services
but may, under certain circumstances, be covered as inpatient services depending on the patient's
condition. When a hospital places a patient under observation but has not formally admitted the
individual as an inpatient, the patient initially is treated as an outpatient. According to CMS's 'Intermediary Manual Part 3,' Chapter II, section 3112.8, observation services are covered only when
provided by the order of a physician or another individual authorized by State licensure laws and
hospital staff bylaws to admit patients to the hospital or to order outpatient tests. Observation services are outpatient services that are paid on an hourly basis and can last up to 48 hours. Inpatient
services are paid under a DRG at a much higher rate. This review will determine whether Medicare
payments to hospitals for renal dialysis services were appropriate."

From the 2008 OIG Work Plan: Medicare Payments for Observation Services Versus Inpatient
Admission for Dialysis Services (http://www.oig.hhs.gov)

- *Inpatient only services performed in an outpatient setting:* Certain procedures are
  designated to be provided in a hospital (acute care facility) only. If the provision of
  these services are reported having occurred in outpatient setting instead, the claim
  might be denied and then charged directly to the beneficiary (patient). In some
  cases, this may be reported with the specific intention of improperly changing

the reimbursement level. As you learned in the section about reporting Place of Service codes earlier in this chapter, some fees differ based on the location at which the service is performed.

- *Misuse of Modifiers 25 and 59:* For those of you who have studied procedure coding, you already know how tricky using modifiers can be with CPT codes. These two modifiers are more delicate to understand and apply accurately. This does not excuse using them improperly. Over the last few years, Modifier 25, in particular, has been over-reported and, therefore, is an identified point of investigation.

Modifier 25 reports a "significant, separately identifiable evaluation and management service by the same physician on the same day of the procedure or other service" (CPT 2008). This modifier can only be appended to an E/M code that is determined by documentation of the key components, as identified in the CPT book, as it would be determined during any other patient encounter. Modifier 25 identifies that this evaluation happened to occur on the same day as a procedure or service performed by this physician for this patient.

> **EXAMPLE** Corrine has an appointment for Dr. Ellis, a dermatologist, to remove several skin tags. After Dr. Ellis completes the procedure, Corrine asks to discuss her concerns about the mole on her cheek and skin cancer—a diagnosis she has had previously. Dr. Ellis takes a complete history, examines her mole, and examines her skin full body. This E/M would be reported with 99213-25 EXPANDED PROBLEM-FOCUSED OFFICE VISIT, SEPARATELY IDENTIFIABLE, because it was performed on the same day as 11200 REMOVAL OF SKIN TAGS, UP TO 15 LESIONS.

Modifier 59 reports a "distinct procedural service." This might be an additional procedure, the same procedure on a different anatomical site, or other additional service that is not usually provided to the same patient on the same day.

> **EXAMPLE** Randy was in an accident at the glass shop where he worked. Dr. Jerome had to remove a splinter from his right eye and repair a laceration in the conjunctiva of his left eye. This would be reported as 65205, 65270-59.

CASE STUDY

FINDINGS

Forty percent of code pairs billed with Modifier 59 in FY 2003 did not meet program requirements, resulting in $59 million in improper payments. Medicare allowed payments for 40 percent of code pairs that did not meet the following program requirements:

(1) The services were not distinct from each other, or
(2) The services were not documented.

Specifically, Modifier 59 was used inappropriately with 15 percent of the code pairs because the services were not distinct from each other.

Office of the Inspector General (http://www.oig.hhs.gov)

Qui Tam

Also mentioned briefly in chapter 4 are *Qui Tam* lawsuits. This provision, under the federal False Claims Act, empowers private citizens to watch out for interests of the government and the public.

It's The Law

". . . the FCA provides that private parties may bring an action on behalf of the United States. 31 U.S.C. 3730 (b). These private parties, known as "qui tam relators," may share in a percentage of the proceeds from an FCA action or settlement. Section 3730(d)(1) of the FCA provides, with some exceptions, that a qui tam relator, when the Government has intervened in the lawsuit, shall receive at least 15 percent but not more than 25 percent of the proceeds of the FCA action depending upon the extent to which the relator substantially contributed to the prosecution of the action. When the Government does not intervene, section 3730(d)(2) provides that the relator shall receive an amount that the court decides is reasonable and shall be not less than 25 percent and not more than 30 percent."

31 U.S.C. 3730 (b) False Claims Act
(http://www.cms.hhs.gov/smdl/downloads/SMD032207Att2.pdf)

This is the recourse that every individual has when they are faced with a health care facility that refuses to abide by the law. This is not tattling. This is standing up for what is right and honest. You learned in the previous section that if you are participating, even in ignorance, you can be found guilty and might be fined and/or sent to jail. You can be a part of the problem or a part of the solution.

The FCA includes a financial reward for any individual who helps the government stop fraud. Participants in *qui tam* lawsuits have been awarded millions of dollars.

CASE STUDY

NEW JERSEY HOSPITAL COMPANY SETTLES *QUI TAM* LAWSUIT ALLEGING MEDICARE FRAUD FOR $265 MILLION

June 15, 2006—St. Barnabas Corp., the largest healthcare provider in New Jersey, has agreed to pay the federal government $265 million to settle two Medicare fraud lawsuits brought by three whistleblowers under the False Claims Act and other charges brought by the federal government.

The *qui tam* (whistleblower) cases involved a supplemental Medicare payment system known as "outliers." Medicare provides outlier payments to hospitals to give them an incentive to treat Medicare inpatients whose care requires unusually high costs. The whistleblowers alleged St. Barnabas inflated those costs from 1995 to 2003 to increase its outlier payments.

(http://www.oig.hhs.gov/publications/docs/hcfac/hcfacreport2006.pdf)

Certainly there is concern for an individual who takes a stand against illegal behavior, and the FCA includes provisions to protect these brave persons. So, someone thinking about reporting illegal behavior in the facility in which they work would not have to worry about retribution during the length of the investigation and the trial.

"The FCA provides protection to *qui tam* relators who are discharged, demoted, suspended, threatened, harassed, or in any other manner discriminated against in the terms and conditions of their employment as a result of their furtherance of an action under the FCA. 31 U.S.C. 3730 (h). Remedies include reinstatement with comparable seniority as the *qui tam* relator would have had but for the discrimination, two times the amount of any back pay, interest on any back pay, and compensation for any special damages sustained as a result of the discrimination, including litigation costs and reasonable attorneys' fees." (http://thomas.loc.gov)

Physician Quality Reporting Initiative (PQRI)

Within the Healthcare Common Procedural Coding System (HCPCS) is a section for Category II codes. These codes are not used for reporting services and procedures, as described by those codes found: Category I—Regular CPT codes; Category III—Emerging technology codes; or HCPCS, Level II codes—for ancillary services such as durable medical equipment and medical supplies.

Category II codes enable a health care office to report certain behaviors or actions that may be taken for the patient's well being that would not be reported separately otherwise. For example, a dermatologist or family practitioner should ask patients with a current diagnosis, or history, of melanoma if they have any new or changing moles, and document this in their encounter notes. The normal reporting requirements would only show the appropriate evaluation and management office visit code and not specifically include this discussion. However, adding category II code 1050F HISTORY OBTAINED REGARDING NEW OR CHANGING MOLES to that same claim form (with a zero dollar value) enables CMS's computers to assess how often physicians are investigating this very important evaluation on their patients who may be at high-risk for melanoma.

The use of Category II codes to participate in the Physician Quality Reporting Initiative (PQRI) is voluntary. To encourage more physicians to participate, CMS has added a bonus payment for those who achieve the reporting goals set forth.

It's The Law

Section 101 of the 2006 Tax Relief and Health Care Act of 2006 (TRHCA) created the 2007 Physician Quality Reporting Initiative (PQRI), which establishes a financial incentive for eligible professionals to participate in a voluntary quality-reporting program. Eligible professionals who successfully report a designated set of quality measures on claims for dates of service from July 1 to December 31, 2007, may earn a bonus payment, subject to a cap, of 1.5 percent of total allowed charges for covered Medicare physician fee schedule services during that same period.

The Centers for Medicare and Medicaid Services (CMS), authorized under Title 1 (http://thomas.loc.gov)

To comply with PQRI, each physician's office should choose one or two of the most applicable performance measures described in Appendix H in the CPT book, or online at http://www.ama-assn.org/go/cpt. To continue with our example, this physician might choose to focus on melanoma and participate in PQRI with only three measures:

1050F HISTORY OBTAINED REGARDING NEW OR CHANGING MOLES
2029F COMPLETE PHYSICIAL SKIN EXAM PERFORMED
5005F PATIENT COUNSELED ON SELF-EXAMINIATION FOR NEW OR CHANGING MOLES

As long as the physician includes these details in his or her encounter notes, the coding specialist can be notified to include this code on those charts, as appropriate.

Mandatory Reporting Circumstances

Each state has its own specific requirements for mandatory reporting. Essentially, these all relate to individual health-related conditions that, at some point in time, may impact the entire community. Most of these laws are designed to enable the government agencies to assist their residents in averting further tragedy.

Domestic Violence, Abuse, and Neglect

It's The Law

"Chapter 39 of the Florida Statutes mandates that any person who knows, or has reasonable cause to suspect, that a child is abused, abandoned, or neglected by a parent, legal custodian, caregiver, or other person responsible for the child's welfare shall report immediately such knowledge or suspicion to the central abuse hotline of the Department of Children and Families."

(http://www.flsenate.gov/Statutes)

Those typically required under state laws include physicians, osteopaths, chiropractors, nurses, health personnel engaged in the admission, examination, and care or treatment of children, health professionals, and mental health professionals, among others. And notice that this Florida statute, like most others, specifically identifies that the report is to occur when there is *"reasonable cause to suspect."*

This puts your health care facility, your department, and you in the forefront for watching out for children. In addition, most mandated reporting laws also include suspicion of abuse or neglect of senior citizens, women, and other residents who may be harmed by another.

Complying with these laws can be difficult emotionally. You may find resistance from your clinical staff, or even within yourself, prompted by fear. What if you are wrong? In some cases, the resistance comes from concern for being judgmental about another family's choices. What business is it of mine? Other questions may arise, as well, such as: What if the child is lying? What if that woman really is clumsy? Older people do bruise easily? Health care individuals may witness or be told by patients about situations that are so horrific it is too difficult to believe. It can be almost psychologically painful to be faced with a child telling you that his head is cut because his mother hit him with something, and much easier to believe the mother's explanation that he fell off his bicycle.

You must remember that you do not have the power to put anyone in jail or take anyone's children away. You are not confirming anyone's guilt. Filing a report about suspected domestic violence and/or child or elder abuse will only spur an investigation.

Communicable Diseases

It's The Law

"By law, Oregon clinicians must report diagnoses (confirmed or suspected) of the following infections, diseases, and conditions. Both clinical and lab-confirmed cases are reportable. The parallel system of lab reporting does not obviate the clinician's obligation to report. Some conditions (e.g., Uncommon Illnesses of Public Health Significance, animal bites, HUS, PID, pesticide poisoning, disease outbreaks) are rarely if ever identified by labs. In short, we depend upon clinicians to report."

(http://www.oregon.gov/SOLL)

An **epidemic** or **pandemic** occurs when one person passes along an illness to those around them. This can happen unknowingly, like an individual who passes along the flu virus by shaking someone's hand, or two people having unprotected sex because they believe they are healthy, yet one transfers a sexually transmitted disease (STD) to the other. The transference of other conditions may occur when a person knows better but does something risky anyway out of foolishness or greed, such as a restaurant worker who is in too much of a hurry to cook the chicken thoroughly, and the customer develops salmonella as a result. You are also aware that there are some who create biological weapons in an attempt to infect others with the intention of harming them.

Regardless of the reason, as members of the health professional community, it is our legal and ethical obligation to do what we can to stop the spread of disease before it gets to epidemic or pandemic proportions. This is why the law requires the health care facility to report signs, symptoms, and confirmed diagnoses of any disease or condition that is considered **contagious**. A list of diseases on one state's mandatory report list can be seen in Figure 7-3.

Anthrax***	Giardiasis
Botulism***	Gonorrhea
Brucellosis	Haemophilus influenzae**
Campylobacteriosis	Hantavirus*
Chancroid	Hepatitis A
Chlamydia infection	Hepatitis B
Cryptosporidiosis	Hepatitis C (new infections)
Cyclospora infection	Hepatitis D (delta)
Diphtheria***	HIV infection and AIDS
Escherichia coli (Shiga-toxigenic)	Legionellosis

Figure 7-3 Specific etiologies that must be reported to state health agencies

Leptospirosis*
Listeriosis
Lyme disease
Malaria
Measles (rubeola)**
Meningococcal disease**
Plague***
Polio**
Rabies**
Rubella**
Pertussis
Q fever
Salmonellosis (including typhoid)
Shigellosis
Syphilis
Taenia solium/Cysticercosis*
Tetanus*
Trichinosis
Tuberculosis
Tularemia
Vibrio infection**
Yersiniosis

OTHER CONDITIONS

Animal bites
Arthropod-borne infection (any)
Hemolytic uremic syndrome (HUS)
Lead poisoning*
Marine intoxications***
Outbreak of disease (any)***
Pesticide poisoning**
Pelvic inflammatory disease (PID) (acute, non-gonococcal)*
Uncommon illness of potential public health significance (any)***

TIMING OF REPORTS

***Immediately—day or night
**Within 24 hours
*Within 1 week
If unspecified, report within 1 working day

Figure 7-3 (Continued)

Health information management professionals are responsible for ensuring that documentation of the official report is in the patient's record. If it is not, you must query the clinician and get the documentation that the report was made, including date, time, and the agency to which the condition or situation was reported. In those situations where you find a physician or other attending professional refusing to report, you will need to do it yourself, and in some states, report the physician for failing to comply with the law.

Chapter Summary

Many aspects of the health care industry depend upon the accurate reporting of data. This includes information that is used to determine reimbursement as well as grants for research projects to discover future tests, procedures, and cures, and funding for government-supported agencies and programs, such as Medicare and Medicaid. It is easy to understand why so many different laws would be enacted to ensure this information is reported correctly.

CHAPTER REVIEW

Multiple Choice Questions

1. The code sets used to report diagnoses and procedures are
   a. AHIMA and AAPC.
   b. ICD-9-CM and CPT.
   c. CPT and ICDR.
   d. HCPCS and DNR.

2. Any of the following, except one, might occur when using an incorrect place of service code:
   a. Payment is sent to another facility.
   b. The claim may be denied.
   c. The claim is paid at an improper rate.
   d. An investigation for fraud may ensue.

3. Reporting several codes instead of one combination code is called
   a. upcoding.
   b. balance billing.
   c. unbundling.
   d. clustering.

4. Billing "incident to" means that the service was performed
   a. at the scene of an accident.
   b. after a global period.
   c. by a non-physician clinician under the supervision of a physician.
   d. by a second physician during the course of another treatment plan.

5. The NPI on the claim form should be that of the
   a. primary care physician who referred the patient.
   b. attending physician who performed the procedures.
   c. consulting physician who recommended the procedures.
   d. facility where the procedures were performed.

6. Should a false claim be filed, the person culpable under the federal False Claims Act is
   a. the physician.
   b. the coder.
   c. the biller.
   d. all of the above

7. An example of upcoding would be reporting
   a. a motorized wheelchair when a cane was provided.
   b. three different vaccine injections when one combination vaccine was given.
   c. a treatment provided to a patient who was never actually treated.
   d. a procedure performed by non-physician professional.

8. DRG creep is the hospital version of what other fraudulent activity?
   a. unbundling
   b. upcoding
   c. clustering
   d. balance billing

9. A suit filed by private citizens on behalf of the government is called a
   a. due diligence lawsuit.
   b. fiscal intermediary.
   c. supeona duces tacum.
   d. *qui tam* lawsuit.

10. Reporting PQRI involves using
    a. ICD-9-CM codes.
    b. Category II codes.
    c. HCFA regulators.
    d. POA indicators.

11. Most states require health care professionals to report suspicion of
    a. domestic violence.
    b. child abuse.
    c. neglect of children or the elderly.
    d. all of the above

12. The law requires the reporting of any disease or condition considered to be
    a. genetic.
    b. hereditary.
    c. contagious.
    d. chronic.

13. The federal False Claims Act only applies to services provided in a
    a. hospital.
    b. ambulatory care center.
    c. physician's office.
    d. all of the above

14. The False Claims Act, like many health care laws, identifies the guilty party as one who
    a. knowingly makes a false record.
    b. causes a false record to be made.
    c. should know a false record is being made.
    d. all of the above

15. Complying with mandatory report laws is _____ under HIPAA's Privacy Rule.
    a. permitted
    b. forbidden
    c. questionable
    d. permitted with patient's signed consent

Research and Discussion Projects

1. Review the federal False Claims Act and its impact on the submission of claim forms to third-party payers.
   a. Discuss procedures you might enact in your facility to avoid violating this law.

   _____

   _____

_____

_____

b. Explain the roles of the physician, the nurse, the coder, and billing professionals in the process of reporting health care encounters.

_____

_____

_____

_____

_____

2. Explain why you believe the *qui tam* statute was included in the law.

_____

_____

_____

_____

3. Explain why physicians' offices should participate in PQRI.

_____

_____

_____

_____

4. Discuss the importance of mandatory report laws in the cases of:
   a. abuse and neglect of children and the elderly
   b. domestic violence
   c. diagnosis of sexually transmitted diseases
   d. diagnosis of communicable diseases

_____

_____

_____

_____

Chapter 8

Creating Policies and Procedures

Learning Outcomes

- Identify the components of policy development
- Explain the purpose of creating policies and procedures
- Detail the role that policies play in a compliance program
- Describe the role that penalties play in a compliance program

Key Terms

authenticate / to verify something is genuine or credible
compelling / attracting attention or compassion; motivation for someone to do something or make something happen
contingency / alternate; something that occurs only when an original fails
rationale / the underlying purpose or reason
violate / to treat with a lack of respect; behavior defiant to a law or contract

Chapter Case Study

"July 2007: In Florida, a doctor was sentenced to 78 months in prison and ordered to pay $504,000 in restitution and forfeit an additional $705,000 after a jury found her guilty on all counts of an 89-count indictment including 44 charges of health care fraud. The female physician, who practiced dermatology, billed Medicare as if she performed highly complex surgical closure procedures when she actually only performed simple surgical stitches or no procedure at all." *(http://www.oig.hhs.gov)*

Introduction

In previous chapters, you learned about the various laws and regulations that impact health care facilities of all sizes and structures. Whether a multi-facility health care system or a single physician's office, these businesses have one thing in common—they all need organizational structure. Company policies and procedures provide this structure for everyone.

Components of Policy Development

Let's go through the process of creating a policy to use as an active example of how one goes about developing rules of behavior for a particular organization. In a large organization, such as a hospital, policies are developed by designated committees and ultimately approved by the board of directors. The process in small health care practices may place this responsibility on the office manager or an outside consulting firm. Whoever is charged with this duty, it must be done for the benefit of the entire organization, as well as those individuals who work within that facility.

Figure 8-1 shows an outline of the components that should be addressed in your policy and procedures manual.

Our example policy will be created to govern release of patient information.

1. Policy topic
2. Policy rationale
3. Individuals affected by the policy
4. Procedural compliance
5. Preferred behaviors
    a. Contingency behaviors
6. Oversight responsibilities
7. Policy review and update
8. Consequences for non-compliance
    a. Governmental penalties
    b. Facility penalties

Figure 8-1 Components of Policy Development

Policy Topic

The policy manual that you create must address all elements of required and expected behaviors, and the topics must be itemized. No one policy will cover everything, even when limited to one department. Therefore, the place to begin will be to identify each and every issue that will require a formal company policy.

There are particular things to take into consideration as you create this list.

1. **Don't assume.** Not everyone was brought up the same way or taught the same things. What this means is that you cannot assume everyone has your same strong work ethic, or any type of ethics at all. Complying with HIPAA's Privacy Rule may be second nature to you, but others have never heard of HIPAA or may have been provided with misinformation.

2. **The policy must be enforceable.** You will address how to enforce these policies later on in this chapter. However, you must have an unambiguous, written policy accessible to all staff in order to be able to enforce the policy. Legally, and ethically, there must be evidence that the individual knows and understands the rules before you can punish them for non-compliance.

Figure 8-2 provides you with a checklist that can be used as a launching point for creating your policy topic list.

The following list provides an example of the types of policies and procedures that may be included in a manual for health information services. The titles and content of the policies and procedures may vary by facility or corporation. Some of the policies and procedures are listed more than once for cross-referencing purposes.

Abbreviations

Access to Automated/Computerized Records

Access to Records (Release of Information) by Resident and by Staff

Admission/Discharge Register

Admission/New Patient Procedures

- Facility Procedures—Establishing/Closing the Record
- Preparing the Medical Record
- Preparing the Master Patient Index Card
- Re-Admission—Continued Use of Previous Record
- Re-Admission—New Record

Amendment of Clinical Records

Audit Schedule

Audit and Monitoring System

- Audit/Monitoring Schedule
- Admission/Readmission Audit
- Concurrent Audit
- Discharge Audit
- Specialized Audits (examples)
- Change in Condition

(Continues)

Figure 8-2 Health Information Policies and Procedures Checklist

- MDS
- Nursing Assistant Flow Sheet
- Psychotropic Drug Documentation
- Pressure Sore
- Restrictive Device/Restraint
- Therapy

Certification, Medicare

Chart Removal and Chart Locator Log

Clinical Records, Definition of Records and Record Service

General Policies

- Access to Records
- Automation of Records (See also Computerization)
- Availability
- Change in Ownership
- Completion of Records
- Confidentiality
- Indexes
- Ownership of Records
- Permanent and Capable of Being Photocopied
- Retention
- Storage of Records
- Subpoena
- Unit Record

Purpose/General Instructions for Keeping Clinical Records, Completing and Correcting Records

Willful Falsification/Willful Omission

Closing the Record

Coding and Indexing, Disease Index

Committee Minutes Guidelines

Computerization and Security of Automated Data/Records

Confidentiality—See Release of Information

Consulting Services for Clinical Records and Plan of Service

Content, Record (the list provided is not all inclusive and should be tailored to the facility/corporation)

- General
- Advanced Directives
- Transfer Form/Discharge Plan of Care
- Discharge Against Medical Advice

Figure 8-2 *(Continued)*

- Physician Consultant Reports
- Medicare Certification/Recertification
- Physician Orders/Telephone Orders
- Physician Services Guidelines and Progress Notes
- Physician History and Physical Exam
- Discharge Summary
- Interdisciplinary Progress Notes

Copying/Release of Records—General

Correcting Clinical Records

Data Collection/Monitoring

Definition of Clinical Records/Health Information Service

Delinquent Physician Visit

Denial Letters, Medicare

Destruction of Records, Log

Disaster Planning for Health Information

Discharge Procedures

- Assembly of Discharge Record
- Chart Order on Discharge
- Completing and Filing Master Patient Index Card
- Discharge Chart Audit
- Notification of Deficiencies
- Incomplete Record File
- Closure of Incomplete Clinical Record

Emergency Disaster Evacuation

Establishing/Closing Record

Falsification of Records, Willful

Fax/Facsimile, Faxing

Filing Order, Discharge (Chart Order)

Filing Order, In-house (Chart Order)

Filing System

Filing System, Unit Record

Forms Management

Forms, Release of Information

Forms, Subpoena

Guide to Location of Items in the Health Information Department

Guidelines, Committee Minutes

(Continues)

Figure 8-2 *(Continued)*

Incomplete Record File

Indexes

- Disease Index and Forms for Indexing
- Master Patient Index
- Release of Information Index/Log

Inservice Training Minutes/Record

Job Description:

- Health Information Coordinator
- Health Unit Coordinator
- Other Health Information Staff (if applicable)

Late Entries

Lost Record—Reconstruction

Master Patient Index

Medicare Documentation

- Certification and Recertification
- Medicare Denial Procedure and Letter
- Medicare Log

Numbering System

Ombudsman, Review/Access to Records

Omission, Willful

Order of Filing, Discharge

Order of Filing, In-house

Organizational Chart for Health Information Department

Orientation/Training of Health Information Department

Outguides

Physician Visit Schedule, Letters, and Monitoring

Physician Visits, Delinquent Visit Follow-up

Quality Assurance

- Health Information Participation
- QA Studies and Reporting

Readmission—Continued Use of Previous Record

Readmission—New Record

Recertification, or Certification (Medicare)

Reconstruction of Lost Record

Refusal of Treatment

Release of Information

Figure 8-2 (Continued)

- Confidentiality
- Confidentiality Statement by Staff
- Copying/Release of Records—General
- Faxing Medical Information
- Procedure for Release—Sample Letters and Authorizations
- Redisclosure of Clinical Information
- Resident Access to Records
- Retrieval of Records (sign-out system)
- Subpoena
- Witnessing Legal Documents

Requesting Information

- From Hospitals and Other Health Care Providers
- Request for Information Form

Retention of Records and Destruction after Retention Period

- Example Statement for Destruction
- Retention Guidelines

Retrieval of Records

Security of Automated Data/Electronic Medical Records

- General Procedures
- Back-up Procedures
- Passwords

Sign-out Logs

Storage of Records

Telephone Orders

Thinning

- In-house Records
- Maintaining Overflow Record

Unit Record System

Figure 8-2 *(Continued)*

Policy Rationale

The new policy must be created for a reason important to the organization as a whole and the **rationale** for the policy should be explained to those affected by it. The underlying intention may be to establish an orderly and legally compliant organization.

This is the case, for example, when policies are created directing staff to be at work at a specified time. Other policies are written to protect employees; for example, those that direct staff to wear gloves when handling specimens. And, of course, federal or state laws prompt other policies to be put into place.

Understanding the rationale of a policy is critical to compliance. When those required to follow a rule do not comprehend its essence, they can lose respect for its importance, as well as for the repercussions of failing to abide by it. This can lead them to ignore the policy or make attempts to shortcut compliance. You have heard them. "This rule is stupid, why should we follow it?" Very often, this is the result of a manager failing to take the time to help them see the underlying issues.

Let's examine the rationale for our example policy. The legal basis for creating an internal policy about releasing patient information is HIPAA's Privacy Rule. You learned in chapter 5 that in almost all circumstances, your facility should have a consent form (Figure 5-6) signed by the patient.

In addition to the legal reason for this policy, there are ethical factors involved as well. No matter how **compelling** an individual's story might be, it is not a health care professional's job to get in the middle of personal relationships. When you expect staff to follow a policy, it can help to open their perspectives to see all sides of a concern.

> **EXAMPLE** Roger Corrigan comes into your office and asks for a copy of his wife's health care records. You know from her file that they have been married for ten years. He states that his wife asked him to pick up the copies because she is applying for a new insurance policy and needs to submit the information with her application.

This seems very innocent, and, actually, rather kind of Mr. Corrigan to do this favor for his wife. He is so nice and you want to help him. There is no signed consent in the file, but what harm could it do to give him her records? There are several possible scenarios underlying this action of generosity by Mr. Corrigan.

1. His story is true, and he really is a nice guy doing his wife a favor.
2. His story is partially true. She is applying for new insurance; however, she did not ask him to pick up her records, because she has not yet told him about her recent diagnosis. She is waiting for the right time because he has a heart condition and she is worried about his reaction to the news. He suspects something is wrong and, rather than talk to her, wants to find out for himself by getting her records.
3. His story is not true at all. They are currently going through a bitter divorce and he wants her health records to look for a reason he can win full custody of the children.
4. His story is not true at all, and there can be a thousand reasons why he wants to **violate** her confidentiality.

The truth is that you don't know what the truth is. So you explain to Mr. Corrigan about HIPAA and the Privacy Rule, and that the law clearly states that you cannot release Mrs. Corrigan's information without her express permission. He flies into a rage. What should you do now? The answer to this question is exactly why having a law is not enough; each office and facility must have an established policy and/or procedure to guide their staff in difficult situations, just like this one.

When you provide the rationale for the policy, you support your staff in situations like this. Most individuals would not think beyond, "What a nice, thoughtful husband," and even though it is against policy, they would think, "What harm could it do?" Look at number two or number three in the list of potential scenarios. The harm could be that he has a heart attack. The harm could be that she loses custody of her children unfairly.

Individuals Affected by the Policy

Not every policy will affect every staff member. Policies regarding the safe handling of specimens will not directly apply to the health information management department, and procedures regarding the flow of information through the office will directly apply to both clinical and administrative personnel.

On the surface, it might appear that a policy regarding the release of patient information would only be of interest to HIM. However, anyone with access to patient records should be aware and responsible. Therefore, the entire staff should be helped to understand this policy. After all, how can you expect the front desk manager to abide by this rule if he knows nothing about it? He might take Mr. Corrigan at face value and feel good about providing him with a copy of Mrs. Corrigan's information and helping a patient. Instead, he actually violated a federal law and possibly placed Mrs. Corrigan in danger.

This is an excellent example of how a policy may appear on the surface to relate to only one department, but, in reality, is something about which everyone in the office should be thoroughly educated.

Procedural Compliance

As stated previously, policies are designed to direct individual behaviors. This portion of the policy needs to tell the members of your organization how to behave in the described situations. This portion of the policy must be clear and specific to assure that individuals will have no question about what behaviors are expected of them. While you may respect all members of your group and believe them to be intelligent, this is no time for giving them blanks to fill in themselves. Each person will interpret things in his or her own way, and the odds are against you getting everyone to respond the way he or she should.

Therefore, your policy regarding being at work on time must include the specific time—8:30 a.m., 9:00 a.m.—whatever is appropriate. In addition, the policy's explanation of expected behaviors will need to include **contingency** behaviors. "If tardiness is unavoidable, then the staff member must call his or her supervisor as soon as possible."

Our example policy identifies that no records can be released without a consent form signed by the patient. A contingency plan will need to address those circumstances when a patient is unable to sign the form and needs the records.

Preferred Behavior

Back to our release of information policy. You already learned in chapter 5 that the preferred behavior is to obtain a release of information form signed by the patient. This portion of the procedural compliance section of the policy should include a sample copy of the form (not everyone will know what it looks like), as well as specific information about how to find the form in the office (Form 123 in the forms folder on the shared hard drive; in the bin marked ROI in the administrative office on the first floor; in the reception area, top drawer of filing cabinet number one).

Next, the policy must explain what should happen once the signed form has been acquired. Should it go into the patient's file, be sent to the records department to have the record pulled and copied, or should a copy be made, with the original going one place and the copy going another? The answer to this will depend upon the internal systems in your facility. Before moving forward with this policy, be certain to investigate the current procedures. Don't just assume that it is a good system just because they have been "doing it this way for years." Creating a new policy is an opportunity to improve things and make them easier to comply with. Talk with staff and get their suggestions for improving the process, or, at least, get their specific complaints so you can understand what they do not like about the current system. When people don't like a process, feel that it takes too much effort, or find that it interferes with doing their job, they are more likely to violate or ignore the rules. The policy will be a greater success if you can enable compliance within the flow of the office, rather than attempt to force the issue and cram it down their throats. Therefore, if one complaint is that it is too much trouble or takes too much time to go into the system and print out a form each time it is needed, don't argue. Make copies and place them in a drawer nearby. Often, the littlest adjustment in a process makes all the difference in the world.

The policy should include a requirement for photo identification to be presented, copied, and attached to the form. This provides your facility with an extra level of protection, proving that you went the extra step to assure that the information was, indeed, being given to the patient. Most facilities have too many patients for them to be recognizable by the staff member, so the policy must cover those situations. Even if the individual asking for the identification knows the patient, the policy can be used to support the effort.

When the individual is requesting their personal records and cannot come into the office personally, your office is legally allowed to permit the patient to submit the release form using a fax or electronic mail. If you want to have your policy be extra cautious, or if for some reason the file in the office does not have the patient's signature for comparison, you can require the form to have a notarized statement that the signature is authentic. This policy serves the patient while still protecting the facility.

It's The Law

"Under the Privacy Rule, a covered entity may use or disclose protected health information pursuant to a copy of a valid and signed Authorization, including a copy that is received by facsimile or electronically transmitted."

(http://www.hhs.gov)

Contingency Behaviors

When creating a policy, it is important to recognize the fact that, in everyday life, not everything goes according to plans. The world is not rigid. Especially within a health care facility, there are times when unexpected things happen. Helping individuals know what to do when the unusual happens will support compliance with the policy. This is why it is wise to establish a contingency policy.

What should a staff member do in an emergency when a signed release form cannot be obtained? Let's go to HIPAA and see if the law provides us with any guidance.

The Office of Civil Rights, Department of Health and Human Services, HIPAA Compliance Assistance, Summary of the HIPAA Privacy Rule reports that there are situations in which a health care facility (covered entity) can release information without the signed consent.

It's The Law

"Permitted Uses and Disclosures. A covered entity is permitted, but not required, to use and disclose protected health information, without an individual's authorization, for the following purposes or situations: (1) To the Individual (unless required for access or accounting of disclosures); (2) Treatment, Payment, and Health Care Operations; (3) Opportunity to Agree or Object; (4) Incident to an otherwise permitted use and disclosure; (5) Public Interest and Benefit Activities; and (6) Limited Data Set for the purposes of research, public health or health care operations. Covered entities may rely on professional ethics and best judgments in deciding which of these permissive uses and disclosures to make."

(http://thomas.loc.gov)

The law itself provides the health care facility with several different contingency plans upon which you can develop your internal policy. From this one section of the law, you can establish additional sections to your policy.

What about when the patient is unable to come in, unable to get to a fax machine or notary public, and needs his records for an appointment with another physician, perhaps a specialist? This is what is meant by the second condition for permitted use and disclosure in the law.

It's The Law

"Treatment is the provision, coordination, or management of health care and related services for an individual by one or more health care providers, including consultation between providers regarding a patient and referral of a patient by one provider to another."

Uses And Disclosures For Treatment, Payment, And Health Care Operations [45 CFR 164.506] (http://thomas.loc.gov)

This portion of the law states that your facility can release the information to the other physician. While you do not have the documentation needed to release the information to the patient because his or her identity cannot be authenticated, your facility does have a way to **authenticate** another covered entity—a physician's office, clinic, or other type of health care facility. You learned about this in chapter 6 (Identity confirmation).

As long as the health care professional can be confirmed to be legitimate by data from a state or national official database, you can legally release the necessary information to them. Again, have your policy specify that the authentication of the other professional be printed out and secured in the patient's file. You want to have the evidence that this was actually done. The printout from a state website, for example, will include the date and time of the documentation, providing verification of compliance with the law.

Now, let's go back to our scenario with Mr. Corrigan. Your office can safeguard Mrs. Corrigan's interests and support Mr. Corrigan's kind efforts by explaining the policy and providing Mrs. Corrigan with the options: She can come into the office herself; a form can be sent (to the address in her file) and returned; or she can contact the office with the information for the insurance company to which she is applying, and your office can send the record directly to them. (Remember that insurance carriers are covered entities under HIPAA, just like health care facilities.) In any regard, unless Mrs. Corrigan signed a release form permitting release to her husband, he has no authority to request release of her records.

How annoying! After all, he is her husband and he should have a right to her health care records because there are no secrets between husband and wife. Really? Remember, it is not a health care professional's responsibility to get in the middle of people's personal relationships. As indicated before, they may be getting a divorce. He may hurt her based on information in her file. The same is true in other personal relationships, such as between a parent and child. You, or any other member of the staff, do not know the intricacies of other relationships, and it is not your business to get in between these two individuals. *Everyone* deserves the right to confidentiality. The law guarantees this and it is not up to you to waive that right.

Oversight Responsibility

One individual, or one category of individuals (job title), must be named responsible for assuring the policy is complied with during the course of day-to-day operations. This does not refer to the compliance officer, who has overall responsibility for all compliance issues throughout the entire department or organization. This refers to the person(s) responsible for assuring this specific policy is followed.

This point person for our release of information policy will be the one to receive the signed form, pull the patient's chart, compare signatures on the form and in the file to assure authenticity (yes, someone might forge the signature to get to the information illegally), and then process the request. This would also be the individual responsible for verifying the status of another covered entity, should the request identify information be disclosed to another health care professional.

Policy Review and Update

Facility policies have to co-exist, peacefully if possible, with your entire staff. Therefore, the internal process for developing and updating policies should be one in which employees have input, preferably before, during, and after implementation. The intention is not to provide a free-for-all in the policy development. This would create an impossible situation because no one policy will ever make everyone happy. However, you want to ensure that your policy development encompasses multiple perspectives. It is much easier for the nursing staff to provide insights on the impact of a certain policy on the clinical staff than for someone in administration to make a prediction or assumption.

It is recommended that the facility have a written process for approving new policies and procedures prior to implementation. Some will need to be approved by the organization's attorneys, while others will be approved by the board of directors. The appropriate groups, in addition to the participating staff members, are ultimately responsible for compliance with the laws, so it is a good idea to identify each area of accountability.

In addition, a list of steps should be published for requests to update or dispute a policy. Providing these opportunities to staff members to interact with the process is a critical sign of respect for their professionalism and their desire to comply. Chances are that very few individuals will avail themselves of this opportunity, but it is important that it be offered.

Consequences for Non-Compliance

Virtually every law and regulation, whether federal or state, clearly explains the consequences for failing to adhere to the rule. The reason for this is connected to an understanding of human behavior. A percentage of your staff, like a portion of the general population, will follow the policy or the law because that is the right thing to do. Another percentage does not care, rejects rules and regulations, and will never comply. However, a large percentage of individuals need motivation of some kind to follow the rules. Some just need to understand and agree, while others comply out of fear of the consequences. Think about how many people might do something wrong, such as rob a bank, if they didn't have to worry about getting caught and going to jail. This goes back to basic human behavior modification, such as what parents use when trying to teach their young children the difference between right and wrong: reward and punishment.

Governmental Penalties

HIPAA's Privacy Rule includes both civil and criminal penalties for failing to protect an individual's protected health information, as prescribed by this law.

It's The Law

"Civil Money Penalties. HHS may impose civil money penalties on a covered entity of $100 per failure to comply with a Privacy Rule requirement. That penalty may not exceed $25,000 per year for multiple violations of the identical Privacy Rule requirement in a calendar year;

"Criminal Penalties. A person who knowingly obtains or discloses individually identifiable health information in violation of HIPAA faces a fine of $50,000 and up to one year imprisonment. The criminal penalties increase to $100,000 and up to five years imprisonment if the wrongful conduct involves false pretenses, and to $250,000 and up to ten years imprisonment if the wrongful conduct involves the intent to sell, transfer, or use individually identifiable health information for commercial advantage, personal gain, or malicious harm. Criminal sanctions will be enforced by the Department of Justice."

(http://thomas.loc.gov)

Facility Penalties

Your health care facility needs to establish its own consequences for violating this policy. This is a level of protection for your staff as well as the organization. The actions that the company may take should be strong enough to effectively deter individuals from thinking about failing to follow the rules. This portion of your policy is part of reducing liability and minimizing potential losses for the organization, as you learned in chapter 1 of this textbook. Your office wants to empower the policy to ensure compliance or to correct a violation before it ever gets as far as the state or federal authorities.

Generally, it is recommended that you include staged disciplinary actions for failing to comply with a company policy, particularly when it is backed by a governmental regulation. Of course, your facility will need to go through each individual policy to determine appropriate actions. Needless to say, violating a policy to call in when one is going to be late to work should not carry the same penalty as that for selling patient information to a tabloid.

The punishment should fit the crime, and first level offenses should be dealt with in a way to encourage learning and correction rather than retribution.

Levels of disciplinary actions used by some facilities include:

- Verbal warning
- Written warning
- Additional training/education
- Suspension with pay (most often used for the time frame from identification of violation through an investigation to determine guilt or innocence)
- Suspension without pay
- Termination

The published consequences for violating a specific policy must be applied equally to all members of the staff. There can be no favoritism, no waivers. Once one person gets away with non-compliance, the ability to enforce a policy is diminished and, at times, erased, and at other times, this behavior by the administration may increase your organization's liability.

There will be more about enforcement in a later chapter of this book.

Creating a Manual

Once all of the policies have been written and approved, they must be published so all staff members can access them. You are certainly familiar with the standard employee manual.

In addition to the printed version, it is a good idea to have these policies uploaded to your facility's intranet. This should be in a password-protected section so that only employees can see them. Electronic versions of policy manuals are great because they can be equipped with a search engine. This will make it easier for everyone to find a specific policy when they are unsure how to proceed in a particular situation.

Chapter Summary

It can be difficult, sometimes, to remember that not everyone knows what you know. Managers are responsible for guiding their staff in their professional endeavors. This includes helping them to know and understand how to behave in all circumstances that they may encounter during their time at work. Nothing can be assumed.

CHAPTER REVIEW

Multiple Choice Questions

1. An official policy should include the
   a. name of the person who wrote the policy.
   b. legal reason for the policy.
   c. number of words in the written version.
   d. address for Congress.

2. One reason a health care facility would need to create official policies is
   a. to educate staff members.
   b. to provide directives for employee behavior.
   c. to protect the interests of the organization.
   d. all of the above

3. Facilities excluded from the need to create a policy manual are
   a. hospitals with more than 200 employees.
   b. clinics with fewer than 30 employees.
   c. facilities that do not charge patients (i.e., a free clinic).
   d. No facilities are excluded.

4. Staff members that must abide by facility policies include
   a. everyone in the facility.
   b. only full-time employees.
   c. full-time and part-time employees.
   d. only clinicians.

5. Policies, as discussed in this text, are designed to direct
   a. budget consideration.
   b. resource allotment.
   c. individual behaviors.
   d. organizational structure.

6. A contingency behavior is one that addresses circumstances
   a. outside of the usual.
   b. during an audit.
   c. involving patients without insurance.
   d. that are day-to-day.

7. The individual named responsible for compliance of a certain policy is in charge of
   a. verification.
   b. report statistics.
   c. oversight.
   d. maximization.

8. After a policy is implemented, a facility should do a
   a. poll of employees.
   b. policy process review.
   c. due diligence.
   d. covert investigation.

9. The policy must include a clear explanation of the
   a. bonuses for compliance.
   b. promotion time frames.
   c. consequences for non-compliance.
   d. names of all employees involved.

10. Penalties may include
    a. fines.
    b. jail or prison time.
    c. termination.
    d. all of the above

11. All policies should include all of these elements except
    a. a rationale.
    b. contingency behaviors.
    c. penalties for non-compliance.
    d. the date the policy was created.

12. Writing policies may be the responsibility of the
    a. manager.
    b. compliance director.
    c. board of directors.
    d. any of the above

13. Policies should be
    a. consistent.
    b. unambiguous.
    c. a and b
    d. open for interpretation.

14. Facilities should provide their staff with the
    a. written process for approving policies.
    b. opportunity to write their own policies.
    c. chance to vote for the policies they like.
    d. legislative report that created each law.

15. Penalties for non-compliance should
    a. be the same for all violations.
    b. be progressive, so the punishment can fit the crime.
    c. never be implemented.
    d. be different for each employee.

Research and Discussion Projects

1. Pick a law or regulation from any of the previous chapters in this book and write a complete policy.

   _____

   _____

   _____

   _____

2. Compare and contrast your policy with those of other students in your class.
   a. Did you notice anything missing?
   b. Do you believe the policy would be effective?

   _____

   _____

   _____

   _____

Chapter 9

Education and Training

Learning Outcomes

- Identify the various types of training programs
- Explain the six components of a training program
- Distinguish the learning styles of adults
- Understand the importance of motivating your audience
- Describe the reasons why staff should be educated about reporting non-compliance

Key Terms

continuing education units (CEU) / the education—via coursework, seminar, or reading—beyond initial formal training, such as a degree or certification, that is required each year to keep a professional current on his or her industry

methodology / formats of organization or technique

proficient / having a great skill or being excellent at performing a task

suffice / to be enough; a sufficient quantity

trade journals / magazines written and published for a specific group of professionals

webinars / seminars and courses where participants attend using a specific site on the Internet that provides a speaker and a presentation, often in PowerPoint

Chapter Case Study

"On June 22, 2007, Kieran Denne, Nicholas Posillico and Robert Maurer, Jr. were indicted by a federal grand jury in Central Islip, New York. They were charged with defrauding insurance companies and the

federal Medicare program out of $2.5 million. The three operated Bay Shore
Bay Shore and Patchogue Physical Therapy in Patchogue. They were each cha
health care fraud for both billing the insurance companies and the governmen
never performed on clients, or billing for services that were supposedly provi
pist but were actually provided by a massage therapist. Deneen was also char
justice for hiding billing and treatment records that had been subpoenaed. L
licensed physical therapists. Maurer is a licensed massage therapist. Part of
charges that the defendants submitted claims for physical therapy supposedly provided by Deenen
when the work was actually performed by Maurer." (http://www.oig.hhs.gov)

Introduction

Health care facilities have a responsibility as well as a tremendous liability to their patients, third-party payers, and the government, built on what their staff members know. This is obvious when it comes to the clinicians who treat the patients hands-on. However, it is also true of every member of the team. Whether you are discussing the front office personnel and the manner with which they check in patients or the health information management staff and their ability to code and bill for optimal reimbursement, the life and success of the organization depends upon each person knowing their job and having the proper skills and abilities.

The same confidence has to be established when it comes to complying with the laws and regulations that govern health care services. As you learned earlier in this book, these laws are applicable to those staff members who "know, or are supposed to know." In addition, some laws go the extra step, such as HIPAA, and include an educational mandate in their scope.

It's The Law

HIPAA's Privacy Rule states:

"Workforce Training and Management. Workforce members include employees, volunteers, trainees, and may also include other persons whose conduct is under the direct control of the entity (whether or not they are paid by the entity). A covered entity must train all workforce members on its privacy policies and procedures, as necessary and appropriate for them to carry out their functions. A covered entity must have and apply appropriate sanctions against workforce members who violate its privacy policies and procedures or the Privacy Rule."

(http://thomas.loc.gov)

It is a mistake for any business to assume that each member of the staff has been educated on every applicable law or regulation. Perhaps someone who didn't have all the facts trained them and so they were, therefore, given misinformation. Or they worked in a facility that believed that it didn't have to comply with the laws because it was unlikely to be the target of an investigation. Even if someone has been trained, the laws may have changed since they learned them. This is why most professional licenses and certifications require annual **continuing education units (CEU)** to be earned. On-going programs of continuing education are necessary for everyone working in a health care facility of any size.

ning Programs

While the official compliance plan must include educational and training events, this does not mean that the facility must actually host all of them. You can't just hand out the employee handbook and expect that to **suffice**. There are many options for small and large facilities across the country to get their employees the knowledge they need:

- Seminars sponsored by professional organizations' local chapters
- Seminars sponsored by independent consulting companies
- Seminars sponsored by governmental agencies
- State and national professional organizations' conventions and conferences
- Courses (individual and degree-seeking) at local educational institutions

These educational events use varying types of **methodology**:

- In-person courses: onsite at the facility
- In-person courses: off-site at another location
- Online courses: using the Internet or the company's intranet, sometimes called **webinars**
- Audio seminars
- Books and other publications, including **trade journals**
- DVDs and videos

Learning opportunities must be planned for in the budget, as well as in the organizational schedule.

Designing a Training Program

There will be occasions when your facility will need to host a training program. Whether you are planning a HIPAA orientation for new members of your department, an instruction on a new software system, or education about new policies and procedures from Medicare, there are many factors that will go into preparing an effective and efficient program.

The components of development include:

- What
- Who
- When
- How
- Why
- Where

What?

What will be the topic of the session? When you are mixing education with work, most often the best practice is *one thing* at a time. Begin by making a list of policies and regulations that are most important to your team. Keep the list handy so that you can add to it as topics come to mind or you are made aware of new subjects.

Next, go over the list from top to bottom and rate each one based on complexity. These topics are more likely to require longer sessions, and possibly more than one meeting. Other topics are surely going to be easier to grasp and can be dealt with quickly, such as reviewing the new registration process for new patients. Doing this will enable you to create a balanced schedule.

Once your list is complete, review the notifications from national trade organizations and government agencies to match topics on your list to those being covered in upcoming seminars and conferences. You can then schedule staff and budget items appropriately.

Finally, you can prioritize those topics left on your list for internally developed training programs.

Who?

Who should attend this particular training session? Additional training never hurt anyone, and everyone can use a reminder of things they already know, but an effective training is written and planned for a specific group of people. Identify what needs to be covered and who in your department needs to know this information.

Each person in your department is an individual and each comes to you with varying degrees of pre-existing knowledge. Even those with years of previous experience may have forgotten things, or learned things incorrectly. Some may even have developed bad habits at their last employer.

> **EXAMPLE** A seminar on the new Present-on-Admission (POA) indicators is most beneficial to those coding and submitting claims for in-patient services, while a presentation on the Physician Quality Reporting Initiative (PQRI) will be more applicable to those working in a physician's office.

Having the entire staff sit through an hour lecture on something that does not relate to their job or responsibilities is a waste of time, energy, and money.

Remember to include a contingency plan for staff members who are unable to attend the scheduled seminar. People get sick or may be scheduled for vacation that week. Plan ahead and think about how these staff members might make up the learning experience.

When?

When will it take place? Scheduling the training during regular working hours means that you will have to coordinate for the loss of productivity. It is important that making up the work does not avalanche on top of you or your staff. The stress of the perceived pileup of work will weigh heavily on everyone, cause resentment, and will typically be evidenced in poor-quality output once people get back to work. When the number of individuals scheduled for the training is large enough, consider dividing the group. Then one portion can be training while the others continue to work.

Members of each group will typically discuss the details of what they have learned, in essence comparing their notes. When positively based, this magnifies the effect of the training session. Breaking up the department can be particularly beneficial when small cliques exist. You may find some will disrupt the training sessions just to get a laugh or to express their machismo. Splitting them into different training sessions will help to abate these potential trouble spots.

If you schedule the training for off-hours, you will have to find a manner in which to pay your staff for attending. Depending upon your budget parameters, this may not be a problem. However, remember that there are more ways to reimburse employees than with money. You can offer them comp time—equivalent time off at a later date to be taken upon approval. Be certain this is planned for and requests, within reason, are approved.

Mandating attendance at an off-hours training without any type of reimbursement may or may not be a violation of employment laws or union rules, but it certainly is not a respectful way to treat your people. Above and beyond the legal ramifications lies the extraordinary opportunity to enflame bad attitudes, disloyalty, and high turnover. All of these conditions will cost you, your department, and your company money, one way or the other.

How Much Time?

One influential element of when to hold the session(s) will be the expected length of time needed. If the training will be short, you can sponsor a learning lunch and have the company pay for the food. It does not have to be a major, catered event. Depending upon the group, pizza and wings may be met with great appreciation. Be certain to give them enough notice to avoid any personal errand conflicts.

Of course, if the topic of the training is expected, or desired, to produce discussion and excitement in those attending, you may not want to confine the class to a locked-in timetable. For example, you may want to discuss ideas for improving the query process with physicians. It may be counterproductive to get the group excited and ideas flowing, then shut down because a deadline has to be met.

How Many Sessions?

No one can learn to be **proficient** in a new software program with one day of training, and very few individuals can grasp five different appeals processes by reading a policy manual. If the training is going to take several hours, you will need to decide how to best time the sessions. For example, if the topic at hand will take too long for a lunch seminar, think carefully about the content of the training. Perhaps two Wednesdays at lunch in a row will work.

Or will it be best for you to block out a half-day or a full day and get it all done at one time? The answer to this lies in the content of the training. Adult learners need to be given bite-sized pieces of information that are then reinforced with the actual use of this information. Therefore, when retraining staff on a new software program, you will get better results by teaching them one or two things and letting them go and use those new skills before attempting to teach them any more.

How?

The manner in which you present information to others directly affects your audience's ability to learn the information, and how much of it they will retain. When you take time to analyze your own preferred method of learning, you will understand that it makes a difference in how much you actually grasp. Whether you are dealing with training physicians about how to create better documentation, or front desk personnel about the new system to perform eligibility and verification, it is beneficial to everyone involved to have them walk out of the training actually more knowledgeable than they were going in . . . and not just bored and muttering about what a big waste of time that was.

Let's review the options that are available to you:

- *Tell Me:* Auditory learners benefit most from the personal presentation of a knowledgeable individual standing in front of the room lecturing on the points to be shared. This can be easy to accommodate and, if someone on staff has the facts, it may cost you practically nothing. However, there are certain considerations:

  - The speaker must be able to present the information in a positive fashion. Not all people are cut out for public speaking. The smartest person on your staff with regard to the subject at hand may not be the best person to teach your people due to an inability to speak in an acceptable way (not in a monotone; free from speech affectations, such as "er," "umm," "ya know," and other distractions; at a natural volume that can be heard beyond the first row). It would also be great if this individual can speak with some enthusiasm and energy. Who can speak about new Medicare billing regulations with enthusiasm? Good question. Make certain you ask this question before committing to your lecturer.

  - The content of the presentation must be written at an appropriate level for the audience. It is useless to talk over everyone's head just to make the speaker appear to be better educated than everyone else. Of course the speaker is more knowledgeable than the audience—they wouldn't be asked to speak otherwise! Being pompous and stuffy does not impress, and it definitely does not educate. Talking down to your audience accomplishes the same result: a roomful of annoyed, impatient staff members who gain nothing from the time spent.

- *Show Me:* Visual learners need to see images and illustrations of the concepts and information being provided. This may be as simple as including a PowerPoint presentation with the speaker or a demonstration of the issues being discussed. For example, if you are talking about the new EHR system, include an actual demonstration of the software in use. If you are educating your audience about how to code for new procedures now being performed in your clinic, include a picture or a video of the procedure or equipment involved. Something as direct as completing the new Consent to Treat form is best learned when an overhead is used to project the form on a screen, and the staff can actually see what you are talking about as you speak. These learners do not require fancy, expensive films or videos to get the point. They just need a picture or illustration for their minds to grasp.

- *Let Me Do:* These hands-on learners thrive in educational processes that are interactive. It is not that they don't need to hear the lecture or see illustrations of how to enter a new procedure code into the system. These members of your staff need to actually try it themselves to complete the learning. Therefore, after you tell them about the new software program and show them how it is done, you must give them time at a computer terminal and let them actually do it, under supervision, to assure that they get it correctly.

- *Give It To Me and I Will Learn It On My Own:* These do-it-yourselfers prefer to be handed the book or the manual and go off on their own. Generally, this is a very small group in most businesses today. However, they should not be ignored.

To assure the learning process actually occurs, this method of education should include some type of test or other confirmation that the material has been absorbed. Offering a certificate of completion after passing the exam is a tangible way of motivating people to learn.

Some managers will find this all a bother and too much work for a simple training session. The bottom line remains: if it is important enough to train employees, it is important enough to assure that they actually gain knowledge.

Why?

Why do we have to sit through this? You can lead an employee to training, but you can't make them think. If you are going to expend the energy to create a training session—whether it is a short seminar in the break room, or a weekend event at a local hotel—you should expect to see benefits in the workplace. Quality should improve, productivity should improve, liability should go down; whatever your goals are, there should be evidence that the training occurred.

It will be next to impossible to obtain a great, open attitude from 100% of your attendees. However, you can take steps to increase their willingness to learn.

What's in it for me? The answer to this has nothing to do with the extra pay or time off you are going to give them for attending. These things only give them a reason to show up, not to listen. This answer also should not be about the company benefits, such as higher productivity or less potential for governmental fines. That is what is in it for the organization.

Your staff needs to be told, clearly and directly, the benefits that they, as individuals, will gain from this training. It is best to explain these benefits prior to the actual training, but repeat them again at the beginning of the session. Whenever possible, these advantages should be expressed as positive benefits, rather than the absence of something negative. For example, if you are going to present a seminar on HIPAA's Privacy Rule, explain the benefits of personal privacy to help each member of your audience see himself or herself in the picture. When someone else has a big boil on their behind, it is funny. When it happens to you, it is quite a different story.

Connect the dots for them. It is not uncommon for staff members to think in different patterns and perspectives than managerial personnel. Administrators draw certain conclusions from some activities, while many staff members cannot calculate a sequence of events. For example, most managers understand the value of continuing education in their careers for raises, promotions, and future job hunting. Staff members typically need continuing explanation and reinforcement of the future value of attending a seminar or class.

Take the time to not only explain that the content of the meeting will be news they can use; let them know in detail how they will use it and what benefit that usage will provide. For example, let's say that the training for the new computer system is going to begin. Start off by telling them about how the system will decrease their paperwork and make queries to the physician easier. Launch the session with the coders discovering how the system includes a medical dictionary to help them look up terminology they aren't clear about.

Provide booster shots of encouragement and enthusiasm. Keep in mind that most of your employees are not typical diehard students. They will need periodic injections of energy and encouragement to keep them going, especially during long training sessions.

Where?

The actual location of the session is something that has to be carefully thought out, because it will contribute or detract from the event.

1. Begin with deciding whether to hold the meeting onsite or away from the office. Using the conference room down the hall will not incur any budget considerations. However, it can sometimes be difficult to get people's full attention when work is right down the hall. Interruptions may occur as other members of the staff come in, just for second, to ask a question. While a meeting room at a community center or hotel may cost some money, getting out of the office can establish a clearer frame of mind for most attendees.

2. Carefully check the technical requirements for the presentation. Having a projector that just won't work with your laptop, or not having an Internet connection, as you thought you would, will have a dramatic affect on your presentation.

3. Monitor the temperature in the room. If it gets too hot, people will get drowsy and find it more difficult to concentrate. At the same time, a room that is too cold will also be distracting.

4. Try to avoid presentation methods like PowerPoints and videos if that means that your staff will be sitting in the dark for any length of time.

Reporting Non-Compliance

This is not in the wrong chapter. You are going to have to educate your staff on the critical importance of reporting any violation, or suspected violation, of any policy, procedure, law, or regulation. This is serious, and it is something that will require support and repetition of the message.

The psychological issues that some have with reporting another individual's incorrect behavior can go all the way back to childhood, when one might be teased for being a tattletale. This builds up the worry that, should someone inform on another person, they will be ostracized from the group.

Another underlying concern comes from the friendships that develop among co-workers. It can be very difficult for an individual to choose between reporting knowledge of the failure to comply with a policy and betraying a friend, especially if the violation is serious and might result in someone getting fired.

You can combat these concerns by making certain that the reporting system is one that can be used without fear, as you learned in chapter 3. Every manager needs extra eyes to monitor the behaviors of all employees at all times in all sections on all shifts. This is why the reporting system is such an important part of the compliance program. However, more has to be done than putting the system into place. The staff must be educated on the value of the system, the protection to the reporters, and the support of the entire organization for those that help keep the facility honest and legal.

All reports to the hotline will be investigated, and this is a fact that should be included in your training. No one will take it seriously if they come to discover that there is no point in reporting a violation because no one does anything about it. These attitudes foster an environment of dishonest and illegal behaviors, ranging from ignoring patients to stealing office supplies, and worse.

Build an atmosphere of honesty and respect, and help your staff to know, from your words and your actions, that you will stand by them.

Chapter Summary

Individuals come to work for a health care facility with many different experiences. Some may join your staff right out of school, with the most up-to-date information and understanding of new laws and regulations. Others may have worked for organizations with less-than-reputable managers who demanded that employees break the law at every opportunity. The best course for your facility to take is to provide them with quality training and ensure that they know what is expected of them.

CHAPTER REVIEW

Multiple Choice Questions

1. Training your staff on compliance may
   a. cost a great deal of money.
   b. save the facility money by reducing liability.
   c. waste time because employees should already know the material.
   d. be too difficult to schedule.

2. Employees may get their education
   a. on the Internet.
   b. at a convention.
   c. from a book.
   d. all of the above

3. Credible sources for educating employees include
   a. professional organizations.
   b. governmental agencies.
   c. local colleges.
   d. all of the above

4. Training programs should include all except
   a. who should attend.
   b. what the topic should be.
   c. that lunch is paid for by the company.
   d. where the meeting will be held.

5. Programs held during off-hours will require
   a. no additional compensation.
   b. time-and-a-half at their regular pay rate.
   c. baby-sitting services.
   d. some type of compensation.

6. Auditory learners prefer presentations that are primarily
   a. hands-on, interactive sessions.
   b. lecture-based.
   c. examples and illustrations.
   d. book-or manual-based.

7. Most staff members need to know this first:
   a. Where will the session be?
   b. How much will you pay me to attend?
   c. Who else will be there?
   d. What's in it for me?

8. The actual location of the training program should be
   a. somewhere in the office so people don't have to travel.
   b. in a restaurant.
   c. at a resort.
   d. at the most appropriate location for the topic and length of time needed.

9. Reporting systems should be
   a. non-threatening.
   b. optional.
   c. publicly done.
   d. required to include evidence.

10. Anyone reporting an occasion of non-compliance should be assured that they will not
    a. be harassed.
    b. be fired.
    c. be ostracized.
    d. all of the above

Research and Discussion Project

1. Recall a time when you were a customer and experienced an incompetent employee. Did you report this person's bad behavior to the manager, or were you afraid to get someone in trouble? Now relate those feelings to the feelings of a staff member who witnesses a fellow employee breaking a rule or policy. Discuss how you will convince them to report the episode of non-compliance.

   _____

   _____

   _____

   _____

   _____

2. In chapter 8 you wrote a policy for one of the laws or regulations you learned about earlier in this textbook. For this project, design a training program to educate your staff on this new policy. Be certain to address all of the elements of a good training program.

   _____

   _____

   _____

   _____

   _____

Chapter 10

The Internal Audit

Learning Outcomes

- Compare the various types of audits
- Determine the best uses of each type of audit
- Identify the concerns evoked by certain types of audits in particular circumstances
- Enumerate the components of an internal audit
- Explain the benefits of internal reporting

Key Terms

comprehensive / investigation of the entire quantity
concurrent / happening at the same time
covert / covered up; hidden from plain sight
external / brought on by an agency or organization other than the facility being audited
internal / generated from inside
occult / cannot be seen without investigation; deeply hidden
overt / out in the open; obvious
retrospective / looking at the past
sampling / investigation or review of a percentage rather than the whole quantity

Chapter Case Study

"On February 5, 2007, in Los Angeles, CA, James Graf was sentenced to 25 years in federal prison and was ordered to pay more than $20 million in restitution. Graf was found guilty by a federal jury in November 2005 of conspiracy, five counts of mail fraud, 10 counts of misappropriation in connection with a health care benefit program, six counts of money

laundering and one count of obstruction of justice. According to court documents, Graf misrepresented to insurance agents and the public that Employers Mutual's plans were insured through one or more legitimate insurance companies, including Sun Life of Canada, United Wisconsin Life Insurance Company and Golden Rule Insurance Company. Graf bilked customers of Employers Mutual LLC, a company that falsely purported to provide health care coverage to more than 20,000 people across the United States. Instead, people who thought they were insured were left facing more than $20 million in unpaid claims when Employers Mutual was shut down by authorities." (http://www.irs.gov)

Introduction

Once a compliance program is written and implemented, the facility must perform regular audits to ensure that the plan is working in day-to-day operations. In addition to looking for evidence of individual or group violations before they become a federal issue, the audit can illuminate manners in which systems can be improved, and the plan can be made easier to accomplish.

Indicators of Fraud

In every organization, there are situations that can disguise fraudulent activities. Some are easier to spot than others.

1. **Overt** signs: In health care offices, it can be obvious to see that something is wrong fairly easily by looking at the statistics measuring the number of rejections and denied claims. A high number of returned claims is a clear sign that something is very wrong in the internal systems. The issue might be poor documentation, inaccurate superbills, poorly trained or untrained coders, etc. Only an investigation can confirm what the real cause is and reveal how to fix this.

2. **Covert** signs: A more subtle indication that your facility is not getting the reimbursement it deserves or may be filing fraudulent claims can be seen in claims that are paid. An investigation can identify continuing activities including undercoding, upcoding, or other risky activities.

3. **Occult** signs: Outside of anyone's view may be a stream of behaviors that are putting your facility in grave danger. These cannot be easily seen and require a thorough investigation of patient documentation, claims forms, and other relevant reports.

Types of Audits

Audits look into the processes and systems involved in accomplishing tasks in order to assure that policies are being followed. As mentioned previously in this textbook, these audits are done to permit the facility to know about an ethics or legal concern before it becomes the basis for a complaint or an allegation of fraud.

Audits can be:

- *Internal or external:* An **internal** audit is instigated and performed by the organization itself, whereas an **external** audit is initiated and conducted by another organization or agency, such as the Office of the Inspector General or Blue Cross Blue Shield.

- *Concurrent or retrospective:* **Concurrent** audits examine a system in action, as it is happening, whereas **retrospective** audits look at work that has already been done.

This chapter will examine managing internal audits. Chapter 11 will go over the administration of external audits.

EXAMPLE Fesbrook Medical Center will be doing an audit on claims sent to Medicare from their west side office. A *concurrent* audit would evaluate claims being created today, before they are submitted. A *retrospective* audit would review claims sent to Medicare last week or last month.

- *Sampling or Comprehensive:* The scope of an audit may begin with a small, random selection, called a **sampling** audit, or focus on one area and investigate the entire sector, called a **comprehensive** audit.

EXAMPLE Varney Pediatrics Clinic has decided to perform an internal audit on its records department's adherence to release of information consent policies. A sampling audit will be done with orders that, if any irregularities are found, the audit will convert into a comprehensive review.

When a sampling audit is performed, it is important that the number of items reviewed is large enough to be statistically valid. In most cases, the greatest concern is that the number is large enough to capture violations that occur occasionally. If not, then the audit is futile, because the results will be flawed.

Components of an Internal Audit

Conducting an audit is a multifaceted event and requires some project management skills.

The Scope of the Audit

1. *Identify the specific policy, law, or element of compliance to investigate.* Internal audits should focus on one aspect of the responsibilities of the department or section. If the policy is multifaceted, then itemize the detailed criteria for the audit. It is best to keep each audit directed so that both the review and the results are manageable. An audit that attempts to accomplish too much at one time has an increased opportunity for failure. Consider doing several smaller audits rather than one large investigation, unless you have the time and manpower to complete the bigger scope.

   The objectives of the audit should be clearly stated, as they are in the example from an Office of the Inspector General's Office of Audit Services report, shown in Figure 10-1.

Objectives

Our audit objectives were:

- To determine whether the Practice claimed reimbursement for pathology laboratory services in accordance with Medicare Part B medical necessity and documentation requirements from May through December 2004, and
- To analyze the Practice's utilization patterns for pathology services.

Scope

Our review of internal controls was limited to understanding the Practice's patient biopsy process, labeling and recording of biopsy tissue for shipment to its San Antonio laboratory, receipting and recording of tissue samples at the San Antonio laboratory, laboratory processing, bill processing, and receipting of Medicare payments.

Office of the Inspector General (http://www.oig.hhs.gov)

Figure 10-1 Sample audit objectives

2. *Determine if the audit will be concurrent or retrospective.* Identify any recent changes in this sector. Changes in systems, such as the implementation of new software or changes in active personnel, might make a retrospective audit produce irrelevant data by identifying old problems that have already been corrected by the change.

> **EXAMPLE** Harrison, the coder who has been with the office for five years, moved away three months ago; Carmen took over his job two months ago. Therefore, a concurrent audit would reveal how Carmen is doing. There is no value, at this point, in assessing whether Harrison was good at his job.

3. *Determine if the audit will be sampling or comprehensive in scope.* For the most part, a random sampling (performed with statistical accuracy) is very effective for compliance audits. Then if a problem or suspicion of irregularities becomes evident, a more intensive, comprehensive audit can be justified. Figure 10-2 includes a description of the random sampling used in an audit performed by the OIG.

Sampling

We selected and reviewed a random sample of 100 Medicare claims totaling $86,197 that Trail Blazer paid during the eight-month period May through December 2004. We provided the associated medical records to the Program Safeguard Contractor (PSC) for medical review to determine whether the pathology services billed for were reasonable, necessary, and in accordance with Medicare Part B requirements.

We conducted our fieldwork at the Practice's office in Tyler and its laboratory in San Antonio, Texas.

Office of the Inspector General (http://www.oig.hhs.gov)

Figure 10-2 Example of a random sampling audit

The Auditors

4. *Determine the member(s) of the audit team.* Make certain that these individuals are qualified to evaluate the specific elements being audited. For example, if you will be auditing claim forms for coding accuracy, use only certified coders, from another area, to perform the review. Do not ever permit staff members to audit their own work as a part of an official investigation. This behavior should already be incorporated in their daily job performance. You also want to avoid having co-workers investigate each other in an official review. Peer pressure and friendships can skew the accuracy of the results.

   In smaller offices, you may not have qualified staff available to perform an audit. When this is the case, look into hiring an outside professional. Be certain to include funds for these important services in your annual budget. Trade journals might provide, via articles or advertisements, contact information for individuals or companies that provide auditing services. Another option for an outsourced auditor may come from your peers, whom you can contact through the local professional chapters of national trade organizations such as AHIMA and AAPC. A third option involves calling a local, accredited college to speak with the chair of the HIM department.

5. *Assign the team a protected area to perform the review.* For the most part, the patient records and other documentation that will be audited should not leave the premises. Generally, there is too much work involved in copying everything for the auditor to take the documents off property. Therefore, find an office, a conference room, or other area that the professionals involved in this review can use. Assure that they will have privacy and quiet, and that they will be away from any possible harassment.

The Framework of the Audit

6. *Designate a time frame for the audit.* Team members should be given a deadline for handing in a report to the supervisor. Additional time can be granted; however, it is not a good idea to leave the investigation open-ended. If the audit has a wide scope, then the reports should be broken into stages so that you can have evidence of progress, and obtain preliminary data.

   > **EXAMPLE** The audit of all claims including lab services will be conducted November 10 through November 15. The report will be completed and submitted to the office manger no later than November 22.

7. *Establish a format for the audit results report.* Everyone has their own way of doing things. Therefore, it is important that you determine how you want the results of the audit delivered. When this is planned ahead of time, a lot of work can be saved. The first question to consider is: What will you do with the results? If it is to be compared to previous data, you may want to request the information be provided in a spreadsheet format, so it can be easily copied and pasted into a master document. This will make it easier to perform additional analysis so trends can

be identified and/or current, quarterly, or annual, results can be compared with previous audits of the same area. Or you might prefer the results presented with a more descriptive analysis, in a word processing document which can be easily dispersed to those who need to see the information. Specify paper, or electronic, or both. If electronic, specify which software program should be used. Do not assume.

> **EXAMPLE** The report will be written using Microsoft Word and e-mailed to the office manager.

Conducting the Audit

Without question, as the manager, you will need to plan the audits out in advance. As you learned in the previous section, there is a lot of work to do in order to ensure valid results. Should you notify the staff in advance, or have it be a surprise? There are considerations for both sides of this question.

The benefit of notifying the team in advance includes the time it should save the auditors because the records can be pulled and ready for the review. The department, or section, being audited can be given a list of items, such as patient records, copies of claim forms, reports from the clearinghouse, etc. This will enable the auditors to get right to their evaluation without having to take the time to gather the information. This may be an important factor when using an outside professional who is paid by the hour to perform the audit.

One reality of advance notice is that individual behaviors will change. If the audit is to be conducted concurrently, you must take into account that the results will be better than at other times. Most individuals are more careful with their performance when they know someone is watching. Think about how a typical driver's behaviors change when they know a police officer happens to be traveling right behind them. All of a sudden, more than usual, they become intensely aware of the proper way to drive and follow every rule. Once the cruiser turns off the street, the driver relaxes again and goes back to traveling a few miles over the speed limit. This is normal human behavior. You must take this into consideration.

One disadvantage of prior notification also comes from a typical human behavior— that of survival. When given the opportunity, those who know in their hearts that their capabilities and skills are not up to acceptable levels will attempt to cover up their inadequacies. If they are charged with pulling twenty patient records randomly, the choices will not be random at all, but carefully selected to avoid detection. This is one of the basic reasons for sponsoring surprise audits. They generally provide a more truthful snippet of a department or facility.

You can also mix up the methodology of your audits, depending upon exactly what the nature of the audit is and how many will be conducted over a period of time. For example, the Joint Commission will visit a facility a prescribed number of times per year. It is known in advance that some of the visits will be announced in advance, while others are always a surprise. The visit is known when the team walks in the door, and not one moment before. (More about these and other external audits in the next chapter.)

Figure 10-3 shows the step-by-step methodology used for completing an audit performed by the OIG.

Methodology

To accomplish our objectives, we:

- Reviewed applicable provisions of the Social Security Act, Code of Federal Regulations, and the Provider Reimbursement Manual;
- Interviewed staff at the Practice's office and laboratory and gained an understanding of the procedures the Practice used at its office and laboratory;
- Reviewed various contractual documentation regarding arrangement for laboratory services, including the employment of the contracted pathologist, rental of space, and management operations;
- Identified and reviewed a random sample of 100 claims that Trail Blazer paid for the Practice's prostate-related pathology services during the period May through December 2004, to verify compliance with Medicare regulations, and calculated the average number of tissue samples per claim of CPT 88305 the Practice examined;
- Contracted with a PSC to review the Practice's medical records for the 100 sampled claims to determine if pathology services were medically necessary, adequately documented, and performed at the level indicated on the claim;
- Identified claims containing units of CPT 88305 for which Trail Blazer paid to independent laboratories that the Practice used during the period September 2003 through April 2004;
- Identified claims containing units of CPT 88305 that Trail Blazer reimbursed to all other providers during the period May through December 2004; and
- Compared the Practice's average units per claim of CPT 88305 claimed before and after it opened its own laboratory and compared the Practice's average units per claim of CPT 88305 after it opened its own laboratory to the average units per claim of CPT 88305 Trail Blazer paid to all other providers.

We performed our review in accordance with generally accepted government auditing standards.

Office of the Inspector General (http://www.oig.hhs.gov)

Figure 10-3 Step-by-step methodology used for completing an audit performed by the Office of the Inspector General

On-going Internal Measures

Exit Interviews

One of the best inside sources a company can have is a staff member who has decided it is time to move on. This individual already has another job, so there is no concern for their future. While you don't want an exit interview to turn into a gripe session, this recently former employee is in a unique position to share some frontline observations.

The format of this interview should be non-threatening and not intimidating. Therefore, a personal encounter behind closed doors is discouraged. You can mail them a paper survey, such as the one shown in figure 10-4. In this case, include a self-addressed stamped envelope. (It is worth the cost of the stamp to get the viewpoint.) Take advantage of current technology and provide an online survey that can be completed from a computer at home. The safer the person feels, the more honesty you are likely to get. There are many websites on which you can create a survey of this, or any other, nature for free or for a low cost. This way, you can accomplish this without worrying about complex programming or Internet protocol servers.

- Why are you leaving the company?
- Do you have specific concerns that led to your decision to leave?
- Do you already have a new job?
- Were particular incentives offered to you that urged your decision to leave?
- What are the best things you experienced while with this company?
- What specific policies, procedures, or other aspects did you dislike about our company?
- On a scale of 1 to 10, with 10 being the best, how would you rate your relationship with your supervisor or manager?
- Would you share some specifics as to why you chose this rating?
- On a scale of 1 to 10, with 10 being the best, how would you rate the company's management or administration?
- Would you share some specifics as to why you chose this rating?
- What were the favorite aspects of your job here?
- What were your least favorite aspects of your job?
- Do you feel the company, or your management, made doing your job easier, more difficult, or had no impact?
- Would you please share some specifics to explain why you chose that answer?
- Do you feel the description of your job responsibilities was accurately presented at your hiring interview?
- Do you feel you were provided with appropriate management support and feedback about your performance?
- Do you feel you were provided with the tools that you needed to succeed?
- If not, what do you feel was missing?

Thank you for helping us make this company a better place to work.

Figure 10-4 Employee Exit Interview

Once you receive the feedback, regardless of the methodology used to obtain it, you need to take it seriously and use the data. Do not make assumptions that negative comments are merely harbored bad feelings. However, all of it should be taken with a grain of salt, because one person's opinion does not make a total truth.

View this information as containing indicators, not absolutes, of potential trouble spots. If the survey indicates that the supervisor on the B shift is incompetent and takes credit for the ideas of others, don't assume this is true or false. Investigate—quietly and cautiously—but nonetheless use the insights you are garnering to obtain a confirmable truth. You might be amazed at what is going on that you had no idea about.

Internal Reporting

The compliance program must include methodologies for current staff members to report observed violations of policies and procedures. No individual manager can be everywhere at all times, and enlisting your staff as participants in continuing compliance should be engrained in your organizational culture. Every member of your team should know, without a doubt, that this is a facility of honesty and no other behavior will be tolerated.

Just as with the exit interviews, these current staffers need to feel safe enough to be honest. In addition, they need to feel protected from any retribution. The fact that those working in your facility are adult-aged does not guarantee that they will all behave like adults. Assure that childish behaviors are not allowed. Those who report non-compliant activities are not "tattlers," "disloyal," or "traitors." These are the brave individuals who are standing up for your facility, its patients, and its staff.

You learned about this in both chapters 3 and 9, and it is worth repeating, that every report must be investigated. This must be an unbreakable rule; there will be no picking and choosing of what to investigate, no prejudging the validity of a report, or discounting information because it came from someone in the billing department who is always complaining about everything. Just because you don't like someone does not mean that his or her judgment is inaccurate. In fact, these situations should be investigated with the same cautions as any other audit. Therefore, the investigator should not have any knowledge of or history with anyone involved (the individual making the report or any of the individuals involved in the alleged issue). Bias in an audit does not ensure compliance, it only delays the truth from coming out.

> Objectivity is the core of a valid audit.

Results Analyses

Once the audit has been completed, the results must be analyzed so that useful information can be culled. Remember, the point of doing all this work is to obtain clues about how to improve your department or office, and make certain it is all done ethically and legally. If the report is just thrown in a file folder, then the entire audit was just a waste of time.

Skills you gained in statistics courses will be very beneficial. However, don't let your eyes glaze over. You can sift through the data and identify ways to improve without having to use complex formulas involving norm and standard deviations. (More about this in chapter 12.)

Results should be reported in a manner that can be used for improvement by the organization, as shown in Figure 10-5. You will note that this audit has a positive result. Not all audits end with fines and penalties. This gives you an excellent example of the reality that, when facilities comply, there is no need to fear an audit.

During our audit period, the Medicare program had not created any national or local coverage determinations or standards for the number of tissue samples that should be examined for urology patients with prostate-related diagnoses. The PSC medical reviewer stated that medical necessity for biopsies cannot be determined in the absence of national or local coverage determinations by Medicare. However, in the absence of these standards, but within the realm of his professional judgment, the PSC medical reviewer was satisfied that the Practice's claims for pathology laboratory services generally complied with Medicare Part B medical necessity and documentation requirements for 99 of 100 reviewed claims. The one exception was improperly billed and paid due to a clerical error, which was corrected during our audit.

We noted an increase in the number of prostate-related pathology services requested and performed after the Practice opened its own laboratory. Prior to the Practice opening its own laboratory in May 2004, the Practice's physicians requested pathology services from independent laboratories on an average of four tissue examinations per claim. After establishing its own laboratory, the Practice's physicians requested pathology services on an average of 12 tissue examinations per claim. In addition, the Medicare carrier, Trail Blazer Health Enterprises, LLC, reimbursed the Practice for more units of service of CPT 88305, on average, than it reimbursed to other providers for CPT 88305.

The Practice's staff stated that research at the time that they established the laboratory indicated that 12 tissue examinations were the industry standard. The Practice's staff stated that they increased the number of tissue examinations requested to be comparable to the standard industry practice.

This report contains no recommendations.

Office of the Inspector General (http://www.oig.hhs.gov)

Figure 10-5 Results of Review

Chapter Summary

Health care offices, large and small, are busy places in which to work. There are many tasks to complete, and almost every one of them provides an opportunity for ethical and legal violations. The best defense an organization can take to protect itself from these concerns is to keep a watchful eye on all levels of activities in the company. Investigations are necessary to identify problems areas, the causes of the problems, as well as potential solutions. Only then can a facility be assured of its ongoing success.

CHAPTER REVIEW

Multiple Choice Questions

1. Fraud can occur in many ways, including all except
   a. overt.
   b. covert.
   c. manifested.
   d. occult.

2. An internal audit is instigated by the
   a. Internal Revenue Service.
   b. FI in your state.
   c. American Medical Association.
   d. organization's management.

3. *The audit reviewed 100 patient records and claim forms of the 2000 filed during the month of June.* This statement indicates a
   a. sampling audit.
   b. comprehensive audit.
   c. external audit.
   d. concurrent audit.

4. *From April 5 through April 7, the auditors reviewed all claims filed by the south side office between March 1 and March 15.* This statement indicates a
   a. sampling audit.
   b. concurrent audit.
   c. retrospective audit.
   d. external audit.

5. *From April 5 through April 7, the auditors reviewed all claims filed by the south side office between March 1 and March 15.* This statement also indicates a
   a. sampling audit.
   b. comprehensive audit.
   c. external audit.
   d. concurrent audit.

6. Exit interviews are most productive when performed
   a. when the individual gives their notice.
   b. in a non-threatening manner.
   c. with those who have been fired.
   d. on the individual's last day.

7. Internal reporting should always be
   a. discouraged.
   b. limited to management staff.
   c. encouraged.
   d. not permitted.

8. Bias during an audit
   a. ensures compliance.
   b. favors the best staff members.
   c. delays the truth from being revealed.
   d. protects the office from external audits.

9. *Rodman Clinic has an average of 43 percent of their submitted claims denied.* This is an _____ indicator of problems in this facility.
   a. overt
   b. covert
   c. occult
   d. none of the above

10. *The investigation identified that 81 percent of claims filed last month were undercoded.* This is an _____ indicator of problems in this facility.
    a. overt
    b. covert
    c. occult
    d. none of the above

11. *All claims created in Madison Hospital for services performed this month are sent to an auditor for review prior to being forwarded to the third party payer.* This is a(n) _____ audit.
    a. sampling
    b. retrospective
    c. concurrent
    d. external

12. *The manager of Dr. Oppenheim's office hired a professional to come in and perform a coding review of claims.* This is a(n) _____ audit.
    a. internal
    b. external
    c. multi-focused
    d. retrospective

13. Providing staff with advance notification of an audit might
    a. make them too nervous to work.
    b. improve their productivity and quality.
    c. provide opportunity for a cover-up of bad behavior.
    d. b and c only

14. Results of audits should be
    a. evaluated and worked into a plan for improvement.
    b. placed in a file for future consideration.
    c. shredded so no one can read this privileged information.
    d. rewritten to make your department look good.

15. Internal audits should be conducted
   a. on a rare occasion.
   b. when suspicions arise.
   c. when someone gets fired from the department.
   d. on a regular basis.

Research and Discussion Project

Choose a policy or regulation to be audited in your facility or a facility in which you would like to work.

1. Write a detailed description of what you want your auditors to review.

_____

_____

_____

_____

2. Determine if the audit will be concurrent or retrospective.

3. Decide if the audit will be sampling or comprehensive.

4. Identify the members of the audit team.

Chapter 11

External Audits

Learning Outcomes

- Explain the reasons why government and private agencies audit health care facilities
- Identify which agencies audit health care facilities
- Describe how the HIM department should handle receipt of a subpoena
- Enumerate the levels of responsibilities assessed by auditors
- Name the types of appeals available to health care facilities

Key Terms

contempt of court / refusal to comply with a court order

Explanation of Benefits (EOB) / a document, usually sent to a policyholder or insured, explaining charges and payments determined between a provider/facility and the insurance carrier based on the individual's policy details

Provider Remittance Advice (PRA) / a document, similar to an EOB, sent to a health care provider with an explanation of the determinations made regarding particular claims submitted

subpoena / a court order to produce evidence

subpoena duces tecum / an order to deliver specific documents to the court

subpoena ad testificandum / an order for an individual to testify in court

willful ignorance / doing something incorrectly because of a lack of desire to find out how to do the task properly

Chapter Case Study

"On Monday, March 26, 2007, in Los Angeles, CA, Haydee Parungao was sentenced to 57 months in prison and ordered to pay $3.1 million in restitution for her role in a health care fraud scheme. Parungao also structured $613,710 in cash transactions to avoid IRS reporting requirements. The registered nurse worked as an independent contractor for several home health agencies and she claimed to provide in-home nursing services for Medicare patients. Between January 2001 and December 2003, Parungao claimed she made more than 18,000 home health visits. Parungao purported to work every single day during this time period, including every weekend and holiday, averaging 20 visits per day. Parungao operated in cash and did not have a bank account or hold property in her name. She made so many referrals to her home health agencies that she frequently received more that $10,000 in a single pay period. Payments totaling more than $10,000 were systematically divided into two or more checks, with each check written for less than $10,000. Parungao did that to avoid triggering cash transaction reports that would go to the IRS." (http://www.irs.gov)

Introduction

Many individuals engage in fraudulent activities for two reasons: to get huge amounts of money, and because they believe that they will never get caught. In large cities, health care workers feel a sense of anonymity because they are surrounded by millions of people. Those who work in small towns tell themselves that investigators concentrate on big cities because there is more going on there. Personnel in multifacility hospital systems think the many layers of corporate bureaucracy protect them, and those in small physicians' offices think they are operating under the radar because, of course, the big money fraud is to be found in big hospitals. Throughout this textbook, you have learned how wrong all of these thoughts are because no one is safe from discovery.

Investigations Are Worthwhile

No matter what your view of the process, one cannot argue with success. The Health Care Fraud and Abuse Control program recovered approximately $8,850,000,000 in the eight years from 1997 to 2005. That's just under nine billion dollars!

According to the Department of Justice annual report, in the fiscal year 2005 alone, "the federal government won or negotiated approximately $1.47 billion in judgments and settlements" and put almost $1.55 billion back into the Medicare Trust Fund, as well as $63.64 million in federal Medicaid funds.

This issue, of course, is not limited to just Medicare. As the largest third-party payer of health care services, and a federal government program with the power of the federal and state government authorities, CMS has the most to lose from fraud, and the most to gain from successful investigations. That is especially true now, as concern grows over this agency's ability to continue to pay for health care for the upcoming baby boomer group. This organization must do all it can to prevent individuals from stealing from its trust fund and must recoup any monies that have been mistakenly paid out or misappropriated.

However, as stated before in this textbook, all of these rules and investigations are not exclusive to Medicare and those caring for its beneficiaries. They just begin with Medicare. Then the state governments and the private insurers follow suit. This is important to remember, because just as CMS has the HCFAC, Blue Cross Blue Shield, Aetna, Prudential, United, and all the rest of the carriers providing health insurance reimbursement have task forces of their own. There is too much money at stake.

CASE STUDY

In FY 2005, U.S. Attorneys' offices opened 935 new criminal health care fraud investigations involving 1597 potential defendants. Federal prosecutors had 1689 health care fraud criminal investigations pending, involving 2670 potential defendants, and filed criminal charges in 382 cases involving 652 defendants. A total of 523 defendants were convicted. The Department of Justice (DOJ) opened 778 new civil health care fraud investigations, and had 1334 civil health care fraud investigations pending at the end of the fiscal year. DOJ filed complaints or intervened in 266 civil health care cases in FY 2005.

Department of Justice (DOJ) Enforcement Actions (http://www.usdoj.gov)

The Investigating Agencies

As we reviewed in chapter 4, there are many agencies and individuals charged with these investigations. The endeavor to uncover fraudulent health care-related activities involves:

- The policyholders/beneficiaries
- Physicians, suppliers, and other providers
- Private and subcontracted carriers
- Durable Medical Equipment Regional Carriers (DMERC)
- Fiscal Intermediaries (FI)
- Program Safeguard Contractors (PSC)
- The Office of Inspector General (OIG)
- Quality Improvement Organizations (QIO)
- Recovery Audit Contractors (RAC)
- The Federal Bureau of Investigation (FBI)
- The Department of Justice (DOJ)
- The Internal Revenue Service (IRS)
- State attorneys general

Every one of these agencies and organizations is empowered to review a provider's claims.

A United Effort

In a speech given to a congressional committee on July 17, 2007, Timothy B. Hill, Chief Financial Officer, Centers for Medicare and Medicaid Services (CMS), stated the CMS and its companion agencies were focused on a united effort to accomplish:

- *"Early detection*: CMS finds problems quickly, using proactive data analysis, probe reviews of claims, audits and post-payment claims reviews, data matches, and other sources to detect improper payments.
- *Coordination*: CMS works through public and private partnerships to identify and fight fraud and abuse. CMS recognizes the importance of working with contractors, beneficiaries, law enforcement partners, and other federal and state agencies to improve the fiscal integrity of the Medicare trust funds.
- *Enforcement*: CMS ensures that action is taken when fraud and abuse is found. CMS will continue to work with our partners, including the Department of Health & Human Services (HHS)/Office of Inspector General (OIG), Department of Justice (DOJ), State agencies for survey and certification, Medicaid Fraud Control Units (MFCUs), and State Medicaid agencies to pursue appropriate corrective actions such as restitution, fines, penalties, damages, and program suspensions or exclusions."

There are many things that might spur an investigation. All organizations, whether they are a governmental agency such as Medicare or a private company such as Blue Cross Blue Shield, use various sources for information that will prompt a closer look at a health care facility.

The Blue Cross Blue Shield Association identified that, in 2005, 70.2 percent of their corporate and financial investigations were motivated by a report called into their fraud hotline, including those made by patients questioning a recently received Explanation of Benefits (EOB).

In addition, these agencies have the ability to program their computers to review claims and gather particular statistics that will illuminate trends of possible illegal activity. These reports will help to identify areas of concern, thereby requiring more research. This will lead to a request for supporting documentation.

Requests for Documentation

Depending upon the agency and the circumstances in question, the request for supporting documentation may arrive at your office in person (auditors do not typically call ahead), or by mail. They may request a random sampling of case files or they may be very specific, citing the names and identification of individual patients whose records are being investigated. Medicare's guidelines regarding timely submission of requested supporting documentation are shown, in part, in Figure 11-1.

Required Documentation Advisory
Reference: RI - CMC 102507
Published Online: 10/30/2007

The Importance of Timely Submission of Documentation

There has been a recent increase in untimely responses to Additional Documentation Requests (ADRs) related to the submission of medical records. When a claim suspends for medical review, a letter requesting documentation is mailed to the provider/physician from our Medical Review (MR) Department. The provider/physician must in turn submit the requested documentation within 45 days of the date on the ADR letter. Per Medicare guidelines, the ADR gives instructions in reference to sending specific documentation to the Contractor within 30 days. However, Medical Review allows an additional 15 days to this request for documentation. *If the documentation is not received by Medical Review within 45 days, the claim will be denied.*

It is very important and in the providers'/physicians' best interest to be aware of and respond appropriately to these guidelines.

Adhering to the timeliness instructions can prevent unnecessary denials and additional unnecessary provider paperwork and staff time. Please share this information with all appropriate personnel within your offices regarding the importance of responding within the allotted 45 days.

When responding, submit only the documentation that is requested in the ADR letter, as applicable, as well as any additional documentation that may support the service(s) billed and suspended for medical review. By submitting the requested documentation, timely providers/physicians can prevent the need for potential reopenings requiring providers to re-copy and re-submit records to the Contractor.

In the past, providers/physicians have had questions about the timeliness of the medical review of their claims and are thus encouraged to refer to the CMS guidelines which are available at http://www.cms.hhs.gov. To access, select Regulations and Guidance, Manuals, Internet On-Line Manuals, Publication 100-08 Program Integrity Manual, Chapter 3, Section 3.4.1.3. You may also click on the following: http://www.cms.hhs.gov/manuals/downloads/pim83c03.pdf. "For ADR responses that are received within the time frame, contractors must complete claims review and notify the provider/physician within 60 days of receiving documentation." The manual further instructs the contractor that, "For prepay reviews, (e.g. prepay probe review, regular prepay review) the contractor should begin counting with the receipt of each medical record. Each new medical record received should start a new 60 day clock."

Figure 11-1 Importance of timely submission of documentation

It's The Law

"Permitted Uses and Disclosures. A covered entity is permitted, but not required, to use and disclose protected health information, without an individual's authorization, for the following purposes or situations: (1) To the Individual (unless required for access or accounting of disclosures); (2) Treatment, Payment, and Health Care Operations; (3) Opportunity to Agree or Object; (4) Incident to an otherwise permitted use and disclosure; (5) Public Interest and Benefit Activities; and (6) Limited Data Set for the purposes of research, public health or health care operations. Covered entities may rely on professional ethics and best judgments in deciding which of these permissive uses and disclosures to make."

(http://www.dhhs.gov/hipaa)

Some health care professionals think that this may cause the facility to violate HIPAA because the law requires that your facility obtain express permission from the patient in order to release patient charts and records, except . . .

Pay specific attention to permitted disclosure number (5) Public Interest and Benefit Activities. In this section of the law, release of information for health oversight activities is permitted.

It's The Law

Health Oversight Activities

Covered entities may disclose protected health information to health oversight agencies (as defined in the Rule) for purposes of legally authorized health oversight activities, such as audits and investigations necessary for oversight of the health care system and government benefit programs.

HIPAA Privacy Rule 45 C.F.R. § 164.512(d)

When receiving a request for documentation, whether from a PSC, RAC, or any other investigative agency, your staff must be trained to respond promptly. However, this does not mean turning over files to anyone who asks. You will need to establish a policy on the proper actions to take. A suggested policy might include:

1. *Verify the identity of the individual and organization requesting the documentation.* Just because you receive an official-looking letter in the mail does not mean it is authentic. Check your state's website for the appropriate contact phone number. This will depend upon what type of request this is. If it is from Medicare or Medicaid, contact the state's FI; if it is from Blue Cross Blue Shield or a private third-party payer, call the main office within your state. The CMS website also enables you to confirm the name of the PSC or RAC. You might want to contact the facility's legal counsel as well, as an additional safeguard.

2. *Ensure that the documentation is complete and accurate.* If it wasn't done before, then now is the time to find those missing lab reports, transcribe the physician's notes, and collect any other errant paperwork. Make certain any handwritten entries can be read. If not, have the author amend the information and initial and date the re-entry.

3. *Never send originals.* Always send copies (not originals) of everything that you send to the requesting agency.

4. *Respond within the time limit stated on the request.* Even if you have to dedicate an employee or two to this full time, you do not want to send the response late.

5. *Send the response in a traceable manner.* You can use the U.S. Post Office, United Parcel Service, Federal Express, or other mailing services; it does not matter as long as the carrier will provide you with tangible proof of delivery date, time, and the name of the person accepting the package.

CASE STUDY

Issues Identified as a Result of the Probe: **No Response**

Twenty-nine services were denied because the requested medical record documentation was not received. Title XVIII of the Social Security Act, section 1862 (a)(1) prohibits Medicare payment for any claim which lacks the necessary information to process the claim. Failure to submit the requested documentation will result in complete or partial denial of services.

Probe Review Results of Office and Other Outpatient Consultation Services (CPT 99241-99242) in Louisiana
Reference: AR - BAD 032307
Published Online: 4/11/2007

Subpoenas

A **subpoena** is more than a request; it is an order from a court of law requiring evidence to be submitted to the court. Two types of subpoenas that a health information management professional may encounter are: **subpoena duces tecum**, which orders the delivery of specific documents to the court and **subpoena ad testificandum**, which requires an individual to come to court to testify.

This is not something to be ignored, because a failure to comply can be considered **contempt of court**—an illegal act that may result in fines and/or imprisonment. Your facility's legal counsel should be notified immediately upon receipt of any type of subpoena.

HIPAA's Privacy Rule permitted disclosure number (5), Public Interest and Benefit Activities, has you covered.

It's The Law

Required by Law. Covered entities may use and disclose protected health information without individual authorization as required by law (including by statute, regulation, or court orders).

HIPAA's Privacy Rule, 45 C.F.R. § 164.512(a)

Notifications of Error

After the documentation is sent, your facility can expect to receive a notification of the results of the audit.

Notification of Underpayment. Reportedly these actually do exist. This would indicate that the audit performed identified instances in which the third-party payer had not sent your facility enough money originally. After you celebrate, be certain to keep all documentation, including the letter and a copy of the check or notice of the electronic funds transfer (EFT), in a safe place.

Notification of Improper Payment. Odds are that your office is more likely to see one of these. As soon as this notification has been received, it is important that the attending physician for the case or cases that were the subject of the investigation, and the facility's legal counsel, are notified.

There are three levels of responsibility that may be assessed as a result of the audit.

> If the investigation found evidence of both underpayment and overpayment, the underpayment will be deducted from the amount owed.

- *Negligence.* This is considered to be the result of human error. Most often, the facility will be requested to pay back the money originally reimbursed plus penalty, and the case is closed.

- *Reckless disregard for the law.* This assessment implies a certain level of intent. In these cases, the assessment is that the office has an attitude of not caring enough to do things correctly. This is called **willful ignorance**. This may rise to the level of a civil violation of the False Claims Act.

- *Criminal intent.* As discussed earlier in this text, this is the determination of criminal activity most often stemming from repeated episodes of an illegal action.

After errors that resulted in overpayment have been found, the penalties that may be assessed include:

- *Denial of payments:* The review of claims and subsequent denial of claims with the same or similar coding patterns.

- *Return of overpayments:* The requirement to reimburse the agency for any monies paid in error.

- *Criminal actions:* The indictment of criminal charges against all those who cause, know, or should know that false claims were filed.

- *Initiation of civil monetary penalties:* These are penalties assessed when a civil violation, rather than a criminal violation, has been discovered.

- *Administrative sanctions:* These sanctions may be a temporary suspension from the program or exclusion from all future participation in the program. This could mean that the provider found guilty would never be permitted to treat and bill for one of their policyholders.

Figure 11-2 shows a summary of improper payments identified in a RAC investigation.

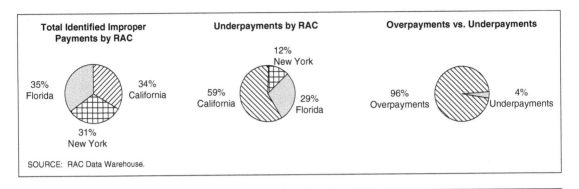

Figure 11-2 RAC-Identified Improper Payments

It's The Law

According to CMS:

"Fraud committed against the Medicare Program may be prosecuted under various provisions of United States Code and could result in the imposition of restitution, fines, and possibly imprisonment.

"Investigation and prosecution of health care fraud are reserved for willful and intentional acts of wrongdoing, substantiated through documented inappropriate billing patterns."

(http://www.cms.hhs.gov)

Appeals

A notification of error does not have to be the end of the case. If you, or your staff, feel that this is a misevaluation, there are appeal options available.

It's The Law

Who May Appeal

CR4019 (Additions to Chapter 29) defines and describes the individuals and entities who have the right to appeal a Medicare contractor's initial determination. (Medicare contractors are carriers, including Durable Medical Equipment Regional Carriers [DMERCs], and Fiscal Intermediaries [FIs], including Regional Home Health Intermediaries [RHHIs].) An individual who has a right to appeal is referred to as a "party."

Related CR Transmittal #: 695 Centers for Medicare and Medicaid Services

The first step that you must take after receiving the audit report is to get the facts on the organization's appeals process. Each organization will most likely differ in the way it handles this course of action.

Once an initial claim determination is made, beneficiaries, providers, and suppliers have the right to appeal Medicare coverage and payment decisions. There are five levels in the Medicare Part A and Part B appeals process.

The levels are:

First Level of Appeal: Re-determination by a Medicare carrier, fiscal intermediary (FI), or Medicare Administrative Contractor (MAC)

Second Level of Appeal: Reconsideration by a Qualified Independent Contractor (QIC)

Third Level of Appeal: Hearing by an Administrative Law Judge (ALJ) in the Office of Medicare Hearings and Appeals

Fourth Level of Appeal: Review by the Medicare Appeals Council

Fifth Level of Appeal: Judicial Review in Federal District Court

(http://www.cms.hhs.gov)

Figure 11-3 CMS Standard Appeals Process for Fee-For-Service Providers

Medicare has a five-level appeal process for hospitals (Part A) and outpatient/physician offices (Part B) audit reports. This same approach is used for challenging individual claim denials. Remember that with Medicare and Medicaid, as identified in the first level of the appeal, you must begin with the FI for the state, because it is the organization responsible for day-to-day operations and processing claims. To illustrate this, take a look at Figure 11-4.

As an example, United Healthcare publishes this instruction so that a health care professional or facility can appeal a decision, a denied claim, or the results of an audit (see Figure 11-5). Remember, an audit is simply a claim or records review for multiple records at one time.

It's The Law

Each "affiliated contractor" (AC)/Medicare administrative contractors (MAC) shall process appeals stemming from a Comprehensive Error Rate Testing (CERT) initiated denial. The AC/MAC shall ensure that the appeal is handled appropriately, as described in other CMS manuals.

Each AC/MAC shall notify the CERT contractor, using the claims status website, when a CERT sampled claim is appealed. Medical records for the appealed CERT claim may be obtained by contacting the CERT appeals coordinator via the appeals page on the claims status website.

Each AC/MAC shall enter all available information for appealed CERT sampled claims by the cut-off date listed on the CERT claims status website calendar. Appeal determinations entered into the CERT appeals tracking system by the specified due date will be reflected in the report.

All cost and workloads associated with §12.3.5 activities shall be allocated to the PM CERT support code (12901). In the case of the DME PSC, the costs and workloads associated with these tasks shall be reported in CMS ART.

Medicare Program Integrity Manual Chapter 12—The Comprehensive Error Rate Testing 12.3.5—
Handling Appeals Resulting From CERT-Initiated Denials (Rev. 204, Issued: 05-25-07;
Effective/Implementation Date: 06-25-07)

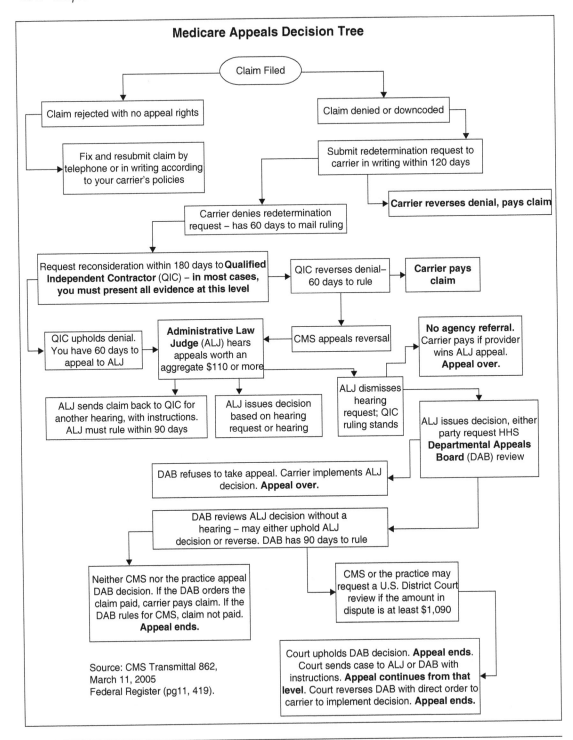

Figure 11-4   Medicare Appeals Decision Tree

If you disagree with a claim adjustment or our decision not to make a claim adjustment, you may appeal by completing the United Healthcare Request for Reconsideration Form, found on http://www.UnitedHealthcareOnline.com.

You may also send a letter of appeal to the claim office identified on the back of the customer's ID card or call the Customer Care number listed on the **EOB**, **PRA** or customer's ID card. Your appeal must be submitted to us within 12 months from the date of processing shown on the EOB or PRA.

If you are appealing a claim that was denied because filing was not timely, for:

- Electronic claims—include confirmation that United Healthcare or one of its affiliates received and accepted your claim.

- Paper claims—include a copy of a screen print from your accounting software to show the date you submitted the claim.

If you disagree with an overpayment refund request, send a letter of appeal to the address noted on the refund request letter. Your appeal must be received within 30 days of the refund request letter in order to allow sufficient time for processing the appeal and to avoid possible offset of the overpayment against future claim payments to you. When submitting the appeal, please attach a copy of the refund request letter and a detailed explanation of why you believe the refund request is in error.

If you disagree with the outcome of the claim appeal, or for any dispute other than claim appeals, you may pursue dispute resolution as described on page 30 of this Guide and in your agreement with us.

(http://www.UnitedHealthcareOnline.com)

Figure 11-5 United Healthcare Claims Appeals

Once it is determined that you have a legitimate reason to appeal a Medicare claim that has been denied, filing CMS 1965 (Figure 11-6) will begin the process.

Chapter Summary

As you have learned throughout this book, there are many government agencies and contractors designated as investigative units to uncover incidents of fraud and abuse of our health care system, and to do everything possible to recover financial losses. This is in the interest of everyone in the United States. The benefits of these investigations are strong and support the concept that virtually all health care providers will be investigated at some point.

Every health care provider has the right of appeal on multiple levels. This begins with the denial of a single claim form, and extends to the ability to challenge the results of any audit.

DEPARTMENT OF HEALTH AND HUMAN SERVICES
CENTERS FOR MEDICARE & MEDICAID SERVICES

REQUEST FOR HEARING
PART B MEDICARE CLAIM
Medical Insurance Benefits - Social Security Act

NOTICE—Anyone who misrepresents or falsifies essential information requested by this form may upon conviction be subject to fine and imprisonment under Federal Law.

CARRIER'S NAME AND ADDRESS	**1** NAME OF PATIENT
	2 HEALTH INSURANCE CLAIM NUMBER

3 I disagree with the review determination on my claim, and request a hearing before a hearing officer of the insurance carrier named above.

MY REASONS ARE: (Attach a copy of the Review Notice. NOTE: If the review decision was made more than 6 months ago, include your reason for not making this request earlier.)

_____

_____

_____

_____

4 CHECK ONE OF THE FOLLOWING

CHECK **ONLY ONE** OF THE STATEMENTS BELOW:

☐ I have additional evidence to submit.
(Attach such evidence to this form or forward it to the carrier within 10 days.)

☐ I do not have additional evidence.

☐ I wish to appear in person before the Hearing Officer.

☐ I do not wish to appear and hereby request a decision on the evidence before the Hearing Officer.

5 EITHER THE CLAIMANT OR REPRESENTATIVE SHOULD SIGN IN THE APPROPRIATE SPACE BELOW

SIGNATURE OR NAME OF CLAIMANT'S REPRESENTATIVE	CLAIMANT'S SIGNATURE	
ADDRESS	ADDRESS	
CITY, STATE, AND ZIP CODE	CITY, STATE, AND ZIP CODE	
TELEPHONE NUMBER	DATE	TELEPHONE NUMBER	DATE

(Claimant should not write below this line)

- -

ACKNOWLEDGMENT OF REQUEST FOR HEARING

Your request for a hearing was received on _____ . You will be notified of the time and place of the hearing at least 10 days before the date of the hearing.

SIGNED	DATE

Figure 11-6 Request for Hearing Part B Medicare Claim

CHAPTER REVIEW

Multiple Choice Questions

1. Health care facilities subject to externals audits include
   a. hospitals.
   b. long-term care facilities.
   c. physicians' offices.
   d. all of the above

2. Fraud is investigated by the
   a. CMS.
   b. DOJ.
   c. IRS.
   d. all of the above

3. The purpose of external audits is to
   a. reclaim overpayments.
   b. identify the competencies of nurses.
   c. increase health insurance coverage.
   d. avoid paying taxes.

4. Governmental investigations may be motivated by
   a. internal audits.
   b. media reports.
   c. a patient's complaints after receiving an EOB.
   d. data glitches.

5. Documentation requested by an external investigator may
   a. not be released without patient written consent.
   b. violate HIPAA's Privacy Rule.
   c. be submitted late, depending upon patient load.
   d. be submitted by the deadline, or a penalty may be assessed.

6. Investigations into fraud and abuse are also referred to as
   a. health care innovators.
   b. health care oversight activities.
   c. HCUP.
   d. restoration.

7. A subpoena duces tecum means that documentation
   a. is not to be disclosed.
   b. is to be read aloud in court.
   c. must be delivered to the court.
   d. should be destroyed immediately.

8. Refusing to follow a subpoena may result in
   a. fines.
   b. jail or prison time.
   c. a or b
   d. none of the above

9. A finding of negligence indicates the auditor believes the errors were
   a. human error.
   b. willful ignorance.
   c. criminal.
   d. reckless disregard of the law.

10. Civil monetary penalties (CMP) can be assessed when
    a. civil violations have been discovered.
    b. criminal sanctions are not strong enough.
    c. the facility has been penalized before.
    d. there is no certified coder on staff.

11. Appealing a Notification of Error from CMS is
    a. not permitted.
    b. a five-level process.
    c. only permitted for hospitals.
    d. only permitted for physicians.

12. Appeals processes _____ for public and private insurers.
    a. are the same
    b. require an attorney
    c. vary
    d. are contempt of court

13. PRA stands for
    a. permission for retrospective audits.
    b. proper remittance advisory.
    c. provider remittance advice.
    d. physician radiological audits.

14. A subpoena ad testificandum means the individual receiving this order must
    a. deliver documentation.
    b. testify in court.
    c. obtain a national certification.
    d. pay an additional fine.

15. When a subpoena is received, HIPAA's Privacy Rule states release of information is
    a. forbidden.
    b. not permitted without written permission from the patient.
    c. permitted.
    d. mandated.

Research and Discussion Project

Go online to any two health care third-party payer websites. You might pick the company with which you have your own health insurance policy, and/or another that you come upon while searching. Just make certain it relates to health care and is a legitimate organization.

1. Compare and contrast their anti-fraud efforts.

   _____

   _____

   _____

   _____

   _____

2. Compare and contrast their appeals processes.

   _____

   _____

   _____

   _____

   _____

3. Compare and contrast the two organizations' anti-fraud efforts. How would you handle an investigation with either of these companies? What would you need to prepare for an appeal?

   _____

   _____

   _____

   _____

   _____

Chapter 12

Keeping the Program Current

Learning Outcomes

- Identify corrective methodologies to improve processes
- Explain how to develop strategies from an audit report
- Determine the importance of updating compliance plans
- Enumerate the benefits of implementing changes to processes

Key Terms

bolstered / supported; encouraged
inaccuracies / elements or components of a claim that are not correct; factual errors
purview / jurisdiction; area of authority or influence
restitution / paying back money received fraudulently

Chapter Case Study

"On April 26, 2007, in Austin, Texas, Rocky L. Lemon of Stillwater, OK, was sentenced to 42 months imprisonment and ordered to pay $4 million in restitution following his guilty pleas to health care fraud and money laundering. Lemon owned and/or operated over 50 nursing homes in Texas and other states through TLC Healthcare, Inc. Lemon admitted that from 1998 until April 2001, he defrauded the Medicare Program and the Texas Medicaid Program by unlawfully diverting Medicare and Medicaid monies to his own personal use. As part of his scheme, Lemon used Medicare and Medicaid monies to finance his purchase of nursing homes. Shortly thereafter, he sold some of the nursing homes and funneled a substantial portion of the net proceeds into his personal bank and brokerage accounts. He also used Medicare and Medicaid funds to engage in other transactions unrelated to fulfilling his obligations to Medicare and Medicaid beneficiaries. In 2001, Lemon abandoned all of his Texas nursing

care facilities, forcing Texas authorities to assume control and management of a number of Lemon's nursing homes. The estimated combined loss to Medicare and Medicaid as a result of Lemon's criminal scheme was approximately $4.2 million." (http://www.irs.org)

Introduction

Regardless of any appeals processes that your office may decide to implement, the audit report can be a very valuable tool for identifying areas needing adjustment, adaptation, or disciplinary actions.

Corrective Action Strategies

Whether the result of an internal or external investigation, the audit report that you receive will itemize the findings discovered by the investigator(s). This document can provide very valuable insights into what areas of your organization need improvements.

Let's use the executive summary of an actual audit (see Figure 12-1) conducted by the OIG in mid-2007 as a working example. From this audit report, you can see how one might develop better strategies for a compliant facility.

Department of Health and Human Services/
Office of Inspector General Office of Audit Services
"Review of Florida Physical Therapist's Medicare Claims for
Therapy Services Provided During 2003" (A-06-06-00078) August 15, 2007

EXECUTIVE SUMMARY:

The objective of this review was to determine whether therapy services provided by a Florida physical therapist during calendar year 2003 met Medicare reimbursement requirements. Of the 100 sampled claims, 96 did not meet Medicare's reimbursement requirements. In total, 494 of the 702 physical therapy services contained in the 100 sampled claims did not meet one or more of the Medicare reimbursement requirements because (1) the physical therapist inappropriately used his provider identification number to bill for services performed or supervised by someone else, (2) the documentation for some therapy services did not meet Medicare requirements, (3) some therapy services were miscoded, and (4) a plan of care did not meet Medicare requirements. The physical therapist did not have a thorough understanding of Medicare requirements and did not have effective policies and procedures in place to ensure that he billed Medicare only for services that met Medicare reimbursement requirements. As a result, the physical therapist improperly billed Medicare and received $10,781 for the 494 services. We recommend that the physical therapist (1) refund to the Medicare program $411,781 in unallowable payments for therapy services provided in 2003 and (2) develop quality control procedures to ensure that therapy services are provided and documented in accordance with Medicare reimbursement requirements. The physical therapist stated that he will address any issues concerning the audit through the Medicare appeals process.

(http://oig.hhs.gov)

Figure 12-1 Executive summary of an audit report

Strategy #1: What you do today IS being scrutinized.

Often, staff members in health care facilities feel safe because they have not been audited yet. A physician once said to this author, "We must be doing things correctly, because we haven't received any notices." This is a very dangerous philosophy. Improper behaviors can be **bolstered** by the lack of immediate punishment, and you can see from every case example in this text that time is an irrelevant concept to the investigators. As you can see in Figure 12-1:

> *"Review of Florida Physical Therapist's Medicare Claims for Therapy Services Provided During 2003 dated August 15, 2007"*

Of course, August 2007 is the date the final report was filed. However, the actual audit took place in 2006—three years after the questionable claims were filed (2003). It is very unlikely that a facility will file a claim on Monday and have auditors show up on Friday of the same week asking about that one claim. The investigation begins and continues for quite some time before the facility knows about it. This should be a motivating factor to take any corrective actions necessary—now!

Strategy #2: Accuracy is more important than speed.

You must implement and enforce actions and processes that encourage the accuracy of claims, not the speed with which they are filed. In Figure 12-1, you see:

> *"Of the 100 sampled claims, 96 did not meet Medicare's reimbursement requirements."*

Yikes! This is a strong indication that something is seriously wrong with this office's coding and billing department. A result like this would easily justify extending a sampling audit into a comprehensive review. There are several corrective actions that can be taken knowing this poor performance is occurring in your office. The audit goes into detail about the **inaccuracies**, providing you with specific concerns to address. Let's discuss the findings identified in Figure 12-1.

> *(1) The physical therapist inappropriately used his provider identification number to bill for services performed or supervised by someone else*

The first thing that the manager should look into is how or why this actually happened. Did the therapist herself direct the billing staff members to use her number? This would lead you to the fact that documentation was inaccurately processed through the office. Or did a member of the billing department unknowingly believe that the NPI was for the entire health care staff, when in reality each clinician should have her own number? This behavior needs to stop immediately. Other clinicians in the office should be directed to apply for their own ID numbers or the office should refuse to file claims for services performed by them. You, your staff, and your entire office—including the physician or health care professional—are responsible and liable for this. Therefore, your office must create the policy and strictly implement it.

(2) The documentation for some therapy services did not meet Medicare requirements

Notice that this does not state that the services themselves did not meet the requirements, but that the *documentation* did not meet the requirements. You might begin with chapter 6 in this textbook, "Compliance With Documentation." However, you must take this a step further, especially when your facility provides specialty services, such as neurosurgery, dermatology, or physical therapy. Take the time to go to the websites for your various third-party payers and download their documentation requirements. It doesn't take long, and you will find that the majority of the requirements have much in common with each other. If your office works with a large number of carriers, begin with those organizations with which you file the most claims, and work your way down the list.

Once you have established the requirements, write a policy that outlines the elements needed, or create a checklist. Remember, you want to make it easy for everyone to comply. Do not be intimidated and feel that it is not your place to tell the physician or provider what to write. That happens to be true. You are not permitted to direct clinicians to write or not write something in the patient's chart. Your guidelines should be more in line with helping the providers understand what details are important to document. Watch the way you word these instructions. You do not want to be guilty of coding for coverage.

(3) Some therapy services were miscoded

This discovery made by the auditors is clearly a directive that your coding personnel need additional training. Many seminars are available from the national organizations, such as AHIMA and AAPC, as well as independent companies. Local area colleges and online schools can provide training, too. There are many books published on specific areas of coding, as well. If there is concern regarding the cost of this additional education, you must remind your facility's administration about the amount of money that has been lost, and will continue to be lost, due to denied claims, and the future monies that will be paid out in fines and penalties. Add in the cost of the time it may take personnel to recode and resubmit claims, as well as the lost interest on monies delayed to the facility due to the extended length of time it is taking to get proper reimbursement, and the total cost to the facility is typically far greater than the price of training. There are virtually no offices or facilities anywhere that do not get a positive financial return on the investment of additional education for their coding staff members.

(4) A plan of care did not meet Medicare requirements

This is the one item in the report that lies solely with the health care provider and is not within your **purview**. However, if the clinician had been acting within published standards of care, this would certainly be an opportunity for appeal. Discuss this issue with the provider involved with this case and develop a course of action.

One thing to note: the report indicates that, out of all the elements being challenged in this audit report . . .

"494 of the 702 physical therapy services contained in the 100 sampled claims"

This is identified as a single event. The report states "a plan of care"—one plan, out of the entire pack of investigated records.

Strategy #3: *The effort to create and maintain a compliance plan is worthwhile.*

Also in Figure 12-1, you will see the report states:

" . . . did not have effective policies and procedures in place to ensure that he billed Medicare only for services that met Medicare reimbursement requirements."

Remind the administration of your facility that filing a claim for reimbursement for a service or treatment that is known, or should be known, to be uncovered or invalid is fraud. Doing this leaves the impression that you are trying to fool the third-party payer into paying your facility for services for which it does not deserve to be paid. Perhaps the computer or the claims adjuster will make a mistake and pay us anyway! Think of this as the equivalent of sending an invoice to a patient for services already paid for by the insurance company just to see if the patient will actually pay you. After all, some will justify, the patient should know what the insurance company will cover and what they will not. If they pay as well, that is their error. This is not ethical and not legal.

In addition, remember what you learned in chapter 1 of this text. Having a compliance plan in action may have reduced the fines and penalties that resulted from this audit. Actually, had an effective compliance plan been in place, this audit may not have happened at all!

Strategy #4: *Good compliance policies add to the facility's bottom line.*

Figure 12-1 states:

"As a result, the physical therapist improperly billed Medicare and received $10,781 for the 494 services."

The bottom line: the audit discovered that the health care office received $10,781 as a result of its fraudulent claims processes. That's almost eleven thousand dollars they received to which they were not entitled. However, this eleven thousand dollars of wrongful revenue will result in a cost to the office of . . .

"We recommend that the physical therapist (1) refund to the Medicare program $411,781 in unallowable payments for therapy services provided in 2003"

The office received almost eleven thousand dollars and got to keep and use that money for three or four years. Now, that money is going to cost them four hundred and one thousand dollars over and above returning the original funds! That averages out to a cost of one hundred thousand dollars a year to use ten thousand dollars. This is not considered to be good business practice from anyone's standpoint.

You may think this is a typographical error, but it is not. The number of records included in the sampling audit is mathematically calculated. The results found in the audit are then calculated back out to match the original number.

> **EXAMPLE** *Evante Medical Center filed a total of 1000 claims. The sampling audit was determined to be 50 records, or 5%.*
>
> *1000 records divided by 20 = 50 records to be reviewed*
>
> *The audit discovered $7000 in improperly paid claims received in those 50 records. Therefore, the $7000 is considered to be 5% of the total overpayments, equaling an approximation that the Medical Center actually received $140,000 improperly.*
>
> *$7000 found multiplied by 20 = $140,000 received incorrectly.*
>
> **Restitution**, *fines, and penalties will be based on the $140,000.*

CASE STUDY

"We used the Office of Inspector General, Office of Audit Services (OAS) RAT-STATS variable appraisal for stratified samples to estimate the amount of unallowable program payments. We reported the estimate of unallowable program payments at the lower limit of the 90-percent two-sided confidence interval in accordance with OAS policy."

From the Methodologies Section of the same report (Figure 12-1)

In addition to a current compliance plan potentially reducing some of these fines and penalties assessed in this, and other, cases, think about the internal audit component of your compliance plan, as discussed in chapter 10. Imagine the benefits to this organization had it performed an internal audit and corrected the items identified in this report *before* this external audit occurred. It may have avoided the investigation all together.

Updating The Plan

There are many ways that you can keep current and know about changes that may affect the policies and internal systems. This might seem like an overwhelming task at first. However, most of the time, your plan should be updated at least once a year, or when any new legislation goes into effect. When you organize a system for staying on top of new legislation and keep your sources easily accessible, this will not be complex at all.

State-Specific Updates

Each and every facility must comply with both federal and state legislation. In addition to states having their own specific laws, there are also state versions of federal laws that may change your organizational policies and/or procedures.

State-Specific Health Insurance Carriers

There are certain insurance companies that offer nationwide coverage for their policyholders; however, they actually divide their company into sub-divisions, state by state. In most cases, you will be submitting claims for services from your facility to the state association or division, rather than the national organization. These websites also provide important updates and information on their policies and processes for claims submission, appeals, and other key factors.

> **EXAMPLE** Blue Cross Blue Shield Association
> http://www.bcbs.com/
> Blue Cross Blue Shield of South Carolina
> http://www.southcarolinablues.com/bcbs/bcbs_redo.nsf

Fiscal Intermediary Updates

Many fiscal intermediaries (FI) encourage providers to sign up for newsletters or other notifications. Sign up and they will e-mail you information as it becomes available.

> **EXAMPLE** From First Coast Service Options—the Medicare FI for the State of Florida
> FCSO eNews—Electronic Mailing List Service:
> Join our eNews mailing list and receive urgent or other critical information issued by your Florida Medicare Carrier & Intermediary, First Coast Service Options, Inc. (FCSO). By signing up, you will receive periodic messages advising you of updates to the provider website and/or: key program alerts, seminar schedules, publications availability, educational tips, critical program changes, etc. Sign up today and select the desired interest group(s).
> (http://www.floridamedicare.com/header/106670.asp)

Federal Updates

The federal government and all of its agencies and departments are required to keep you informed of changes occurring in current and upcoming laws and regulations.

The Department of Health and Human Services

The Department of Health and Human Services of the federal government is the umbrella portal to all things related to health care in our national structure.

> **EXAMPLE** Department of Health and Human Services
> Policies & Regulations
>
> * Health Information Technology Standards
> * Health Information Privacy (HIPAA)
> * Laws & Regulations
> * Policies & Guidelines
> * Review Boards
> * Testimony
>
> (http://www.hhs.gov/policies/index.html)

CMS Updates

The CMS website also publishes quarterly updates for easy access to the latest information.

> **EXAMPLE** Welcome to the Centers for Medicare & Medicaid Services' (CMS) Quarterly Provider Update (QPU). By publishing this Update, we intend to make it easier for providers, suppliers, and the general public to understand the changes we are proposing or making in the programs we administer (for example, Medicare, Medicaid, and the State Children's Health Insurance Program [SCHIP]).
>
> CMS publishes this update at the beginning of each quarter to inform the public about the following:
>
> * Regulations and major policies currently under development during this quarter.
> * Regulations and major policies completed or cancelled.
> * New/Revised manual instructions.
>
> (http://www.cms.hhs.gov/quarterlyproviderUpdates)

Office of the Inspector General Updates

The annual OIG work plan outlines key areas into which this federal government agency will focus investigations. The plan is published on the OIG website in October of each year for the following calendar year.

It may appear that the OIG focuses only on the non-compliance of those who provide health care services to Medicare and Medicaid beneficiaries, but that is not true. The HCFAC, under HIPAA, expands the jurisdiction of health care oversight activities.

It's The Law

"Our work is authorized by the Inspector General Act of 1978 (Public Law 95-452), as amended. Congress created OIGs to be independent and objective units within Federal departments and agencies for the purposes of: (1) conducting audits and investigations of programs and operations; (2) coordinating and recommending policies to promote economy, efficiency, and effectiveness in the administration of programs; (3) preventing and detecting fraud and abuse; and (4) keeping the Department Secretary or agency administrator and Congress informed about the necessity for corrective action."

(http://oig.hhs.gov/publications/workplan.html)

Office of Civil Rights (OCR)

HIPAA compliance, along with other important polices and regulations, is monitored by the Office of Civil Rights within the Department of Health and Human Services. Updates and best practices are also accessible from this website: http://www.hhs.gov/ocr

The Joint Commission Updates

The Joint Commission regulates hospitals, nursing homes, and other similar facilities. Those of you working in a Joint Commission-accredited organization should have its website bookmarked. In addition, it has a newsletter for which you can sign up that will provide short, manageable updates that you can incorporate, as appropriate, into your office work systems.

While it may not have authority over your physician's office, its guidelines can still provide important direction. The Joint Commission has a specific area on its website for physicians, nurses, and pharmacists, along with other specialized areas. These reports and programs can provide you with important information on issues that are current priorities.

EXAMPLE The Joint Commission's "For The Physician" area:

The ACS National Surgical Quality Improvement Program (ACS NSQIP) is the first nationally validated, risk-adjusted, outcomes-based program to measure and improve the quality of surgical care. The program employs a prospective, peer-controlled, validated database to quantify 30-day risk-adjusted surgical outcomes, which allows valid comparison of outcomes among all hospitals in the program. Medical centers and their surgical staff are able to use the data to make informed decisions regarding their continuous quality improvement efforts.

(http://www.jointcommission.org/Physicians/md_pi.htm)

Specialized Health Care Organizations Updates

Virtually every area of health care has its own national trade organization. These associations focus on laws and regulations, as well as best practices, for their individual sectors of the industry.

Health Information Management

Two primary organizations for health information management professionals, AHIMA and AAPC, maintain excellent websites that include compliance and regulatory updates, in addition to providing important networking with others in this particular sector of the industry. AHIMA's website offers members access to its Communities of Practice (CoP), providing hundreds of chat rooms and discussion areas for the exchange of ideas and policies and procedures.

Both of these organizations and their websites can provide you with important support for creating and implementing compliance plans, as well as continuing education, certification exams, etc.

EXAMPLE American Health Information Management Association (AHIMA)

http://www.ahima.org

American Academy of Professional Coders

http://www.aapc.com

Physician Associations

In addition to the American Medical Association (AMA) website, you can access updates and compliance policy information directly applicable to your specific type of physician facility. Every specific area of health care has an association. Google the type of specialty, use the plus sign, and type the word "association" and you will be provided with the current website for that national organization.

EXAMPLE pediatrician + association = American Academy of Pediatrics

http://www.aap.org

American Medication Association

http://www.ama-assn.org

American Association of Orthopaedic Surgeons

http://www.aaos.org

American Academy of Family Physicians

http://www.aafp.org/online/en/home.html

Facility Organizations

Health care facilities also have organizations that represent their interests and particular perspectives in the industry.

EXAMPLE The American Hospital Association has a portion of its website dedicated to compliance issues.

http://www.aha.org/aha/advocacy/compliance/index.html

The American Association of Ambulatory Surgery Centers

http://www.aaasc.org

The American Association of Homes and Services for the Aging (nursing homes) http://www.aahsa.org

Chapter Summary

Once your compliance plan is written and in place, make certain that, at least once a year, the compliance officer or compliance committee makes the time to review and update any policies and procedures that have been found to be less than effective, or need to be altered because of a change in legislation or regulations.

CHAPTER REVIEW

Multiple Choice Questions

1. Corrective action strategies may be developed from the results of
   a. internal audits.
   b. external audits.
   c. staff and patient input.
   d. all of the above

2. Audits performed by the OIG review
   a. coding practices.
   b. documentation requirements.
   c. accounting practices.
   d. a and b only

3. Good compliance plans
   a. cost too much to write.
   b. protect the assets of the organization.
   c. endanger the staff by highlighting errors.
   d. are too complicated to implement.

4. Once written, compliance plans should be updated every
   a. thirty days.
   b. six months.
   c. year.
   d. five years.

5. Updates to the compliance plan may come from
   a. government agencies.
   b. insurance carriers.
   c. national health care organizations.
   d. all of the above

6. _____ is a good example of a good source for compliance update information.
   a. *WebMD*
   b. The American Health Information Management Association
   c. *The New York Times*
   d. *Health* magazine

7. _____ is *another* good example of a good source for compliance update information.
   a. The American Academy of Family Physicians
   b. The Good Health Source
   c. Nutritional Guidelines USA
   d. Sun City Nursing Homes

8. Updates to the compliance plan should come from all except
   a. the federal government.
   b. the state government.
   c. the Office of Healthcare Compliance.
   d. a fiscal intermediary.

9. When a sampling audit discovers an overpayment, the auditors may
   a. only get back the amount of the overpayment discovered.
   b. calculate the amount discovered to apply to the total.
   c. divide by twelve.
   d. multiple by five.

10. The audit results may affect the processes in the way
    a. the physician documents encounters.
    b. coders interpret documentation.
    c. billing is submitted.
    d. all of the above

11. CMS' Quarterly Provider Update includes all except
    a. regulations currently under development.
    b. new or revised manual instructions.
    c. new pricing information.
    d. regulations completed or cancelled.

12. The Office of Civil Rights is the best source for correct information on
    a. Medicare compliance.
    b. HIPAA compliance.
    c. coding information.
    d. patient safety regulations.

13. External audits performed by agencies, such as OIG, occur
    a. retrospectively.
    b. concurrently.
    c. internally.
    d. comprehensively.

14. In order to request documentation for an audit, the OIG or RAC must
    a. issue an subpoena.
    b. pay for the flight to Washington, D.C.
    c. officially request the information.
    d. reimburse office staff for participating.

15. Information on the Joint Commission website applies only to
    a. hospitals.
    b. physicians' offices.
    c. long term care facilities.
    d. all of the above

Research and Discussion Project

1. Identify the type of facility in which you work or would like to work. Go to the Internet
   and list all the sources you might use to keep your compliance plan up to date.

   _____

   _____

   _____

   _____

   _____

2. Make note of any specific areas or links provided on the websites that would make it easier
   for you to check up-to-date information.

   _____

   _____

   _____

   _____

3. Copy or print out a change or update that you find. This information may not be more
   than six months old.

4. Compare and contrast the information from each of the websites you found in step 1. Is
   there overlap or duplication? Which sites have identified important elements that no other
   site had?

   _____

   _____

   _____

   _____

   _____

Chapter 13

Enforcement: Dealing with Non-Compliance

Learning Outcomes

- Identify the various levels of disciplinary action
- Explain the components of a due process notification
- Describe the elements required on a disciplinary action form
- Discern the appropriate punishment for each level of violation

Key Terms

alleged / suspected, but not yet proven as a fact

arduous / difficult, strenuous, hard work

due process / the system or processes of justice; the sequence of events that lead to a finding of guilt or innocence

infractions / acts that break the rules; actions of non-compliance with policies and procedures

reiteration / a repetition of the same thing again

repercussion / consequence; ramification

vet / to carefully examine something or to scrutinize an action to determine correctness

Chapter Case Study

"On October 16, 2006, in Los Angeles, CA, Lourdes 'Lulu' Perez, a registered nurse who once owned the two largest home health agencies in California, was sentenced to 46 months in prison for her role in defrauding Medicare out of $40 million and for filing false tax returns that concealed

her ill-gotten gains. Additionally, Perez was sentenced to three years of supervised release and ordered to pay $6,127,374 to Medicare and $874,336 to the IRS; she has already re-paid approximately $34 million to the government. According to court documents, Perez orchestrated a scheme in which her companies obtained patients by paying illegal kickbacks to marketers; doctors and patients then billed Medicare for services that were not medically necessary, and in some cases not performed at all, and created false medical records to support the fraudulent claims and avoid detection of the fraud by Medicare contractors. The scheme ran from October 2002 until September 2003, when federal authorities seized more than $20 million in assets from Perez and Medicare suspended further payments to her agencies." (http://www.oig.hhs.gov)

Introduction

In chapter 1, you learned that one of the benefits of implementing a compliance plan is the confirmation to all staff members that the company is an honest one that expects legal and ethical behavior from its members. Assuring that these staff members are held accountable for following the plan is the glue that holds the moral fiber of the company together. Every policy must have an appropriate **repercussion** for failure to comply, and that consequence must be put into practice equally.

Disciplinary Action Policies

Your health care facility must publish a description of all levels of disciplinary actions that may be invoked when a staff member has allegedly violated a company policy or procedure.

The repercussions for non-compliance should be included in the original compliance plan and the policies and procedures manual. Not only are individuals entitled to know what the penalty will be if they choose to break a rule, but, by publishing the level of punishment in advance, it may act as a deterrent. The organization should follow all steps of **due process**, the system of justice as set out by this section of the compliance plan, to avoid any perceptions that disciplinary actions are being applied unequally.

Due Process

Once a violation has been identified and connected to a specific employee, the disciplinary action policy should be put into effect. This must include notification to the staff member, as well as any applicable administrative or managerial individuals, of the concern.

The notice should include:

1. *The description of the policy or law with which the staff member is **alleged** to have failed to comply.* You want to be very specific to assure that all conversations and evaluations do not veer off topic. For example, if the concern is that one particular coder has been found to be coding inaccurately, the assessment of this situation must focus solely on this concern, and not that the same employee

comes to work late frequently. One thing has nothing to do with the other when determining sanctions for lower-than-acceptable performance in coding. Only at an annual performance review would it be appropriate to consider all of the actions of the staff member.

> **EXAMPLE** Gigi is suspected of violating our facility policy that states that a copy of photo identification must be taken from anyone requesting patient records and attached to the signed release-of-information consent form.

2. *A statement or summary of what evidence or information led to the allegation that this employee violated this policy.* If the source of information regarding the alleged wrongdoing came from a report made by other staff members, the names of the individuals should be protected to prevent harassment. If the source is an audit report, or a remittance advice (RA) from a third-party payer, then the cases or claims should be listed.

> **EXAMPLE** A patient filed a complaint stating that our facility released a copy of her medical records to her ex-husband's girlfriend without her permission. There is no copy of a photo identification card in the file, and the signature on the consent form is illegible and does not match the patient's signature on other documents in the file.

3. *The process that will be enacted to determine if disciplinary action needs to be taken, and, if so, at what level, and the member(s) of management that will be involved in this process.* Once the allegation has been confirmed, this section of the plan should make it clear to everyone involved what steps will happen next, and who will be responsible for accomplishing these tasks.

> **EXAMPLE** Stacy, the department manager, will gather all documents and records relating to this complaint and present the evidence to the executive board. The executive board of the facility will then review all files and records relating to this incident and make a determination of what action, if any, should be taken.

4. *The employee's right to defend or explain his or her actions.* This should be a **reiteration** of what is already in the employee manual; however, it is worth repeating here so there is no confusion or ambiguity.

> **EXAMPLE** The staff member has the right to attend the meeting with the executive board and present his or her explanation of the incident, along with any other documentation or evidence in his or her possession that may be related to this concern.

5. *The determination and implementation of disciplinary action.* The original notice should itemize what potential disciplinary actions might be assessed if the employee is found to have violated the policy or rule.

> **EXAMPLE** The executive board has determined that Gigi did, in fact, violate the facility policy by failing to obtain a copy of photo identification, which is required in order to prevent release of patient information to an unauthorized individual. She is suspended without pay for two weeks pending an investigation into other records she has handled. Should any other violations be illuminated by the audit, the employee faces termination.

6. *The employee's right to appeal the implementation of the disciplinary action.* Medicare and Blue Cross Blue Shield give you the right to appeal, and your facility should provide a staff member the right to appeal a disciplinary action if they feel it was assessed unfairly. In the close-knit community of a workplace, it may be difficult to prevent personality differences from mixing with compliance issues. There should be a way that this individual can be heard by a third-party that is known to be objective and unbiased, such as a supervisor from another area of the facility.

> **EXAMPLE** The staff member may petition the executive board, in writing within 30 days, to appeal this decision. The letter should clearly detail the case at hand, reiterate any and all evidence that applies to this case, and any and all explanations as to why the actions that were determined to be against policy may have been justified.

This may sound like a court of law procedure, and it should. Internal disciplinary actions should follow legal system strategies to protect the employees and the organization itself. This entire textbook is about following proper rules and regulations. Part of this includes the protection of employees' rights guaranteed by federal and state employment laws. In addition, just like our system of justice in the United States, it would be sadly ironic if the compliance plan instituted by your office was used to illegally harass an innocent staff member because of personality issues and not, in truth, because of his or her failure to comply with policies.

The entire process should be designed and maintained to **vet** the daily behaviors of staff, protect good employees, and help to identify those who might present a legal danger to the organization. Health information management professionals already understand the critical importance of documentation, and these circumstances are no different. Use a standardized Disciplinary Action Report (Figure 13-1) throughout your facility for inclusion in the staff member's employee file.

Levels of Action

Certainly, everyone would agree that the punishment should fit the crime. Some violations may occur because the staff member was assumed to know the right behavior and evidently needs additional training or education. However, if the infraction happens again, then this employee did not learn the lesson the first time, and a message to the employee and other staff members must clearly be sent. Yet, there are other **infractions** that should be grounds for immediate termination without any second chances to endanger your facility.

Sample DISCIPLINARY ACTION FORM

EMPLOYEE:_____   POSITION:_____

SUPERVISOR:_____   DEPARTMENT:_____

Policy or Procedure Allegedly Violated: _____

Date(s) of Incident_____   Time of Incident:_____

Description of Alleged Violation:

_____

_____

_____

_____

_____

Action Plan:

_____

_____

_____

_____

_____

If Employee Fails to Comply with Above Stated Action Plan:

_____

_____

TYPE OF ACTION taken at this meeting: Date: _____
- ☐ Verbal Counseling (Dept. File Only)
- ☐ Written Warning
- ☐ Suspension: From _____ To: _____
- ☐ Termination: Effective _____

I acknowledge receipt of this disciplinary action and that its contents have been discussed with me. I understand that my signature does not necessarily indicate agreement.

_____   _____
Employee Signature   Date

_____   _____
Manager/Supervisor Signature   Date

_____   _____
Human Resources Representative   Date

Figure 13-1 Sample disciplinary action form

Begin by establishing the various levels of disciplinary action:

1. *Warning.* This is the lowest level of disciplinary action. The nature of the warning is that of a private talk between supervisor and staff member identifying the behavior of concern and offering suggestions to the employee as to what corrections might be made. The documentation in the staff member's record would need to be nothing more than a notation identifying:

    a. The time and date the warning was given;

    b. The suggestions made to the employee; and

    c. The employee's response.

    This is typically reserved for first time, minor infractions, such as coming in late several times or failing to file lab reports in patient charts in a timely fashion.

2. *Informal Disciplinary Action*: The level of disciplinary action most often used for behaviors that are believed to be correctable. The implementation of this action might require the employee to take a seminar or go through retraining. The employee record should include:

    a. A signed, completed disciplinary action form that includes:

        i. The date and time of the issuance of the additional education requirement;

        ii. A deadline for completing the training;

        iii. Specification of what disciplinary action would be put into effect if the employee does not comply by the deadline; and

        iv. The signatures of both staff member and the manager.

    A certification of completion, or some other credible evidence, should be attached to the disciplinary action form to close the event. If not, then a second disciplinary action form should be initiated to implement the subsequent action for failure to comply with the corrective action.

3. *Punitive Action*: This penalty would be used for a violation that is not quite severe enough to terminate someone's employment, but stern enough to be taken seriously. Examples of punitive actions include:

    a. Suspension with pay (this might be used to protect the facility while an investigation looks into the facts to determine responsibility),

    b. Suspension without pay,

    c. A demotion, or

    d. Exclusion from a company benefit (such as an annual bonus).

    Implementing punitive action should require the supervisor or manager to include a copy of a detailed written report of the violation, the investigation, copies of the evidence of wrongdoing, and any other records about employee actions that resulted in the application of this punishment.

4. *Termination*: Firing someone is always difficult, and an action most managers try to avoid. This can be more **arduous** when the employee is well liked or is in a sympathetic position, such as being a single parent. As a manager, you must remember your responsibility is not to any one individual but to the entire

organization. When one person consistently violates office policies and procedures, and refuses to learn from opportunities to improve their work, this person endangers everyone who works there, as well as the patients who are cared for by the facility. A person is not paid an annual salary to be a lunch buddy or to share coffee breaks. They have been hired to do a very important job, and that job must be performed ethically and legally. Every termination must be supported by documentation placed in the employee's file, as indicated in number 3 above:

a. A detailed written report of the specific policy or policies that were violated,

b. Complete identification of the source or sources of the information that led to the allegation,

c. Details on the investigation that ensued,

d. Copies of all evidence of wrongdoing,

e. An outline of previous warnings or notifications given to the employee on previous occasions regarding this behavior, and any other records of employee behaviors that resulted in the decision to terminate his or her employment. Whether or not the laws in your state require showing cause for termination, you should do it anyway. The file should hold clarification that there was no retaliation or personal vendetta, but that this staff member violated the written policies of the office.

Once the levels have been established, you can go through all of the policies to decide which level of infraction should be assigned to which level of disciplinary action.

> **EXAMPLE** A violation of HIPAA, such as talking to a patient in front of others in the waiting room, may require just a warning the first time. However, being overhead talking about a patient, by name, in a restaurant is grounds for immediate termination.

Additional Factors

Before assessment of punishment can be made, the determination of the staff member's level of negligence should be determined.

1. *Confirmation of knowledge*: One of the most dangerous things anyone in health information management can do is assume. This is why each health care facility must fulfill its corporate responsibility to publish a policies and procedures manual and reinforce this knowledge with training, as discussed in chapter 9 of this textbook. Be certain that your staff knows exactly what behaviors are expected of them and what the repercussions are should they fail to comply with the rules. Even on those occasions when you hire someone with many years of experience, you cannot be certain that the person's former employer taught him or her the importance of complying with federal and state laws.

2. *Series of violations*: Your facility is a workplace, and your employees should be expected to behave like adults, in a professional manner. Included in this expectation is the desire and ability to correct one's own behavior when it is found to be ineffective or improper. Therefore, once a warning has been issued and the

employee has been clearly notified of behaviors that are not appropriate, corrective actions should be evident and improvements should be seen. When this is not the case, and the same mistakes continue to be made, the employee is obviously negligent in his or her obligation to exert his personal best for this employer.

3. *Disruption of facility systems*: It is bad enough when an employee's poor performance or failure to comply with company policies negatively affects his or her own productivity. But when these behaviors interfere with other staff members' ability to perform to their ethical and legal best, the problem rises to an even higher level of negligence.

Chapter Summary

Most individuals find the disciplining of an employee to be one of the most difficult actions they have to take. However, it is important to assure that all individuals in your organization take the policies and procedures seriously. In order to accomplish this, violations must be met with consequences.

CHAPTER REVIEW

Multiple Choice Questions

1. All policies should have known _____ for non-compliance
   a. specific consequences
   b. vague statements
   c. occasional punishments
   d. employee-determined results

2. Repercussions for non-compliance should be
   a. decided by a committee.
   b. based on the individual.
   c. published in the policy manual.
   d. different based on seniority.

3. The audit report indicates that Filene has been coding for coverage on claims she submits for her friends who come to this clinic. This is an alleged
   a. ethical violation.
   b. legal violation.
   c. moral violation.
   d. human error.

4. Evidence in the due process evaluation of Filene's violation (from question 3) will include
   a. a statement from her friends.
   b. copies of the patient record and claim forms.
   c. Filene's pay stubs.
   d. all of the above

5. The notice of due diligence to Filene should include
    a. her right to a lawyer.
    b. her right to defend herself.
    c. her date of employment.
    d. her last promotion.

6. Informal disciplinary actions should include
    a. a termination date.
    b. a demotion or suspension.
    c. the employee's written apology.
    d. a plan for improvement.

7. Punitive action might be
    a. termination.
    b. suspension without pay.
    c. request for retraining.
    d. a warning.

8. If an investigation must be completed to determine employee guilt or innocence, it is recommended that the employee be
    a. suspended with pay.
    b. suspended without pay.
    c. told to clean out the inventory closet.
    d. terminated.

9. The disciplinary action should be more severe when there has been a
    a. confirmation of knowledge.
    b. series of violations.
    c. misspelling of terms.
    d. first offense.

10. A warning is
    a. the lowest level of disciplinary action.
    b. severe punishment for serious infractions.
    c. evidence of wrongdoing.
    d. testimony in court.

11. A complaint from a patient should immediately cause the action of
    a. termination.
    b. suspension.
    c. investigation.
    d. appeal.

12. Employees who are terminated after being found guilty of a wrongdoing should have
    a. no recourse.
    b. access to a published appeal process.
    c. one month's severance pay.
    d. three references.

13. A disciplinary action should always be
    a. applied equally to all staff.
    b. documented.
    c. final.
    d. a and b only

14. An employee who has violated a policy more than once should be considered for
    a. retraining.
    b. a promotion.
    c. termination.
    d. a raise.

15. Enforcement of consequences for non-compliance is a key component of
    a. legal compliance.
    b. ethical compliance.
    c. an organizational attitude of honesty.
    d. all of the above

Research and Discussion Project

1. Review different policies that might be created for any of the laws and regulations identified in this textbook and assign one or more disciplinary actions to the violation of each policy. Refer to chapter 5, "Compliance: Consent," chapter 6, "Compliance: Documentation," and chapter 7, "Compliance: Reporting."

   _____

   _____

   _____

   _____

   _____

2. Explain why a "due process" letter is important to issue.

   _____

   _____

   _____

   _____

3. Pair up with another student or friend and go through a role-playing exercise. One should play the role of a manger and the other an employee who has allegedly violated a company policy. Identify the policy and practice, discussing the violation with the "employee." How will you explain the situation? What will you do if the "employee" gets upset and starts to yell? What will you do if the "employee" starts to cry? What punishment is fair to both the organization and the "employee"?

Appendix A

Health Care Compliance Association (HCCA)
Certified in Healthcare Compliance (CHC) Examination
DETAILED EXAMINATION CONTENT OUTLINE

The outline on the following pages spells out the areas and tasks that will be tested on the HCCB CHC Certification Examination. The examination will be scored on participants' responses to 100 multiple choice questions spread across all subject areas.

EXAMINATION CONTENT OUTLINE	*Essentials of Health Care Compliance* Chapter
1. Standards, Policies, and Procedures	
A. Conduct a review of polices and procedures	8
B. Consult with appropriate and competent legal resources	2, 4
C. Ensure appropriate coding policies and procedures	7, 8
D. Ensure that appropriate billing and audit tools exist	7, 10, and 11
E. Ensure maintenance of policies and procedures that address overpayments	6, 7
F. Integrate mission, vision, and values with code of conduct	2
G. Maintain compliance plan and program	1, 3, 12
H. Ensure that a non-retaliation policy exists	9
I. Oversee internal and external compliance audit policies and procedures	10, 11

J. Ensure maintenance of a record retention policy	6
K. Maintain a code of conduct	2
L. Ensure maintenance of a conflict-of-interest policy	3
M. Ensure maintenance of appropriate confidentiality policies	3, 4
N. Ensure maintenance of appropriate privacy policies	4, 5
O. Ensure maintenance of policies and procedures to address regulatory requirements (e.g., EMTALA, CLIA, Anti-Kickback, research, labor laws)	4, 6, 8
P. Ensure maintenance of appropriate policies on interactions with other health care industry participants (e.g., hospitals/physicians, drug representatives, vendors)	4, 8, 9
Q. Develop policies and procedures that address the compliance role in quality-of-care issues	6, 8
R. Ensure maintenance of a policy on gifts and gratuities	8
S. Ensure maintenance of standards of accountability for employees at all levels	9
T. Maintain a compliance manual	8
U. Ensure maintenance of policies on waivers of co-payments and deductibles	4, 8
V. Propose appropriate governance policies related to compliance	1, 4

2. Compliance Program Administration	
A. Administer and plan a compliance budget	3
B. Report compliance activity to the governance board/committee	1, 2, 3
C. Coordinate operational aspects of a compliance program with the oversight committee	1, 2, 3
D. Collaborate with others to institute best business practices	2, 3

E. Coordinate organizational efforts to maintain a compliance program	1, 2
F. Recommend that the scope of the compliance program be in keeping with current industry standards	12
G. Ensure that the compliance oversight committee's goals and functions are addressed	2, 3
H. Evaluate the effectiveness of the compliance program on an ongoing basis	11, 12
I. Maintain knowledge of current regulatory changes and interpretations of laws (e.g., literature and conferences)	4, 8
J. Maintain the credibility and integrity of the compliance program	4, 8
K. Recognize the need for outside expertise	1, 2
L. Manage a compliance education program	9
M. Ensure that the organization has defined the responsibilities, purpose, function, and authority of the compliance officer	2
N. Ensure the governing board understands its responsibility as it relates to the compliance program	2
O. Ensure that the role of counsel in the compliance process has been defined	2
P. Delineate the responsibilities, purpose, and function for all compliance staff	2
Q. Allocate staffing for the compliance function	2
R. Ensure compliance risk assessments are conducted	3
S. Participate in the development of internal controls	3, 4, 5, 6, 7, 8
T. Incorporate relevant aspects of the OIG work plan into compliance operations	4
U. Integrate the compliance program into operations	8
V. Develop an annual compliance work plan	8

3. Screening and evaluation of employees, physicians, vendors, and other agents	
A. Ensure the organization has processes in place to identify and disclose conflicts of interest	6, 7, 8
B. Include compliance in all job descriptions	9
C. Use compliance as an element of job evaluation	9
D. Conduct background checks on relevant personnel in accordance with applicable rules and laws	3, 4, 8
E. Conduct compliance-sensitive exit interviews	10
F. Include a sanction list review in professional credentialing activities	10
G. Monitor government sanction lists for excluded individuals/entities (e.g., OIG, GSA, SDN, SDGT)	10

4. Communication, education, and training on compliance issues	
A. Disseminate relevant fraud alerts and other relevant guidance material	9
B. Communicate compliance information throughout the organization	9
C. Develop appropriate compliance training for all applicable individuals (e.g., orientation, remedial)	9
D. Distill complex laws and regulations into a format employees can understand	4, 8, 9
E. Educate staff on compliance policies	9
F. Ensure that employees understand their obligation to accurately document activities	9
G. Ensure that there is a process in place for employees to understand the compliance aspects of their job responsibilities	9
H. Promote a culture of compliance throughout the organization	1, 3, 9
I. Encourage employees to seek guidance and clarification when in doubt	9

J. Participate in continuing education to maintain professional competence	9
K. Track participation in ongoing compliance training programs	10
L. Conduct general compliance training for all employees, physicians, vendors, and other agents	9
M. Conduct risk-specific training for targeted employees	9
N. Provide the human resources department and management with training to help them recognize compliance risks associated with employee misconduct	9

5. Monitoring, auditing, and internal reporting systems	
A. Protect anonymity and confidentiality within legal and practical limits	5
B. Publicize the reporting system to all employees, physicians, vendors, and others	9, 10
C. Monitor for violations of applicable laws and regulations	10, 11
D. Authorize independent investigations when necessary	11
E. Conduct organizational risk assessments	10
F. Develop action plans based on risk assessments	12, 13
G. Operate system(s) to enable employees to report any non-compliance (e.g., a hotline)	9
H. Address compliance concerns expressed by employees through internal reporting	9, 12
I. Monitor and enforce compliance-related policies and procedures	10, 11, 12, 13
J. Conduct compliance audits	10
K. Engage in routine monitoring of compliance-related activities	10, 11
L. Monitor compliance audit results (e.g., track, trend, evaluate, benchmark)	12

M. Develop an annual compliance audit plan	10
N. Address audits conducted by external entities	11
O. Monitor compliance with governance policies	4, 8, 12

6. Discipline for non-compliance	
A. Recommend disciplinary action when non-compliance is substantiated	13
B. Ensure discipline is proportionate to the violation	13
C. Ensure discipline is consistent with policies and procedures	13
D. Ensure discipline is enforced consistently throughout all levels of the organization	13
E. Ensure recommended disciplinary action is documented	13
F. Recommend appropriate action for individuals and entities that have been excluded from government programs	13
G. Ensure that compliance-related violations are addressed in disciplinary policies	13
H. Coordinate with management to ensure appropriate corrective action is taken	13

7. Investigations and remedial measures	
A. Communicate noncompliance through appropriate channels	9
B. Develop corrective action plans in response to noncompliance	13
C. Monitor the effectiveness of corrective action plans and modify as needed	12
D. Incorporate any necessary changes to reduce risk	12
E. Respond to inquiries promptly, thoroughly, and discretely	12, 13

F. Initiate policies and education to respond to identified problems or vulnerabilities	9, 12
G. Conduct fair, objective, and discrete investigations	10, 11
H. Cooperate with government inquiries and investigations	12
I. Investigate matters related to noncompliance	10
J. Maintain records on compliance investigations	11
K. Negotiate with regulatory agencies	11
L. Disclose overpayments to payors	7
M. Coordinate voluntary disclosures with legal counsel	7
N. Coordinate investigations to preserve applicable privileges	1, 11

Appendix B

Abbreviations and Acronyms

A/P	accounts payable
A/R	accounts receivable
AAPC	American Academy of Professional Coders
AAPCC	average adjusted per capita cost
AAHC	American Accreditation Healthcare Commission
AAHP	American Association of Health Plans
AAMT	American Association of Medical Transcriptionists
AAPPO	American Association of Preferred Provider Organizations
AB	allowed benefit
ABC	activity-based costing
ABMS	American Board of Medical Specialties
ABN	Advance Beneficiary Notice
AC	ambulatory care
ACCP	Approval Committee for Certificate Programs
ACF	adult care facility
ACG	adjusted clinical groups
ACHE	American College of Healthcare Executives
ADA	Americans with Disabilities Act
ADC	average daily census
ADL	activities of daily living
ADM	alcohol, drug, or mental disorder
ADS	alternative delivery system
ADT	admission, discharge, transfer
AG	attorney general
AHA	American Hospital Association
AHC	alternative health care
AHIMA	American Health Information Management Association
AHPB	adjusted historic payment base
AHRQ	Agency for Healthcare Research and Quality
AIDS	acquired immune deficiency syndrome

AIMS	abnormal involuntary movement scale
AKA	above-knee amputation
ALJ	administrative law judge
ALOS	average length of stay
ALS	advanced life support
AMA	American Medical Association
AMA	against medical advice
ANSI	American National Standards Institute
AOA	Administration on Aging
AOB	assignment of benefits
APC	ambulatory payment classification
AP-DRG	all patients-diagnosed related group
APG	ambulatory patient group
APR	adjusted payment rate; also average payment rate
APR-DRG	all patients refined–diagnosis related group
APS	attending physician statement
APT	average admissions per thousand
ARA	associate regional administrator
ASC	ambulatory surgery center
AUR	ambulatory utilization review
BBA	Balanced Budget Act (of 1997)
BBRA	Balanced Budget Refinement Act (of 1999)
BCBS	Blue Cross Blue Shield
BIC	beneficiary identification code
BKA	below-knee amputation
BL	black lung
BLS	basic life support
BME	Board of Medical Examiners
BMT	bone marrow transplant
CAC	Carrier Advisory Committee; also computer-assisted coding
CAH	critical access hospital
CAP	capitation or correction action plan
CARF	Commission on Accreditation of Rehabilitation Facilities
CAT	computerized axial tomography; also, CT scan
CBO	Congressional Budget Office; also Central Billing Office
CBSA	core-based statistical area
CC	chief complaint and complications/comorbidities
CCI	correct coding initiative
CCN	correspondence control number
CCS	certified coding specialist
CCU	critical care unit or cardiac care unit
CDE	certified diabetic educators
CDHP	consumer-driven health plan
CDT	current dental terminology
CEO	chief executive officer

CEPA	coding certificate program assessment
CERT	comprehensive error rate testing
CF	conversion factor
CFO	chief financial officer
CFR	code of federal regulations
CHAMPUS	Civilian Health and Medical Program of the Uniformed Services
CHAMPVA	Civilian Health and Medical Program—Veterans Administration
CHIME	College of Health Information Management Executives
CHIN	Community Health Information Network
CHIP	Children's Health Insurance Plan
CICU	coronary intensive care unit
CIM	coverage issues manual
CIO	chief information officer
CIS	clinical information system
CLIA	clinical laboratory improvement amendments
CMD	contractor medical director
CMG	case-mix group
CMHC	community mental health center
CMI	case-mix index
CMO	chief medical officer
CMP	civil monetary penalties; also comprehensive medical plan
CMN	Certificate of Medical Necessity
CMR	comprehensive medical review
CMS	Center for Medicare and Medicaid Services
CMT	certified medical transcriptionist
CNM	certified nurse midwife
COA	certificate of authority
COB	coordination of benefits
COBRA	Consolidation Omnibus Budget Reconciliation Act
COC	certificate of coverage
CON	Certificate of Need; also CN
COP	conditions of participation
CORF	comprehensive outpatient rehabilitation facility
COS	clinical outcomes system
CP	clinical psychologist
CPHA	Commission on Professional and Hospital Activities
CPO	care plan oversight
CPC	certified professional coder
CPR	cardiopulmonary resuscitation and computerized patient record
CPT	*Current Procedural Terminology*
CQI	continuous quality improvement
CRD	chronic renal disease
CRNA	certified registered nurse anesthetist
CSO	clinical service organization and chief security officer
CSW	clinical social worker
CTO	chief technology officer
CWLA	Child Welfare League of America

CWW	Clinic Without Walls
CY	calendar year
DAW	dispense as written
DBLC	data base life cycle
DBMS	data base management system
DCA	deferred compensation administrator
DCI	duplicate coverage inquiry
DEFRA	Deficit Reduction Act of 1984
DHHS	Department of Health and Human Services
DHSQ	Division of Health Standards and Quality
DME	durable medical equipment
DMEMAC	durable medical equipment Medicare administrative contractor
DMEPOS	durable medical equipment prosthetics, orthotics, and supplies
DMEPSC	durable medical equipment program safeguard contractors
DMERC	durable medical equipment regional carrier
DNFB	discharged, no final bill report
DNR	do not resuscitate
DOA	dead on arrival
DOB	date of birth
DOJ	Department of Justice
DOL	Department of Labor
DOS	date of service
DPAHC	durable power of attorney for health care
DRG	diagnosis-related group
DSM-IV	*Diagnostic and Statistical Manual—4th edition*
DUR	drug utilization review
DX	diagnosis
EAP	employee assistance program
ECF	extended care facility
ECG	electrocardiogram; also EKG
ED	Emergency Department
EDI	electronic data interchange
EDMS	electronic document management system
EEG	electroencephalogram
EFT	electronic funds transfer
EHR	electronic health record
EIN	Employer Identification Number (tax ID)
EKG	electrocardiogram; also ECG
E/M	evaluation and management
EMC	electronic media claims
EMDS	essential medical data set
EMR	electronic medical record
EMS	emergency medical systems
EMT	emergency medical technician
EMTALA	Emergency Medical Treatment & Active Labor Act

ENT	ear, nose, throat
EOB	explanation of benefits
EOC	episode of care
EOI	evidence of insurability
EOM	end-of-month
EOY	end-of-year
EPO	exclusive provider organization
EPSDT	early and periodic screening, diagnosis, and treatment
ER	emergency room
ERA	electronic remittance advice
ERISA	Employee Retirement Income Security Act of 1974
ERN	electronic remittance notice
ESRD	end-stage renal disease
F&A	fraud and abuse
FBI	Federal Bureau of Investigation
FCA	False Claims Act; also FFCA—federal False Claims Act
FCN	financial control number
FEHBP	Federal Employees Health Benefits Plan
FEP	Federal Employee Program
FFS	fee-for-service
FI	fiscal intermediary
FLSA	Fair Labor Standards Act
FOP	field of practice
FOIA	Freedom of Information Act
FPL	federal poverty level
FR	*Federal Register*
FSA	flexible spending account
FTE	full-time equivalents
FTP	file transfer protocol
FY	fiscal year
FYE	fiscal year-end
GAAP	generally accepted accounting principles
GAF	geographic adjustment factor
GAO	Government Accountability Office
GASB	Government Accounting Standards Board
GPCI	geographic practice cost index
GPO	Government Printing Office
H&P	history and physical
HAC	hospital-acquired conditions
HAZMAT	hazardous materials
HBP	hospital-based physician
HCFA	Health Care Finance Administration
HCFAC	Health Care Fraud and Abuse Control program
HCPCS	Healthcare Common Procedure Coding System

HCQIP	Health Care Quality Improvement Program
HCUP	Healthcare Cost and Utilization Project
HEDIS	health plan employer data and information set
HEENT	head, eyes, ears, nose, throat
HFAP	Healthcare Facilities Accreditation Program
HHA	home health agency
HHRG	home health resource group
HHS	U.S. Department of Health and Human Services
HI	health insurance
HIAA	Health Insurance Association of America
HIM	health information management
HIMR	Health Insurance Master Record
HIPAA	Health Insurance Portability and Accountability Act
HIPDB	Healthcare Integrity and Protection Data Bank
HIPPS	Health Insurance Prospective Payment System
HIQH	Health Insurance Query for Home Health Agencies
HIS	healthcare information system
HIT	health information technology
HIV	human immunodeficiency virus
HL7	Health Level Seven
HME	home medical equipment
HMO	health maintenance organization
HPSA	health professional shortage area
HRSA	Health Resources Services Administration
HSA	Health Service Agreement
HSP	health service plan
IBNR	incurred but not reported
ICD	*International Classification of Diseases*
ICF	intermediate care facility
ICN	internal control number
ICR	intelligent character recognition
ICU	intensive care unit
IDR	intelligent document recognition
IDS	integrated delivery system
IDTF	independent diagnostic testing facility
IHS	Indian Health Service
IL	independent laboratory
IME	independent medical evaluation
IOM	Internet-Only Manual; also Institute of Medicine
IP	inpatient
IPF	inpatient psychiatric facility
IPO	integrated provider organization
IRB	Institutional Review Board
IRF	Inpatient Rehabilitation Facility
IRR	internal rate of return
IS	information systems

ISO	International Standards Organization
ISN	integrated service network
IT	information technology
IVR	integrated voice response system
JCAHO	Joint Commission on Accreditation of Healthcare Organizations, now the Joint Commission
KC	knowledge clusters
LAN	local area network
LCER	limiting charge exception report
LFS	laboratory fee schedule
LLP	limited-license practitioner
LMRP	Local Medical Review Policy
LMS	learning management systems
LOS	length of stay
LPN	licensed practical nurse
LTAC	long-term acute care hospital
LTC	long-term care
LTCH	long-term care hospital
LVN	licensed vocational nurse
MA	medical assistant
MAC	monitored anesthesia care; also maximum allowable cost
MCC	major co-morbidity/complication
MCM	Medicare carriers manual
MCO	managed care organization
MCR	medical cost ratio
MCS	Multi-Carrier System (Medicare Part B)
MD	medical doctor
MDC	major diagnostic category
MEI	Medicare Economic Index
MEDPAR	Medicare Provider Analysis and Review
MED-PARD	Medicare Participating Physician/Supplier Directory
MFS	Medicare fee schedule
MIM	medical intermediary manual
MIP	Medicare Integrity Plan
MIS	management information system
MPI	Master Patient Index
MPFSDB	Medicare Physician Fee Schedule Database
MR	medical review
MRI	magnetic resonance imaging
MRN	medical record number
MRUR	medical review/utilization review
MSA	Medical Savings Account
MSN	Medicare summary notice
MSO	management service organization

MSP	Medicare secondary payer
MSP RAC	Medicare secondary payer recovery audit contractor
MTD	month-to-date
NAR	nursing assessment record
NCD	national coverage decision
NCHS	National Center for Health Statistics
NCP	National Coverage Provision
NCQA	National Committee on Quality Assurance
NCVHS	National Committee on Vital and Health Statistics
NDC	National Drug Code
NEC	not elsewhere classified
NH	nursing home
NICU	Neonatal Intensive Care Unit
NIH	National Institutes of Health
NGC	National Guidelines Clearinghouse
NLM	National Library of Medicine
NOC	not otherwise classified
NONPAR	non-participating provider (Medicare)
NOS	not elsewhere specified
NP	nurse practitioner
NPA	Non-Par Approved; also National Prescription Audit
NPDB	National Practitioner Data Bank
NPI	national provider identifier
NPP	non-physician practitioner
NPN	non-par not approved
NSC	National Supplier Clearinghouse
NSF	national standard format; also non-sufficient funds
NUBC	National Uniform Billing Committee
NUCC	National Uniform Claim Committee
OAS	Office of Audit Services
OASIS	outcome and assessment information set
OB/GYN	obstetrics/gynecology
OBRA	Omnibus Budget Reconciliation Act
OCE	outpatient code editor
OCFAA	Office of Civil Fraud and Administration Adjudication
OCIG	Office of Counsel to the Inspector General
OCR	optical character reader or optical claims recognition
OEI	Office of Evaluations and Inspections
OER	outcomes and effectiveness research
OI	Office of Investigations
OIG	Office of the Inspector General
OMB	Office of Management and Budget
OMP	Office of Management and Policy
OON	out-of-network
OOP	out-of-pocket costs
OP	outpatient

OPD	outpatient department
O/P	overpayment
OPL	other-party liability
OPPS	outpatient prospective payment system
OR	operating room
ORF	outpatient rehabilitation facility
OSHA	Occupational Safety and Health Administration
OT	occupational therapy
OTC	over-the-counter
OV	office visit
PA	physician assistant; also professional association
PAC	Political Action Committee
PACE	programs of all-inclusive care for the elderly
PACU	post-anesthesia care unit
PAI	patient assessment instrument
PAR	participating provider (physician)
PAT	pre-admission testing
PAYERID	payer identification number
PC	professional component
PCA	progressive corrective action
PCN	primary care network
PCP	primary care provider (physician)
PDA	personal digital assistant
PDR	*Physician's Desk Reference*
PEC	pre-existing condition
PEP	partial episode payment
PEPP	payment error prevention
PERT	program evaluation review technique
PHC	public health clinic
PHI	protected health information
PHR	personal health record
PI	program integrity
PICU	Pediatric Intensive Care Unit
PIM	program integrity manual
PIN	physician identifier number
PM	program memorandum
PMR	proportionate mortality rate
PO	purchase order; also physician organization
POA	present-on-admission
POC	plan of care
POS	place of service; also point of service
PPE	professional practice experience
PPO	preferred provider organization
PPPM	per patient per month
PPR	periodic performance review
PPS	prospective payment system
PRN	provider remittance notice

PRO	peer review organization
PSC	program safeguard contractors
PSDA	Patient Self-Determination Act
PSI	payment status indicator
PSRO	professional standards review organization
PT	physical therapy
PX	procedure
QA	quality assurance
QIO	quality improvement organization
QM	quality management
QMB	qualified Medicare beneficiary
RA	remittance advice
RAC	recovery audit contractors
RAI	resident assessment instrument
RAP	request for anticipated payment
RAVEN	resident assessment validation and entry
RBRVS	resource-based relative value system
RBRVU	resource-based relative value unit
RC	reasonable charge; also reasonable and customary
R/D	research and development
RFID	radio frequency identification
RFP	request for proposal
RHC	rural health clinic
RHIA	registered health information administrator
RHIO	regional health information organization
RHIT	registered health information technician
RM	risk management
RN	registered nurse
ROI	release of information; also return on investment
ROS	review of systems
RVS	relative value scale
RVU	relative value unit
RX	prescription
SAG	state attorney general
SCHIP	State Children's Health Insurance Program
SDP	single-drug pricer
SDS	same-day surgery
SLP	speech language protocol (therapy)
SMFCU	State Medicaid Fraud Control Units
SNF	Skilled Nursing Facility
SNODENT	systemized nomenclature of dentistry
SNOMED	systemized nomenclature of medicine
SOAP	subjective, objective, assessment, plan
SOI	severity of illness
SPR	standard paper remittance

SSA	Social Security Administration
SSI	Supplemental Security Income
SSN	Social Security number
STD	sexually transmitted disease
STP	standard treatment protocol
TAF	Taxpayers Against Fraud
TAN	treatment authorization number
TANF	Temporary Assistance for Needy Families
TC	technical component
TEFRA	Tax Equity and Fiscal Responsibility Act of 1983
TIN	taxpayer identification number
TOS	type of service
TPA	third-party administrator
TRICARE	new name for CHAMPUS
TQM	total quality management
UACDS	Uniform Ambulatory Care Data Set
UB	uniform bill form
UCC	Urgent Care Center
UCDS	uniform clinical data set
UCR	usual, customary, reasonable
UHDDS	uniform hospital discharge data set
UM	utilization management
UMLS	Unified Medical Language System
UPIN	unique physician identification number
UR	utilization review
USAO	United States attorneys' office
USC	United States code
VA	Veterans Administration
VE	voluntary effort
VoIP	voice-over Internet protocol
VRS	voice recognition software
WC	Workers' Compensation
WHO	World Health Organization
YTD	year-to-date

DO NOT USE ABBREVIATION LIST FROM THE JOINT COMMISSION

U	Unit, mistaken for 0 (zero)
IU	Internal Unit, mistaken for IV (intravenous) or 10 (ten)
QD, qd	Daily, mistaken for every other day
QOD, qod	Every Other Day, mistaken for every day
MS	Morphine Sulfate, mistaken for magnesium sulfate
MS 04	Magnesium Sulfate, mistaken for morphine sulfate

Appendix C

Professional Associations

AAAHC	American Association for Ambulatory Health Care
AAHC/URAC	American Accreditation Healthcare Commission
AAHP	American Association of Health Plans
AAHSA	American Association of Homes and Services for the Aging
AAMC	Association of American Medical Colleges
AAMT	Association of American Medical Transcriptionists
AAP	American Academy of Pediatrics
AAPC	American Academy of Professional Coders
AARC	American Association of Respiratory Care
AARP	American Association of Retired Persons
ACC	American College of Cardiology
ACHE	American College of Healthcare Executives
ACIP	Advisory Committee on Immunization Practices
ACOG	American College of Obstetricians and Gynecologists
ACPE	American College of Physician Executives
ACR	American College of Radiology
ACS	American College of Surgeons -or-
	American Cancer Society
ADA	American Diabetes Association -or-
	American Dental Association
AFDC	Aid to Families with Dependent Children
AHA	American Heart Association -or-
	American Hospital Association
AHCA	American Health Care Association
AHCPR	Agency for Health Care Policy and Research
AHIMA	American Health Information Management Association
AHRA	American Healthcare Radiology Administrators
AHRMM	Association for Healthcare Resource & Materials Management
AHRQ	Agency for Healthcare Research and Quality
AMA	American Medical Association

AMCRA	American Medical Care and Review Associates
AMIA	American Medical Information Association
AMRA	American Medical Records Association
ANA	American Nurses Association
ANSI	American National Standards Institute
AOA	Administration on Aging -or- American Osteopathic Association
AONE	American Organization of Nurse Executives
AOTA	American Occupational Therapy Association
APA	American Psychiatric Association
APHA	American Public Health Association
APTA	American Physical Therapy Association
ARC	American Red Cross
ASAE	American Society of Association Executives
ASC	Accredited Standards Committee
ASDVS	American Society for Directors of Volunteer Services
ASHE	American Society for Healthcare Engineering
ASHES	American Society for Healthcare Environmental Services
ASHFSA	American Society for Healthcare Food Service Administrators
ASHHRA	American Society for Healthcare Human Resources Administration
ASHRM	American Society for Healthcare Risk Management
ASQ	American Society for Quality
ASTM	American Society for Testing and Materials
BC/BS	Blue Cross Blue Shield Association
BME	Board of Medical Examiners
CAP	College of American Pathologists
CARF	Commission on Accreditation of Rehabilitation Facilities
CDC	Centers for Disease Control and Prevention
CHA	Catholic Health Association -or- Center for Health Affairs
CHAMPUS	Civilian Health and Medical Program of the Uniformed Services
CHAMPVA	Civilian Health and Medical Program of the Veteran's Administration
CHAP	Community Health Accreditation Program
CHIME	College of Health Information Management Executives
CMS	Centers for Medicare and Medicaid Services (formerly HCFA)
COA	Council on Accreditation for Children and Family Services
CPHA	Commission on Professional and Hospital Activities
DEA	Drug Enforcement Agency
DOJ	U.S. Department of Justice
EEOC	Equal Employment Opportunity Commission

FAH	Federation of American Hospitals
FDA	U.S. Food and Drug Administration
FEMA	Federal Emergency Management Agency
FHA	Farmers Home Administration -or- Federal Housing Administration
FTC	Federal Trade Commission
GAO	General Accounting Office
HCFA	Health Care Financing Administration
HFMA	Healthcare Financial Management Association
HHS	U.S. Department of Health and Human Services
HIAA	Health Insurance Association of America
HIDI	Hospital Industry Data Institute
HIMSS	Healthcare Information Management Systems Society
HRSA	Health Resources and Services Administration
IHI	Institute for Healthcare Improvement
IMD	Institute for Mental Disease
IOM	Institute of Medicine of the National Academy of Sciences
ISMP	Institute for Safe Medication Practices
IRS	Internal Revenue Service
JAMA	Journal of the American Medical Association
JAR	Joint Annual Report of Hospitals
JCAHO	**... now** The Joint Commission; formerly the Joint Commission on Accreditation of Healthcare Organizations
JCR	Joint Commission Resources
MedPAC	Medicare Payment Advisory Commission
NAACCR	North American Association of Central Cancer Registries
NACHRI	National Association of Children's Hospitals and Related Institutions
NAHQ	National Association of Healthcare Quality
NBRC	National Board for Respiratory Care
NBME	National Board of Medical Examiners
NCCMERP	National Coordinating Council for Medication Error Reporting and Prevention
NCHS	National Center for Health Statistics
NCHSR	National Center for Health Services Research
NCQA	National Committee for Quality Assurance
NCVHS	National Committee on Vital and Health Statistics
NDMS	National Disaster Medical System
NFPA	National Fire Prevention Association
NHSC	National Health Service Corp

NIH	National Institutes of Health
NIOSH	National Institute for Occupational Safety and Health
NLRB	National Labor Relations Board
NPDB	National Practitioner Data Bank
NPSF	National Patient Safety Foundation
NPSP	National Patient Safety Partnership
NRC	Nuclear Regulatory Commission
NRHA	National Rural Health Association
OCR	U.S. Office of Civil Rights
OHS	U.S. Office of Homeland Security
OIG	Office of Inspector General
OMB	U.S. Office of Management and Budget
OPO	Organ Procurement Organization
ORHP	Office of Rural Health Policy
OSHA	Occupational Safety and Health Administration
PHS	Public Health Services
ProPAC	Prospective Payment Assessment Commission
Qsource	Center for Healthcare Quality
SHSMD	Society for Healthcare Strategy & Market Development
UAN	United American Nurses
UNOS	United Network for Organ Sharing
URAC	Utilization Review Accreditation Commission
USP	United States Pharmacopeia
VA	Veterans Administration
WHO	World Health Organization
WIC	Women and Infant Children program

Appendix D

Professional Designations

ANP	advanced nurse practitioner
ARPN	advanced practice registered nurse
ART	accredited record technician
CADAC	certified alcohol and drug abuse counselor
CCA	certified coding associate
CCS	certified coding specialist
CCS-P	certified coding specialist—physician-based
CHC	certified in healthcare compliance
CHFP	certified healthcare financial professional
CHPS	certification in healthcare privacy and security
CMA	certified medical assistant
CMT	certified medical transcriptionist
CNA	certified nurse assistant
CNM	certified nurse-midwife
CNO	chief nursing officer
CPC	certified professional coder
CPC-H	certified professional coder—hospital
CRNA	certified registered nurse anesthetist
CTR	certified tumor registrar
DC	doctor of chiropractic
DDS	doctor of dental surgery
DO	doctor of osteopathy
DPM	doctor of podiatric medicine
DSC	doctor of surgical chiropody
DVM	doctor of veterinary medicine
EMT	emergency medical technician
FACHE	fellow of the American College of Healthcare Executives
GP	general practitioner
LPC	licensed professional counselor
LPT	licensed physical therapist

LPN	licensed practical nurse
LVN	licensed vocational nurse
MD	medical doctor
MHA	master of hospital (health) administration
MHSA	master of health services administration
MPA	master of public administration
MPH	master of public health
MSN	master of science in nursing
MSW	master of social work
ND	doctor of naturopathic medicine
OD	doctor of optometry
OTR	occupational therapist registered
PA	physician assistant
RHIA	registered health information administrator
RHIT	registered health information technician
RN	registered nurse
RPh	registered pharmacist
RRT	respiratory therapist
RT	radiology technologist

Appendix E

Reference Websites

Agency for Healthcare Research and Quality	http://healthit.ahrq.gov
American Academy of Professional Coders	http://www.aapc.com
American Association of Ambulatory Surgery Centers	http://www.aaasc.org
American Association of Homes and Services for the Aging (nursing homes)	http://www.aahsa.org
American Health Information Management Association	http://www.ahima.org
American Health Lawyers Association	http://www.healthlawyers.org
American Health Quality Association	http://www.ahqa.org
American Hospital Association: Compliance Index	http://www.aha.org/aha/advocacy/compliance/index.html
American Medical Association	http://www.ama-assn.org
Blue Cross Blue Shield Association	http://www.bcbs.com
Center on Medical Record Rights and Privacy, Health Policy Institute, Georgetown University	http://hpi.georgetown.edu/privacy
Centers for Medicare and Medicaid Services	http://www.cms.hhs.gov
Coalition Against Insurance Fraud	http://www.insurancefraud.org
Code of Federal Regulations (CFR)	http://www.gpoaccess.gov/cfr
Comprehensive Error Rate Testing (CERT)	http://www.cms.hhs.gov/CERT
Correct Coding Initiatives	http://www.ntis.gov/products/cci.aspx
Department of Health and Human Services	http://www.hhs.gov

Directory of Open Access Journals	http://www.doaj.org/doaj?func=findJournals
Federal Bureau of Investigation (FBI)	http://www.fbi.gov
Federal Emergency Medical Treatment and Active Labor Act (EMTALA) (Patient Anti-Dumping Law)	http://www.emtala.com
Federal False Claims Act	http://www.cms.hhs.gov/smdl/downloads/SMD032207Att2.pdf
Federal Register: False Claims Act	http://www.oig.hhs.gov/authorities/docs/06/waisgate.pdf
Federal Register	http://www.gpoaccess.gov/fr
FindLaw: Health Laws	http://www.findlaw.com/01topics/19health/index.html
Florida Health News	http://www.floridahealthnews.org
Fraud Digest	http://frauddigest.com
Government Printing Office	http://www.gpoaccess.gov
Health Care Compliance Association	http://www.hcca-info.org
Healthcare Financial Management Association	http://www.hfma.org
Health Care Fraud Report	http://www.bna.com/current/hfr/tope.htm
Healthcare Integrity and Protection Data Bank	http://www.npdb-hipdb.com
Health Care Procedure Coding System (HCPCS)	http://www.cms.hhs.gov/medicare/hcpcs
Health Data Management	http://www.healthdatamanagement.com
Health Ethics Trust	http://www.corporateethics.com/
Health HIPPO	http://hippo.findlaw.com/hippofra.html
Health Insurance Portability and Accountability Act (HIPAA)	http://www.hhs.gov/policies/index.html
Institutes of Medicine	http://www.iom.edu
Internal Revenue Service: Examples of Healthcare Fraud Investigations	http://www.irs.gov/compliance/enforcement/article/0,,id=174637,00.html
International Classification of Diseases-10th revision (ICD-10)	http://www.cdc.gov/nchs/about/otheract/icd9/abticd10.htm
Joint Commission	http://www.jointcommission.org
Law by State: Cornell University Law School	http://www.law.cornell.edu/states
Library Spot	http://www.libraryspot.com
Mayo Clinic	http://www.mayoclinic.com
Medicaid Fraud Control Units	http://oig.hhs.gov/publications/mfcu.html
MedicineNet	http://www.medterms.com

Medline Plus	http://www.nlm.nih.gov/ medlineplus
Medscape	http://www.medscape.com
Merck Manual	http://www.merck.com
National Association of Medicaid Fraud Control Units	http://www.namfcu.net
National Center for Health Statistics	http://www.cdc.gov/nchs
National Committee for Quality Assurance	http://www.ncqa.org
National Committee for Vital and Health Statistics	http://www.ncvhs.hhs.gov
National Guideline Clearinghouse	http://www.guideline.gov
National Health Care Anti-Fraud Association	http://www.nhcaa.org
National Health Law Program	http://www.healthlaw.org
National Health Policy Forum	http://www.nhpf.org
National Institutes of Health: Legal, Ethical, and Safety Issues	http://clinicalcenter.nih.gov/ participate/patientinfo/legal.shtml
National Library of Medicine	http://www.nlm.nih.gov
National Practitioner Database	http://www.npdb-hipdb.com
Occupational Safety and Health Administration	http://www.osha.gov
Office of Civil Rights	http://www.hhs.gov/ocr
Office of the Inspector General	http://www.oig.hhs.gov
Pay-For-Performance—Medicare	http://www.cms.hhs.gov/apps/ media/press/release .asp?counter=1343
Qui Tam	http://www.usdoj.gov/usao/pae/ Documents/fcaprocess2.pdf
Qui Tam	http://www.megalaw.com/top/ quitam.php
Tricare	http://www.tricare.mil
THOMAS (congressional legislative information)	http://www.thomas.gov
United States Department of Justice	http://www.usdoj.gov
United States Department of Labor	http://www.dol.gov
United States Sentencing Commission	http://www.ussc.gov/guidelin.htm
WebMD	http://www.webmd.com
World Health Organization	http://www.who.int/en

Glossary

acronym: A word or term formed by the grouping of initials or parts of the words in a phrase

administrative laws: Rules created by authorized agencies

advance directive: A document in which an individual states his agreement to or refusal of future health care services

age of majority: When a person is no longer considered a minor; the age of 18

alleged: Thought to have happened, but not yet proven

allocation: Assignment of equipment, supplies, manpower, and/or money to various tasks, departments, or other sectors of an organization

allowances: From the FSG, a lessening of penalties or punishments assessed for an organization found guilty of fraud

ambiguity: Something that can be interpreted in more than one manner

analyze: To study something in great detail with the intent of better understanding its contents

arduous: Difficult, strenuous, hard work

audit: An official review of work product for correctness

auspices: The realm of responsibility of a job, department, or an organization

authenticate: To verify something is genuine or credible

bolstered: Supported; encouraged

buy-in: A conscious agreement by all of those affected by the terms of the policy or procedure

Certificate of medical necessity (CMN): A document, signed by the attending physician, that supports a medical reason for a patient requiring equipment, such as a wheelchair or cane

Civil laws: Laws that deal with the rights of individuals

CMPL: Civil monetary penalty laws

Coding for coverage: Reporting a code based on what the third-party will pay rather than accurately reporting what occurred with the patient

Compelling: Attracting attention or compassion; providing motivation for someone to do something or make something happen

Compliance: The act of obeying, or following rules

Comprehensive: Investigation of the entire quantity

Concurrent: Happening at the same time

Consent for treatment: A written authorization, signed by the patient or guardian, for the physician or health care facility to provide services and treatments

Conspiracy: Plans between two or more people to commit a crime

Contagious: Transferred from one individual to another

Contempt of court: Refusal to comply with a court order

Contingency: Alternate; something that occurs only when an original fails

Continuing education units (CEU): Education, via coursework, seminar, or reading, to keep a professional current on their industry, required each year beyond initial formal training such as a degree or certification

Covert: Covered up; hidden from plain sight

Criminal laws: Laws that protect individuals' health, safety, and welfare

Defendants: Persons or organizations accused of wrongdoing in a civil or criminal legal action

Determine: To decide something conclusively

Disseminate: To disperse or spread information

Documentation: The process of providing tangible, written (hand-written, typed, or computerized) details

Do Not Resuscitate (DNR) order: A form expressing that, should the patient go into cardiac arrest, he or she does not wish to be resuscitated or have any heroic measures taken to save his or her life

Due diligence: In criminal law, the proof that everything possible and reasonable was done to prevent the act from happening

Due process: The system or processes of justice; the sequence of events that lead to a finding of guilt or innocence

Durable medical equipment (DME): Health care equipment designed to assist a patient with continued care, such as a nebulizer, or with improved quality of life, such as a wheelchair. These items are long-lasting or can be used for more than one patient

Electronic health records (EHR): The creation and maintenance of patient charts in a computerized system

EOB: a document, usually sent to a policyholder or insured, explaining charges and payments determined between a provider/facility and the insurance carrier based on the individual's policy details

Epidemic: Disease that spreads more quickly and more extensively within a population than is statistically reasonable

Ethical: In agreement with accepted moral conduct

Evaluation and management (E/M) code: A procedure code that reports physician services for assessing a patient's condition, determining a treatment plan, and continued supervision of care

Express consent: Written consent that is specific and signed by the individual

External: Brought on by an agency or organization other than the facility being audited

Federal Register: The daily publication for rules, proposed rules, and notices of the federal government

Fraud: Using dishonesty or inaccurate information with the intention of wrongly gaining money or other benefit

Health care surrogacy: An individual named to speak for a patient regarding procedures and treatments when that patient is unable to communicate his or her wishes

Implement: To put into action

Implied consent: A situation where agreement can be reasonably assumed, based on an individual's actions or behavior

Inaccuracies: Elements or components of a claim that are not correct; factual errors

Incarceration: Imprisonment or confinement; putting someone in jail or prison

Informed consent: A regulation mandating the sharing of information with a patient by a health care provider to assist the patient in deciding to agree or refuse treatment

Infraction: The failure to comply with a rule or policy

Integrity: The personal characteristic of high moral principles and professional standards

Internal: Generated from inside

Joint and several: Each individual involved is responsible for the entire amount of the debt, judgment, or penalty

Laws: The rules of behavior as determined by an authority

Living will: A legal document specifying life-saving procedures and treatments that the individual agrees to or refuses in advance of needing those treatments

Methodology: Formats of organization or technique

Mitigating circumstance: An event that partially excuses a wrong or lessens the results

Occult: Cannot be seen without investigation; deeply hidden

Oversight: The responsibility to supervise

Overt: Out in the open; obvious

Pandemic: A widespread epidemic, typically international in scope

Perpetuate: To continue, spread, disseminate

Provider Remittance Advice (PRA): a document, similar to an EOB, sent to a health care provider with an explanation of the determinations made regarding particular claims submitted

Private laws: Regulations dealing with interactions between individuals and each other and/or private businesses

Proficient: Great skill or excellence at performing a task

Propensity: A tendency to demonstrate particular behavior

Public laws: Laws regarding the relationship between the government and its people

Purview: Jurisdiction; area of authority or influence

Query: To ask

Random sampling: The choosing of a specific item or organization solely by chance, using no other determining factors

Rationale: The underlying purpose or reason

Reiteration: Repetition of the same thing again

Relators: Individuals who relate or tell

Repercussions: Consequences or results of one's actions

Respondeat superior: A legal concept assigning responsibility and liability to a supervisor, or person in charge, for the actions of an employee

Restitution: Paying back money received fraudulently

Retribution: Punishment for something someone has done

Retrospective: Looking at the past

Rules of participation: The structure of the agreement between third-party payer and health care provider for reimbursement

Sampling: Investigation or review of a percentage rather than the whole quantity

Sanction: A punishment for failing to obey a law or rule

Statutes: Laws established by a legislative body of the government

Subpoena: A court order to produce evidence

Subpoena ad testificandum: An order for an individual to testify in court

Subpoena duces tecum: An order to deliver specific documents to the court

Superbills: preprinted forms used in health care facilities that contain the diagnosis and procedure codes most often used in that facility

Superconfidentiality: PHI that may not be disclosed without written permission of the patient, except to a governmental agency as prescribed by law

Suffice: To be enough, provide a sufficient quantity

Synthesized: The combining of different ideas into a new, cohesive unit

Trade journals: Magazines written and published for a specific group of professionals

Undbundled: The practice of coding several services individually rather than using one combination code

Veracity: Truthfulness

Vet: To carefully examine something or to scrutinize an action to determine correctness

Violate: To treat with a lack of respect; to show behavior defiant to a law or contract

Webinars: Seminars and courses where participants attend using a specific site on the Internet that provides a presentation, often in PowerPoint, along with a speaker

Willful ignorance: Doing something incorrectly because of a lack of desire to find out how to do the task properly

Index

CPSIA information can be obtained
at www.ICGtesting.com
Printed in the USA
FFHW022233201219
57113191-62687FF

9 781418 049218